# Michigan Bird Watching

## A Year-Round Guide

Copyright © 2004, Bill Thompson, III

All Rights Reserved. No part of this book may be reproduced or transmitted in any form, or by any means, electronic or mechanical, including photocopying, recording, or by any information storage and retrieval system, without permission in writing from the publisher.

Published by Cool Springs Press, a Division of Thomas Nelson, Inc., P. O. Box 141000, Nashville, Tennessee, 37214.

Thompson, Bill, III.
   Michigan bird watching : a year-round guide / Bill Thompson, III, and the staff of Bird watcher's digest.
      p. cm.
   Includes bibliographical references and index.
   ISBN 1-59186-167-5
   1. Bird watching--Michigan. 2. Birds--Michigan. I. Bird watcher's digest. II. Title.
QL684.M5T49 2004
598'.07'234774--dc22

                                  2004029304

First Printing 2005
Printed in the United States of America
10 9 8 7 6 5 4 3 2 1

**Managing Editor:** Billie Brownell
**Interior Designer:** Bill Kersey, Kersey Graphics
**Production Artist:** S.E. Anderson
**Map and Icon Illustrator:** Heather Lynch
**Sighting Notes Illustrator:** Julie Zickefoose

Cool Springs Press books may be purchased in bulk for educational, business, fundraising, or sales promotional use. For information, please email SpecialMarkets@ThomasNelson.com.

Visit the Thomas Nelson website at **www.thomasnelson.com**

# Photography Credits
**Arthur Morris/Birds as Art:** Front cover top photo (sandhill crane); front cover bottom photo (American robin); intro photo page 6 (American robin); Pages 14; 15; 16 (cerulean warbler); 17 (American goldfinch); 19; 20; 21 (downy woodpecker); 26 (sandhill crane)
**Maslowski Photography:** Pages 16 (ruby-throated hummingbird); 21 (pine siskin); 22 (Connecticut warbler); 25 (prairie warbler)
**Tom Vezo:** Pages 17 (Bonaparte's gull); 24 (pileated woodpecker); 25 (piping plover); 26 (spruce grouse)
**Ron Austing:** Front cover featured photo (Kirtland's warbler); Page 24 (Kirtland's warbler)
**Brian Henry:** Back cover bottom photo (Eastern bluebird); Page 23 (great gray owl)
**Gary Meszaros:** Front cover middle photo (golden-winged warbler); 23 (golden-winged warbler)
**Barth Schorre:** Back cover top photo (scarlet tanager); Page 22 (Carolina wren)

# Michigan Bird Watching

## A Year-Round Guide

Bill Thompson, III
and the staff of
**Bird Watcher's Digest**

Cool Springs Press
A Division of Thomas Nelson Publishers
*Since 1798*

www.thomasnelson.com

# Dedication and Acknowledgements

## Dedication

To my parents, Bill and Elsa Thompson, who were bird watching *way* before it was cool and who had the courage and optimism to launch *Bird Watcher's Digest* in the living room of our home back in 1978. Thank you, Mom and Dad, for opening the door to my lifelong passion for birds and bird watching.

To Julie, Phoebe, and Liam (my own little family) who make each day sweeter than the last.

And to my siblings, Andy and Laura, for always being there for me.

## Acknowledgements

There's no such thing as "too many cooks spoiling the broth" when creating a book. From the outset I leaned on and drew upon the talents of publishing professionals and birding experts in creating this book. At *Bird Watcher's Digest*: Deborah Griffith (special editorial blue ribbon), Heather Lynch (map design kudos), Andy Thompson, Ann Kerenyi, Linda Brejwo, Bob Carlsen, Elsa "Catbird" Thompson, Helen Neuberger, Susan Hill, Joyce Abicht, Laura Kammermeier, and Katherine Koch deserve my never-ending thanks for covering for me at *BWD* so I could stay home and write.

Andy Thompson, Charles Kirkwood, and Russell Galen made early and important contributions to the launching of this book.

My deep gratitude to the folks at Cool Springs Press—especially Billie Brownell, Hank McBride, David Dunham, and Roger Waynick—for their enthusiasm, guidance, and support. Thanks also to the many people who helped in the development of this book "behind the scenes"—to Jamie Chavez for her copyediting expertise, to Bill Kersey for his art direction, and to S.E. Anderson for pulling it all together.

Helping me with the content creation were Norma Siebenheller, Howard Youth, and Julie Zickefoose, three peerless bird authors. Without them I'd still be laboring over a smoking-hot laptop.

College football fans might think that people from Michigan and Ohio cannot get along. Fortunately, bird watchers don't have these social hang-ups, so Allen Chartier and I got along wonderfully as he created the "Welcome to Bird Watching in Michigan" chapter of this book.

Allen T. Chartier has been birding in Michigan since the age of 11. He currently serves as the fall season compiler of the *Michigan Bird Survey*, is a past managing editor of the state's journal, *Michigan Birds and Natural History*, and served on the Michigan Bird Records Committee (from 1998 to 2003). Allen is co-editor of the book *A Birder's Guide to Michigan*, published in 2004 by the American Birding Association.

Creating a book requires a lot of "cooks" and I am grateful for everyone's contributions. Any errors or omissions contained herein are the responsibility of the author (me).

Finally, thank *YOU* for reading this book. I hope our paths cross someday in a beautiful natural place where there are lots and lots of birds. What could be better?

—Bill Thompson, III

# Table of Contents

## Welcome to Bird Watching in Michigan    7
    Ecoregions of Michigan   9
    Michigan Bird Watching by Season   14
    Michigan's Ten Must-See Birds   22

        Carolina Wren   22      Pileated Woodpecker   24
        Connecticut Warbler   22      Piping Plover   25
        Golden-winged Warbler   23      Prairie Warbler   25
        Great Gray Owl   23      Sandhill Crane   26
        Kirtland's Warbler   24      Spruce Grouse   26

    Michigan's Ten Best Bird-Watching Spots   27
    Resources for Michigan Bird Watchers   32

## Getting Started in Bird Watching    33
## Feeding and Housing    37
## How to Use *Michigan Bird Watching*    44
## 100 Most Commonly Encountered Birds in Michigan    45
## Resources    146
    Solutions for Common Feeding Problems   146
    Food/Feeder Chart   147
    Nest Box Chart   148
    A Glossary of Common Bird Terms   150
    Frequently Asked Questions   152
    How to Build a Simple Birdhouse   157
    Bird-Friendly Plants for Your Yard   162
    National Organizations for Bird Watchers   166
        (National Organizations, Field Guides, Audio Guides, and Periodicals)

## Index    169
## Meet Bill Thompson, III    176

# Welcome to Bird Watching
## *in Michigan...* Allen T. Chartier

"If you seek a pleasant peninsula, look about you" is Michigan's very appropriate state motto. Consisting of two peninsulas surrounded by the largest freshwater system in the world, the Great Lakes, there is indeed much beauty here.

Michigan offers a great deal of beauty and interest to the bird watcher and nature enthusiast. The state boasts 3,000 miles of shoreline, 11,000 interior lakes, 36,000 miles of rivers and streams, and the largest state forest system in the nation. With these diverse habitats, Michigan is particularly rich in bird species, with 421 species on the official state list.

Although somewhat removed from the middle of the continent, Michigan's birdlife provides a taste of North, South, East, and West. The majority of birds occurring here are decidedly eastern in flavor, but a western influence is evidenced by the state's small breeding populations of clay-colored sparrow, western meadowlark, and yellow-headed blackbird, and by the annual migrations, in small numbers, of more westerly species such as Franklin's gull and Harris's sparrow. Without doubt, Michigan is a northern state, and breeding warblers are well represented, in addition to breeding white-throated, Lincoln's, and Le Conte's sparrows, and hermit and Swainson's thrushes. There is also a far North component to Michigan's birdlife in the presence of boreal breeding species, mainly in the Upper Peninsula, represented by breeding spruce grouse, black-backed woodpecker, gray jay, boreal chickadee, Connecticut warbler, and white-winged and red crossbills. In winter, species from even farther north (including common redpolls, pine grosbeaks, white-winged and red crossbills, and great gray, snowy, boreal, and northern hawk owls) move into Michigan on three- to five-year cycles, or irruptions. In the southernmost portions of Michigan several species occur, some near the northernmost limits of their distributions. These include red-bellied woodpecker, Acadian flycatcher, white-eyed vireo, Carolina wren, cerulean warbler, Kentucky warbler, hooded warbler, and yellow-breasted chat.

Bird migrations are strongly influenced by the presence of the Great Lakes. Waterbirds use the lakes and shorelines as flyways, and Michigan provides a unique opportunity to see a number of otherwise pelagic or Atlantic coastal species as they migrate from their breeding grounds to their oceanic wintering grounds. Hawks and other birds—which avoid crossing large bodies of water, since lift is greater over land—concentrate by the shorelines of the lakes, and afford the bird watcher an opportunity to see thousands of these magnificent raptors. Songbirds migrate mostly at night, but sites along the lakeshores often produce the best opportunities for observing large numbers of migrants. Bird watchers from the southern United States are often surprised to find out that by the time the migrants reach Michigan, most of the breeding warblers, sparrows, and thrushes are in full song as they near their breeding grounds, providing a wondrous dawn chorus on almost any morning in May.

No introduction to bird watching in Michigan would be complete without mentioning our most unique bird, the endangered Kirtland's warbler. The vast majority of the world population of Kirtland's warblers breeds only in the north central Lower Peninsula of Michigan and migrates to the Bahamas for winter. This species is without doubt Michigan's biggest drawing card for attracting bird watchers from around the world, although once here, bird watchers cannot help but notice the great diversity and beauty that Michigan's birds have to offer.

## A Brief History of Michigan Ornithology

The history of ornithology in Michigan is rich and extensive, with many regional and local works in addition to several important statewide publications. The first bird list for the entire state was published by Gibbs in 1879, although there were more localized listings published earlier, including a listing of birds in the Detroit region by Merriam in the 1700s. Gibbs' list was followed by a more detailed account of Michigan's birds by Cook in 1893. This was followed by another thorough reference that updated the list of known species, published by Barrows in 1912. By this time, the last passenger pigeon had long since disappeared from Michigan, the only species now extinct known to have occurred in the state.

The Michigan Bird Survey, a detailed accounting season-by-season of the state's bird records, contributed by a growing band of birders, began in 1957. The survey was published in the state's journal, the *Jack-Pine Warbler* from 1957 to 1989 and 1991 to 1993. From 1994 to the present, the survey has been published in the replacement journal *Michigan Birds & Natural History*.

Between 1983 and 1988, Michigan's birders took to the field in a monumental undertaking to document the breeding distribution of the state's birds. The results were published in *The Atlas of Breeding Birds of Michigan* in 1991. Currently, a second atlas is under way; it aims to document changes in breeding status and distributions from the first atlas.

The Michigan Bird Records Committee was formed in 1988, and currently archives and evaluates records of casual and accidental species, as well as new species for the state list, and reviews these records to determine whether they should be published in the quarterly *Michigan Bird Survey*. The committee also regularly updates the list of accepted Michigan species.

More contemporary ornithologists have also worked in Michigan. Among the more notable is George Wallace who discovered in 1961 that an almost complete die-off of American robins on the Michigan State University campus was due to their ingestion of DDT, which was being used to control Dutch elm disease. In 1955 he published *An Introduction to Ornithology* with Harold D. Mahan.

Josselyn Van Tyne was the first ornithologist to show that North American birds returned to the same wintering areas in the tropics. In 1959, with Andrew J. Berger, he published *Fundamentals of Ornithology*, one of the first modern ornithology textbooks. The Van Tyne Memorial Library, housed at the University of Michigan Museum of Zoology (Bird Division), where he was curator from 1931 to 1952, is named in his honor.

In 1960 Harold F. Mayfield published a thorough life history of the Kirtland's warbler, simply titled *The Kirtland's Warbler*. Mayfield is also responsible for developing a method for determining species nesting success and survivorship, now dubbed the Mayfield Method, which is used extensively in bird conservation studies worldwide.

Finally, Lawrence H. Walkinshaw, a Michigan dentist with a passion for ornithology, is well known as a world authority on his favorite birds, the cranes. In 1949 he published *The Sandhill Crane*, a life history of this species based largely on his eighteen years of observation and research of the species throughout its range in North America and Cuba, including, of course, his home state of Michigan. In 1932 he became the first person ever to band a Kirtland's warbler, and his interest in the species resulted in his publication, *The Kirtland's Warbler: The Natural History of an Endangered Species*, in 1983.

# Ecoregions of Michigan

Glaciation has had a profound influence on the landforms, as well as vegetation cover, throughout Michigan; no portion of the state has escaped the force of glacial activity. The most obvious product of the last (Wisconsonian) period of glaciation was the formation of the five Great Lakes; four of which—Superior, Michigan, Huron, and Erie—surround Michigan, forming two distinct peninsulas. Throughout the state, the topography consists primarily of a variety of glacial formations: broad till plains with a variety of landforms including dunes, ridges, hills, ponds, and small bodies of water.

Much of the state is rather low in elevation and flat, particularly in the southern Lower Peninsula. The only truly mountainous areas of Michigan are in the western Upper Peninsula, including the Huron Mountains west of Marquette, the Porcupine Mountains northeast of Ironwood, and the Keweenaw Ridge along the Keweenaw Peninsula, which juts northward into Lake Superior. These mountainous areas sit on Precambrian bedrock that is part of the Canadian Shield. Michigan's highest point is Mt. Arvon (1,979-foot elevation), located in the Marquette highland west of the Huron Mountains.

In general, Michigan straddles the zone where southern deciduous forests gradually give way to coniferous forests to the north. About midway up the Lower Peninsula, running at about 43 degrees north latitude, or roughly from Muskegon to Saginaw, is a boundary described by early ecologists in Michigan as a "zone of tension." To the north of this zone, conifers are more frequent in forested areas, while south of this zone conifers are infrequent, except in some coastal dune areas. While deciduous forests clearly dominate the southern Lower Peninsula, coniferous forests are not uniformly distributed in the northern Lower or Upper Peninsulas. As travelers move north through the state, it is easy to detect the increasing presence of conifers, as well as the subtle change in deciduous forests. Birches in particular become more common to the north, as they thrive in areas where the soil tends to remain frozen throughout the entire winter. Many southern plants reach the northern limits of their distribution at the tension zone.

Nearly all of Michigan's magnificent forests, which never completely covered the state, were logged in the 1800s, with only a few isolated fragments of virgin timber remaining. Among these fragments of old growth include a virgin stand of white pine at Hartwick Pines State Park and, surprisingly, a patch of about 200 acres of forest on Belle Isle in the Detroit River. Thus, older second growth and successional areas predominate in most of the state. (Successional habit is anything that is changing from less vegetated to more heavily vegetated. This often refers to farm fields that become overgrown, then scrubby, brushy habitat, then recovering woodland, then forest.)

Large portions of Michigan are under cultivation. Most of the southern Lower Peninsula is dominated by agriculture, as well as by human settlements and urbanization. Most of Michigan's large cities, and more than half of the state's more than eight million people are in the southern Lower Peninsula.

## The Great Lakes and Coastlines

One of the most distinctive ecoregions of Michigan certainly must be the Great Lakes, four of which border on the state. These lakes are a great influence on Michigan's bird life. Many islands provide breeding habitat for ground-nesting waterbirds. These include some large colonies of herring and ring-billed gulls and smaller breeding colonies of Caspian, common, and Forster's terns. In the trees on these islands, double-crested cormorants often form large nesting colonies as they have begun to recover from steep declines in the 1960s and 1970s, which occurred due to the pesticide DDT causing their eggshells to grow thin. Lying offshore, these islands provide some measure of protection from predators due to their isolation from the mainland, and closer proximity to food sources of these mainly fish-eating birds.

The open waters of the lakes provide resting and feeding areas for many thousands of migrating diving ducks, sea ducks, geese, swans, loons, grebes, gulls, terns, and, rarely, jaegers. Among the five diving duck species occurring regularly in Michigan, canvasback and greater scaup occur mainly on the Great Lakes in migration. Redhead and lesser scaup migrate on the large lakes but are also found on smaller lakes, and ring-necked ducks occur much more frequently on smaller lakes though sometimes near the shorelines of the Great Lakes. From shore it is possible to see waterfowl only a couple miles away, yet there are often large flocks that occur even farther out. Canvasbacks are one of the specialties of the Great Lakes and in many years the largest counts in North America, sometimes tens of thousands, are found on Lake St. Clair or Lake Erie during the annual Christmas Bird Count.

The sea ducks include three species of scoter, common goldeneye, bufflehead, and long-tailed duck. The Great Lakes provide a migration corridor for these species, as well as a wintering area for many when the lakes don't freeze all the way across. Goldeneyes and buffleheads occur frequently on smaller lakes as well, but the scoters and long-tailed ducks are almost completely confined to the Great Lakes, where their main food is shellfish. The unfortunate introduction of zebra mussels into the Great Lakes ecosystem has at least had one short term benefit, because in recent years large rafts of hundreds of scoters and thousands of long-tailed ducks have overwintered in northern and central Lake Michigan. These species apparently feed on the abundance of this invasive shellfish. The greater scaup seems to have benefited from the presence of zebra mussels as well.

Large groups of red-breasted mergansers in migration, and common mergansers in late fall through winter (ice conditions permitting) can be found on the Great Lakes and shorelines; flocks of thousands of birds are not uncommon. Mergansers feed primarily on small fish, including shiners, minnows, and suckers. Both species can also be found on smaller lakes, where their relative, the hooded merganser, is almost exclusively found, though the common merganser is much more often found on the Great Lakes, especially in winter.

Michigan's more than 3,000 miles of shoreline is longer than that of any state except Alaska. The character of the shoreline varies from rocky to sandy to marshy. Many of the state's dabbling ducks migrate along the shorelines, and breed in the coastal marshes. Migrant shorebirds use most of Michigan's shorelines to varying degrees. Rocky shores attract few shorebirds, mainly small numbers of ruddy turnstone and black-bellied plover. The rare purple sandpiper prefers rocky areas, but is most often found on man-made jetties on Lake Michigan in late fall. Sandy shorelines are found mostly along Lakes Michigan and Huron, where they sometimes attract several species of shorebirds and provide breeding habitat, where undisturbed, for the piping plover, which is listed as a threatened species by the federal government.

## Southern Lower Peninsula

This most intensely settled region of Michigan also provides the greatest diversity of habitat types in the state, though much of it is fragmented. The major cities of Detroit, Flint, Ann Arbor, Lansing, Grand Rapids, Battle Creek, and Kalamazoo provide habitat for only the most tolerant birds, primarily introduced species including mute swan, Canada goose (native populations do not breed in Michigan), ring-necked pheasant, rock pigeon, European starling, house finch, and house sparrow. Native species that are tolerant of cities and agricultural areas include mourning dove, killdeer, red-tailed hawk, American kestrel, downy woodpecker, blue jay, black-capped chickadee, American crow, Carolina wren, American robin, song sparrow, northern cardinal, red-winged blackbird, common grackle, and American goldfinch.

Agricultural areas account for a significant proportion of the land area in the southern Lower Peninsula. Horned larks, field sparrows, vesper sparrows, western meadowlarks, and bobolinks are found in agricultural areas and fallow fields. If these fields are left to regenerate for several years, they can become suitable for less common species including upland sandpiper, and grasshopper and Henslow's sparrows.

These neglected and fallow fields resemble prairie habitats, which are now quite rare in Michigan, and require frequent burning to maintain. Most of Michigan's remaining prairies are in the southwestern corner of the state, and even there they are extremely fragmented. More extensive prairies in the past allowed species like greater prairie-chicken to breed in the state, but by 1981 they had died out. These prairies and grasslands also allowed the brown-headed cowbird to invade the state in large numbers during the last century, which negatively affected many songbirds that had never encountered this species before, and were not adapted to counter their parasitic habits. Most severely affected by the increase in cowbird numbers was the always range-restricted Kirtland's warbler in the northern Lower Peninsula.

The rivers and streams in the southern Lower Peninsula provide riparian forest corridors where woodland birds can find refuge and breeding habitat. Belted kingfishers build their nests in steep banks along these rivers, while eastern phoebes nest under bridges over these streams. A few species found more often in larger stands of deciduous forest can often eke out a living in these narrow corridors of habitat. This habitat also provides feeding and resting areas for migrating songbirds. Riparian areas with southern affinities, which often include stands of sycamore, provide breeding areas for southern bird species such as prothonotary warbler and, much more rarely, yellow-throated warbler. The latter is primarily restricted to the riparian areas of the Galien River in the southwestern corner of the state. The woodlands in southern Michigan support one of the healthiest breeding populations of cerulean warblers in North America.

Successional areas include shrubby fields, shrub wetlands, and early stages of second growth woodlands. Birds found breeding in these habitats include yellow warbler, blue-winged warbler, gray catbird, brown thrasher, swamp sparrow, song sparrow, Baltimore oriole, indigo bunting, and many others.

Nearly all the woodland in Michigan is second growth, and in the southern Lower Peninsula this woodland is dominated by deciduous species. As successional areas mature into woodland, larger areas of forest have provided opportunities for species requiring larger tracts to recolonize areas they inhabited before deforestation, including pileated woodpecker and barred owl, which are now found closer to urbanized areas than previously. These woodlands provide food and shelter for migrating songbirds. Breeding species in these southern deciduous woodlands include wood duck, ruffed grouse, yellow-billed and black-billed cuckoos, downy, hairy, and red-bellied woodpeckers, eastern wood-pewee, great crested flycatcher, Acadian flycatcher, red-eyed vireo, yellow-throated vireo, tufted titmouse, veery, wood thrush, and scarlet tanager.

Marshlands are patchy in distribution in the interior portions of the southern Lower Peninsula, but along the shore of Lake Erie some large areas have been reclaimed. Some portions of the Lake Erie lakeplain provide habitat for a number of rare and threatened plant species; this rare environment is one of the few of its type in the world. Areas of cattail are all too frequently invaded by phragmites and purple loosestrife in this region, which are far less productive for birds. Cattail marshes provide breeding habitat for sora and Virginia rails, common moorhen, American bittern, mallard, blue-winged teal, marsh wren, swamp sparrow, and many other species.

## Northern Lower Peninsula

Larger stands of deciduous and mixed forest, with less agricultural and urban development, characterize the northern Lower Peninsula. The Huron-Manistee National Forest contains a good variety of deciduous, mixed, and coniferous (both wet and dry) habitats, where a number of warbler species can be found breeding. In the western portion (primarily the Manistee section), maples, oaks, and hickories intermingle with red and white pine and cedars, providing a varied habitat for many breeding species. In these areas black-throated blue, chestnut-sided, yellow-rumped, magnolia, and black-and-white warblers, American redstarts, and northern waterthrushes are fairly common. Mourning warblers are widespread but not commonly encountered. Forest floor inhabitants include wood thrush, veery, Swainson's thrush, and ovenbird. In areas where conifers dominate, black-throated green, Blackburnian, and pine warblers, as well as dark-eyed juncos can be found. In addition to the abundance of breeding warblers in this habitat, ruffed grouse, wild turkey, red-shouldered hawk, and barred owl can also be seen.

The eastern portions of the Huron-Manistee National Forest are dominated by stands of jack pines on sandy soil, which are the preferred habitat of the Kirtland's warbler. Although jack pines occur from northern Alberta south through Minnesota and Michigan and east into the Canadian Maritimes, only north-central Michigan provides the Kirtland's warbler with its primary breeding habitat. Occasionally, individuals have been found breeding in Minnesota, Wisconsin, and Ontario, but not in recent years. A few Kirtland's warblers do nest in scattered locales in the Upper Peninsula in drier jack pine plains. Other species that can be found breeding in these areas include Nashville, yellow, yellow-rumped, and black-and-white warblers, Swainson's and hermit thrushes, Lincoln's and clay-colored spar-, rows, and, in the more open areas, Brewer's blackbirds.

Successional areas, which sometimes include alder and conifers, are good breeding areas for eastern towhee and both blue-winged and golden-winged warblers. The golden-winged seems to prefer older shrubby fields, before woodland takes over, and often with a coniferous wetland component. The golden-winged warbler is more specialized than the blue-winged warbler, and is thus being crowded out as the blue-winged has been increasing its range northward. These two species hybridize with each other where they come into contact, which is more of a threat to the less common and more specialized golden-winged warbler. These mixed alder-cedar wetlands are also breeding habitat for white-throated sparrows.

One of the state's best wetland areas occurs along Saginaw Bay. The extensive marshes here provide breeding habitat for many waterfowl, as well as sora and Virginia rails, American coots, black terns, American and least bitterns, and harbor one of the most reliable breeding colonies of yellow-headed blackbird in the state. Large areas of mudflat provide feeding grounds for migrant shorebirds, and the waters of Saginaw Bay host thousands of migrating waterfowl. One of the premier bird watching sites in the Midwest is Tawas Point, where the narrow peninsula provides a resting place for thousands of northbound migrant songbirds in spring, as well as in fall. The trees and shrubs are short due to the sandy soil, so observing migrant warblers here is a pleasant experience, with no complaints of "warbler neck" so common where the trees are taller.

In the northwestern portion of the Lower Peninsula, there are some quality areas of grassland where upland sandpipers, grasshopper sparrows, and bobolinks may be easily found. Also in these areas, Savannah and field sparrows, as well as eastern meadowlarks can be quite common, with an occasional western meadowlark in areas where the grass is shorter.

Along Lake Michigan, the dominant habitat is forested dunes (primarily conifers), a large portion of which have been preserved in the Sleeping Bear Dunes National Lakeshore, some of the tallest sand dunes in North America. This habitat provides breeding areas for one of Michigan's rarest breeding warblers, the prairie warbler, (which occurs in even smaller numbers than Kirtland's warblers). The beaches here and farther to the north provide an undisturbed and protected breeding ground for the piping plover, which is a threatened species. These areas of forested dunes occur along the entire length of Lake Michigan and into the southernmost portions of Michigan, where breeding species from farther north, including black-throated green and Canada warblers, can be found in isolated patches.

Sandy areas also occur along the Lake Huron shore, and piping plovers have been found breeding recently around Alpena. The sandy regions also reach to the tip of Michigan's "thumb," which is typically considered part of the southern Lower Peninsula. Standing on the sandy shores of Lake Michigan or Lake Huron gives one a feeling of standing on the Atlantic seashore. This illusion is reinforced by the huge dimensions of the lakes, both of which are more than fifty miles wide, but also by some of the plants on the beaches. Some species of grass and other plants, including Marram grass, sand reed grass, beach pea, sea rocket, and wormwood are found principally on the Atlantic Coast, but have disjunct populations along the sandy Great Lakes shorelines. A unique feature of these shores is the presence of three localized Great Lakes endemic plants, the Lake Huron tansy, Houghton's goldenrod, and Pitcher's thistle, found nowhere else in the world.

## Upper Peninsula

The Upper Peninsula is truly "up north" for many Michiganians, providing large areas of relatively unspoiled habitat and isolation. The eastern portion of the Upper Peninsula is somewhat different in character from the western portion, being more heavily forested, and more dominated by mixed and coniferous forests. Also, the eastern portion holds a few open areas as well as patches of boreal forest and spruce bogs. The western portion has more open areas as well as a greater proportion of deciduous and mixed forest than the eastern, though there are probably more patches of boreal forest in the western Upper Peninsula.

The eastern Upper Peninsula has received much more attention from bird watchers, so we have a better idea of which birds occur there. The large Hiawatha National Forest consists of much mixed and coniferous forest and wetlands that provide breeding habitat for many warblers also found in the northern Lower Peninsula. The patches of boreal forest are perhaps the most unique feature of the Upper Peninsula, with spruces and cedars dominating, containing isolated bogs that are attractive to a number of species, although there are also anomalous patches of boreal forest in the northernmost portions of the Lower Peninsula. Breeding songbirds in this habitat include olive-sided and yellow-bellied flycatchers, ruby-crowned and golden-crowned kinglets, hermit thrush, and pine siskin. A few less common (and some rare) breeding warblers include Cape May, bay-breasted, palm, and Wilson's, while the bog areas themselves are places where the secretive Connecticut warbler breeds. Other boreal forest inhabitants, found throughout the Upper Peninsula, include spruce grouse, black-backed woodpecker, gray jay, boreal chickadee, and sometimes white-winged and red crossbills.

Throughout the Upper Peninsula there are open areas and jack pine plains where a few Kirtland's warblers have been found nesting. Also, the more open patches provide breeding display grounds for sharp-tailed grouse. In winter these openings and their edges provide hunting grounds for northern owl species, including snowy owl, northern hawk owl, and great gray owl, which invade the Upper Peninsula about once every three to five years when the populations of small northern mammals, especially voles, crashes. These owls must then wander much more widely in search of food. Often accompanying these cyclical irruptions are rough-legged hawks and northern shrikes. Similarly, the cone crop cycle brings what are known as "winter finches" into the Upper Peninsula (and in some years throughout the state). Common and hoary redpolls, red and white-winged crossbills, pine and evening grosbeaks, and pine siskins are the species involved in these population increases, though the siskin, the crossbills, and the evening grosbeak also breed in the northern parts of the state.

Wetlands in the Upper Peninsula are varied and include the previously mentioned spruce bogs, as well as tamarack bogs, alder swamps, cattail marshes, open lakes, and sedge marshes. Common loons and bald eagles often nest on the more isolated and undisturbed lakes. Sedge marshes are home to species that are uncommon to rare elsewhere in Michigan, including yellow rail (listed as threatened in the state), sedge wren, and Le Conte's sparrow. The large man-made wetlands of Seney National Wildlife Refuge provide breeding habitat for Michigan's largest breeding population of trumpeter swans, which were introduced here through the 1990s.

# Michigan Bird Watching by Season

## Spring

March's weather is perhaps the most variable, sometimes being an extension of winter, sometimes heralding the onset of spring, although it usually exhibits characteristics of both seasons. The arrival of male red-winged blackbirds by the first week in March, when they begin defending territories, filling the still brown marshes with their first songs in months, could perhaps be considered a harbinger of spring. But with the possibility for winterlike weather the entire month even in the southern portions, can this really be called spring? The traditional harbinger of spring, the American robin, is also Michigan's state bird; yet robins overwinter here, often quite far north, and in the south, sometimes in flocks of hundreds or thousands.

In contrast, while some birds are tentatively arriving in the southern portions of the state, including an incursion of migrant waterfowl following the ice breakup on the Great Lakes, the north is still firmly in the grip of winter, with some northward movement of northern finches and some raptors. This is a good time to check southern Lake Michigan, Lake Erie, and the Detroit River as thousands of waterfowl can suddenly appear after the ice breakup.

Yet other birds, including great blue heron, great horned owl, red-tailed hawk, mourning dove, gray jay, and horned lark, have actually begun nesting early in March. Toward the end of the month, American woodcocks arrive in the south and begin their courtship flights, and tufted titmice begin breeding. After the vernal equinox, the official beginning of spring in late March, the pace of arriving migrants increases with tree swallows, killdeer, Wilson's snipe, rusty blackbird, and sometimes eastern phoebe typically arriving in the southern regions of the state.

With the receding snow, the skunk cabbage is the only "flower" that is likely to be encountered in March. As the ground thaws and warm all-night rains fill woodland vernal ponds, mole salamanders (tiger, spotted, and blue-spotted) make their annual terrestrial migrations to breed *en masse* in these ponds.

April sees a noticeable increase in migrant arrivals, with many sparrows, kinglets, blue-gray gnatcatchers, and yellow-rumped warblers typically arriving mid-month. This is a good time for loon migration on the Great Lakes, and in the Upper Peninsula the duck migration is in full swing. Spruce and sharp-tailed grouse breeding activity is at its peak this month, making them somewhat easier to see than most other times of the year.

Spring raptor migration reaches its peak in the latter half of the month, with rough-legged hawks passing through sites like Whitefish Point in the Upper Peninsula and broad-winged hawks arriving in the Lower Peninsula. The first few shorebirds arrive at the end of the month, as well as the first scouts of the warblers, thrushes, and ruby-throated hummingbirds. April 15 is a good day to put up your hummingbird feeder in southern Michigan, as the first arrivals are often here on or before this date. American tree spar-

*Eastern phoebe*

rows, which have been resident all winter, usually depart for their more northerly breeding range by the end of the month. Least flycatchers sometimes move into the state during the last week of April.

This is a good time of year to visit wetland areas and shores of the Great Lakes for migrating waterfowl, loons, and grebes. Although woodland areas are still not leafed out, the forest floor blooms in profusion with ephemeral spring wildflowers including bloodroot, spring beauty, hepaticas, Dutchman's breeches, common toothwort, spring cress, red trillium, and large white trillium.

May is the peak of migration throughout the state, with greatest numbers of some species occurring in the southern part of the Lower Peninsula as much as one or two weeks earlier than in the northern Lower Peninsula and the Upper Peninsula. Warblers and thrushes begin to arrive the first week, and most reach their peak mid-month. Cool mornings early in the month will often find Baltimore orioles visiting your hummingbird feeders, so it's a good idea to give them a separate feeder and some orange halves before the first of May. Kirtland's warblers arrive on average around May 10 and begin singing actively by about May 15. Flycatchers and cuckoos arrive later in the month, along with some of the later arriving warblers, particularly Connecticut warbler. Loons and waterfowl continue to migrate along the Great Lakes, especially in the Upper Peninsula. Shorebird numbers build up, at least where there is habitat, through the end of the month. Whimbrels make a fleeting appearance statewide in a narrow window centered around May 25, but most other shorebird species have mostly departed by the end of the month.

Weather affects the number of migrants, especially nocturnal migrants, which will be detected in any given spring. If weather conditions are favorable for migration (south winds overnight with fair weather and clear nighttime skies),

*Baltimore oriole (male)*

many migrants will over-fly much of the region and arrive safely at their breeding grounds. Bird watchers often consider this situation to be a poor spring migration, but it is certainly the best situation for the birds. More often, spring storms move through Michigan, with heavy rain and sometimes strong north winds, with cool temperatures following. Migrants encountering these conditions at night are grounded, where they must find shelter and food to wait out the passage of these weather systems. Under these conditions, bird watchers may find birds nearly everywhere in the morning, and often feeding very near the ground as most insect activity will also be depressed in cooler conditions. This is known as a "fallout" of migrants, and is something that Michigan bird watchers look forward to each spring, keeping a vigilant eye on the weather reports through the month of May. While allowing bird watchers excellent opportunities to observe many colorful migrants at close range in almost any habitat, including urban parks and suburban backyards, such fallouts are stressful to the migrant birds and, if conditions are severe enough, can prove fatal for some. However, migrant birds have been encountering the hazard of weather systems during their migrations for eons with little impact on their populations. Loss of habitat and collisions with human-made structures are newer hazards that the birds haven't adapted to, and these cause far greater mortality than natural forces.

## Summer

*Ruby-throated hummingbird (male)*

With the arrival of June, singing activity of breeding songbirds reaches its peak, while there is a fair number of migrant shorebirds still occupying wetlands and mudflats. Very few waterfowl are migrating, and all those that remain to breed in Michigan have, for the most part, built nests and are incubating eggs. Late migrant songbirds, including black-billed and yellow-billed cuckoos, olive-sided and yellow-bellied flycatchers, and Connecticut warblers may still be present in the southern Lower Peninsula, not yet occupying their breeding grounds. This is a good season to head north for breeding songbirds, or to head to one of the marshes and wetlands for shorebird migration. Summer activity at your bird feeder will likely be reduced, as the winter birds have gone north, and the resident breeders are busy raising young. Visits will likely be limited to the "regulars," including mourning dove, downy and red-bellied woodpeckers, black-capped chickadee, tufted titmouse, white-breasted nuthatch, house finch, and American goldfinch. In cities, feeders will also have plenty of rock pigeons, European starlings, and house sparrows year-round.

By July many passerines are feeding fledged young from their first broods, and by the end of the month singing activity tends to diminish as the parent birds are both busily occupied feeding young. There is an almost imperceptible gap between the northbound shorebirds and the southbound ones, and the first adults of many Arctic breeding species return to Michigan in late July. In northern areas, adult male ruby-throated hummingbirds begin to depart by the end of July. Replacing them at your hummingbird feeders will be adult females and newly

*Cerulean warbler (male)*

*Bonaparte's gull*

fledged youngsters, creating quite a feisty scene as they jostle for feeding spots. Waiting for the peak bloom of thistles, American goldfinches generally begin their nesting activity in July.

Even though the calendar still indicates it is summer, the transition from summer to fall as far as bird activity is concerned occurs in August. Southbound shorebirds arrive in good numbers during this month, as well as a few early Bonaparte's gulls and some early stragglers of northern breeding waterfowl. The peak of red-necked grebe migration, involving thousands of birds, occurs at Whitefish Point in late August. Although it is relatively inconspicuous, songbird migration is often well underway by mid-month, with peak numbers of many warblers, including yellow and Blackburnian, as well as *Empidonax* flycatchers, and warbling vireos. The first migrant thrushes begin moving by mid-August and build in numbers through the end of the month. The migration of common nighthawks typically peaks at the end of the month. Quite a number of breeding species slip out of the state almost undetected, including black-billed and yellow-billed cuckoos, olive-sided and Acadian flycatchers, blue-winged, golden-winged, and cerulean warblers, and yellow-breasted chat. Nearly all of Michigan's Kirtland's warblers depart by the end of August, except for a few stragglers.

Swallow numbers build up through the month, as most species prepare for migrations into September. Purple martins and bank swallows are the earliest to leave, with most gone by the end of August. Ruby-throated hummingbird migration peaks toward the end of the month, and most eastern kingbirds have departed by the end of August. Blue-winged teal build in numbers throughout the month, as they are the earliest of the waterfowl to depart the state and one of the few that does not overwinter. The first few raptors begin their southward migrations toward the end of August, including a few broad-winged and sharp-shinned hawks, northern harrier, osprey, and American kestrel.

*American goldfinch (male)*

# Autumn

Although most of September is still technically summer, with the autumnal equinox falling around the third week, the migrations of many groups of birds are in full swing. Being the peak of migration in general, September is also an excellent month for rarities and vagrant birds to show up, potentially adding spice to a day's bird watching. Most warblers, vireos, and thrushes peak in their migrations this month. Waterfowl migration picks up significantly at both Great Lakes and inland sites. This is an excellent month for migrating loons at Whitefish Point, and numbers of scoters and long-tailed ducks build up through the month. Hawk migration begins and peaks quickly in September; large numbers of broad-winged hawks dominate the skies, with thousands of birds at well-known hawk-watching stations between September 10 and September 20. Most of the sharp-shinned hawks for the season will pass through in September; peak numbers of bald eagles and ospreys also pass through this month. Shorebird migration continues, though numbers of some species begin to decline and species variety is often considerably diminished by the end of September, compared with the peaks of July and August. Ruby-throated hummingbirds continue to migrate out of the state and most will have departed by the end of September, but it is always a good idea to leave your feeder up at least two weeks after you see the last one to help late migrants. It is a myth that leaving your feeders up will prevent hummingbirds from migrating.

Often overlooked by the casual observer, blue jays abruptly begin their southward migration in late September and tens of thousands of birds can be seen each day at coastal locations and hawk-watch sites. Many people think that blue jays do not migrate, and they will often visit feeders year-round, but in fact the summer birds are completely replaced with winter birds from farther north. The blue jay migration, when you're lucky enough to witness it, is truly spectacular. Most backyards only notice a slight increase in blue jays at the feeder in late September without realizing that these are likely migrants moving through.

Gulls also begin migrating through the Great Lakes in autumn, and often some of the more rare species are detected. Those charismatic, raptorial gulls, the jaegers, begin migrating offshore from a few locales on the Great Lakes during September as well, though the weather conditions they prefer can be quite unpleasant for bird watchers—strong northwest winds with cooler temperatures, and sometimes even rain or snow later in October and November.

Toward the end of September northern passerines, including Lapland longspurs, snow buntings, and American tree sparrows begin moving into the Upper Peninsula, and dark-eyed juncos begin moving into the southern Lower Peninsula. In strong irruption years, the winter finches, including pine siskins, common redpolls, pine grosbeaks, white-winged and red crossbills, and evening grosbeaks, will begin to appear at the end of the month in the Upper Peninsula. Bird feeders in the northern parts of the state will attract many of these birds, but be prepared with plenty of sunflower seed, especially for the seemingly ravenous evening grosbeaks. This is a good time to offer high-energy foods, such as suet and peanuts, at your feeders.

With the onset of October, migration of warblers and thrushes begins to wind down, and species diversity is significantly lower by mid-month compared with the peak in September. Typically, orange-crowned, yellow-rumped, black-throated blue, Nashville, and blackpoll warblers are the only species to occur later in October, and orange-crowned actually peaks at this time, being extremely rare even in late September. The last few straggling ruby-throated hummingbirds depart before mid-month. Waterfowl migration is still going strong in October, with the arrival of many species of diving ducks into the southern portions of the state, as well as migrant Canada geese from farther north. Activity at feeders increases with the arrival of white-throated and

*Red-shouldered hawk*

everyone awaits the arrival of the first golden eagle, usually sometime after the fifteenth. Turkey vultures peak in mid-October, with thousands possible on a single day. In late October, appropriate weather conditions are even more important for seeing a good hawk migration. Northwest winds following the passage of a cold front are the best conditions, so avid hawk watchers stay tuned to the weather conditions all fall.

Sparrow migration peaks during this month, with large numbers of white-throated and white-crowned sparrows, as well as song and swamp sparrows. Kinglets and brown creepers, breeders in northern Michigan, begin moving south. American pipits and horned larks move through in peak numbers.

white-crowned sparrows, dark-eyed juncos, and migrant American goldfinches.

Although the big numbers have passed by in September, the species diversity of migrating hawks is greatest in October. On rare occasions, it is possible to see fifteen or more species at one of the hawk-watch sites, particularly at Lake Erie Metropark. The sharp-shinned hawks are past their peak by mid-month, while Cooper's hawks are just reaching peak. Northern goshawks move through in small numbers in October, and in good flight years (they're somewhat cyclical) multiples can be seen some days. Northern harriers seem to lack a peak migration time, with steady numbers from late August through early December, although late October is a good time for the later arriving males to be seen. The dashing falcons, especially peregrines and merlins, peak early in October, while American kestrels dwindle to a very few by the end of the month. October is really the month for the broad-winged buteos. Early in the month, a few straggling broad-winged hawks from the September masses can be seen, while peak numbers of red-tailed and red-shouldered hawks occur in late October. The end of the month is also the time when the beautiful rough-legged hawk begins its migration, and

In November rarer gulls, including glaucous and Iceland gulls, and small numbers of jaegers continue to move along the Great Lakes. More sea ducks, including scoters and long-tailed ducks, and increased numbers of diving ducks move into the Great Lakes, and many will remain until freeze-up. Many sparrows continue to migrate through the state, with significant numbers of American tree sparrows, which will remain through winter. Lapland longspurs and snow buntings migrate in peak numbers throughout the month. In strong irruption years northern finches move into the southern portions of the state, and it is always a pleasant surprise in southern Michigan to attract one of these less common birds to your feeder. Keeping your feeders stocked and clear of snow and ice will increase your chances of attracting grosbeaks, crossbills, siskins, and redpolls. Northern owls, in good irruption years, make their first appearance in the Upper Peninsula by the end of the month.

Hawk migration continues, with decreased diversity and numbers, but with such "high quality" birds as rough-legged hawk, golden eagle, and northern goshawk to be expected, and sometimes in surprising numbers. The end of November is often quite wintry, bird-wise and weather-wise, even in southern portions of the state.

# Winter

Winter has settled in by December in the Upper Peninsula, but in southern portions of the state there is still some southbound movement of birds. Late migrating songbirds, including American pipits, horned larks, Lapland longspurs, and snow buntings, continue to move through, while on the Great Lakes, large numbers of waterfowl may be present until they get frozen out and have to move farther south. Spectacular rafts of canvasback and both greater and lesser scaup can be seen at this time, as well as thousands of common mergansers. Most red-breasted mergansers have moved out before the onset of winter. Glaucous gulls from the north and great black-backed gulls from the east are still moving into and through the state, as well as a few straggling Bonaparte's gulls. In some years, irruptions of winter finches do not begin until late in the season, someimes with birds not reaching the southern Lower Peninsula until late December or even early January. Northern harriers, rough-legged hawks, and a few red-tailed hawks may migrate throughout the month. By the end of December winter-resident passerines are mostly settled in, with a very few late lingering migrant sparrows. Many dark-eyed juncos and American tree sparrows will take up residence near bird feeders throughout the state, along with good numbers of American goldfinches and the typical resident species. Don't be surprised if a winter-resident sharp-shinned or Cooper's hawk occasionally takes advantage of your bird feeders as well, generally preying on the weaker individuals.

Many Michigan bird watchers gather in late December and early January to participate in the annual Christmas Bird Counts that are conducted annually around the state. Started in 1900 by the National Audubon Society as an alternative to the "side hunt"—a Christmas tradition where men and boys competed to shoot the most birds in one day—the Christmas Bird Count is an all-day tallying of every bird seen within proscribed count circles. Most Michigan bird clubs run at least one Christmas Bird Count and they are always in need of additional counters, drivers, and feeder watchers to help cover the count's territory. Beginning birders are always welcomed, too, and this is an excellent way to tap into your local birding community. Most counts run from dawn until dusk, with participants often gathering for a "tally rally" at the end of the day, where warm food and the day's best sightings are shared and enjoyed.

Winter bird watching can be very exciting in your own backyard, especially if some of the winter finch species are "invading" Michigan as they do when the supply of natural foods and seeds is depleted in the north. Some of the much-anticipated winter finch species we look for include pine siskin, common redpoll, evening grosbeak, red and white-winged crossbills, and pine grosbeak. Any of these birds can be attracted to bird feeders well-stocked with sunflower seed or thistle (Niger) seed, but they are even more likely to be found in large stands of conifers, especially ones laden with seed-rich cones. Cemeteries, parks, arboretums, and other places with large stands of mature conifers are likely places to encounter these roving bands of winter finches.

*Dark-eyed junco*

*Downy woodpecker (male)*

In addition to keeping the feeders stocked, winter is an important time to provide your birds with water and shelter. Nest boxes and birdhouses will be used for nighttime roosting by bluebirds, chickadees, titmice, downy woodpeckers, and even screech-owls. Make sure your boxes are placed with the entrance hole facing away from the prevailing wind. Consider caulking the vent holes and lining the interiors with a handful of dried grass to enhance the insulating quality of your birdhouses. A small bird bath equipped with an outdoor water heater (available from wild bird or farm supply stores) will ensure that your backyard birds have access to unfrozen water, even in the coldest weather.

Keeping warm and dry is just as important for the bird watcher as it is for the birds. When venturing out in a Michigan winter, always dress in layers and wear more clothing than you think is necessary. Wise veteran birders always say, "It's colder than you think it is." This is especially true if you will be exposed to direct wind, such as along a lake, or if you will be outside for more than short periods. It's almost impossible to enjoy birding when you are shivering (and it's really hard to hold your binoculars steady, too).

January is truly the middle of winter in Michigan, often with the coldest temperatures of the season and plenty of snow, with the Great Lakes freezing almost entirely in colder years. Wintering gulls, including rarer northern species such as glaucous, Iceland, and Thayer's gulls, move inland to smaller, often frozen lakes, and landfills. Waterfowl are concentrated into smaller areas of open water with common mergansers, diving ducks, and sea ducks predominating. Most dabbling ducks have moved out of the state by December. In modest irruption years, winter finches and northern owls may not arrive until mid-month. This is a good time to make a trip to the Upper Peninsula to look for these species, as well as boreal species such as the gray jay and boreal chickadee.

February often continues cold and snowy, with gulls and wintering waterfowl still dominating the birding scene. The last half of the month typically sees the initiation of the breeding season for great horned owl, mourning dove, and gray jay. The first migrants returning north are found near the end of the month, including northern harrier, horned lark, and male red-winged blackbirds. If the thaw is early, greater numbers of diving ducks, and a few dabbling ducks, move into the Great Lakes. Northern finches and owls, when present in irruption years, will remain through the month, especially in the Upper Peninsula.

As the new year begins, Michigan bird watchers eagerly anticipate the first signs of spring migration among our birds, and the seasonal cycle begins once more.

*Pine siskin*

# Michigan's Ten Must-See Birds

## Carolina Wren
*Thryothorus ludovicianus*

The Carolina is the largest wren found in Michigan, at about 5 1/2 inches in length. It is easily recognized by its rufous-brown upperparts and whitish underparts with a buffy belly, long, pointed, and curved bill, and broad, bright white line over the eye. The very pleasing song, "tea kettle, tea kettle, tea kettle..." is somewhat similar to the northern cardinal or tufted titmouse, but unlike any other wren in the state.

The Carolina wren is an uncommon to fairly common permanent resident, generally found south of Grand Rapids and Flint in the southern Lower Peninsula. It is most easily found in residential areas, but also in wooded areas. Winters with deep snow, most recently during the late 1970s, have eliminated this species completely from the state in the past, but the birds re-colonized by mid-1980s. Single birds have recently reached as far north as the Upper Peninsula during northward movements in fall.

This species is usually easy to find by listening for its song. Most well-wooded parks and residential areas in the southernmost portions of Michigan have resident Carolina wrens. Some places to check include Fairlane Woods at the University of Michigan at Dearborn, the Kleinstuck Preserve near Kalamazoo, and Sarett Nature Center near Berrien Springs.

## Connecticut Warbler
*Oporornis agilis*

This is a large warbler, nearly 6 inches in length, and is almost always found walking on the ground. The back, wings, and tail are olive-green, and the head, throat, and upper chest are all gray, forming a distinct hooded appearance. There is a distinct, complete white eye ring. The lower breast, belly, and under tail are bright yellow. The legs are sturdy and bright pink. The song is a staccato "chippy chuppy chippy chuppy chippy chuppy."

The Connecticut warbler is a rare breeding species in Michigan, but is more often encountered during migration, when it is rare in spring and fall. Its spring arrival is later than that of many other warblers—typically in the last half of May into early June even in the southern portions of the state. In fall, most are detected at banding stations, but they seem to move south in greatest numbers in mid-September. Connecticut warblers breed on the edges of spruce bogs, which are very patchy in distribution in Michigan. They are shy, skulking birds that are more often heard than seen.

Connecticut warblers can be found at many locations in migration, though many sites do not record them every year. Some places that have proven consistent are Kleinstuck Preserve near Kalamazoo, the Nichols Arboretum in Ann Arbor, Fairlane Woods at the University of Michigan in Dearborn, Metro Beach Metropark near Mt. Clemens, and Tawas Point State Park.

# Golden-winged Warbler
*Vermivora chrysoptera*

This is one of our most boldly patterned warblers, with a gray body, a black ear patch surrounded by white, a black throat, bright-yellow crown, and true to its name, broad golden-yellow wing bars. One of our smaller warblers at slightly less than 5 inches in length, the golden-winged warbler is often detected by its "bee buzz buzz buzz" song.

The golden-winged warbler is an uncommon and declining summer resident, most numerous in the northern Lower Peninsula and parts of the Upper Peninsula, arriving in May and departing by mid-September. It is more local than the blue-winged warbler, and its range retracts northward as the blue-winged's expands and hybridizes with it. These hybrids are frequent enough that they too have been given names; Brewster's warbler, which is more frequently encountered, and Lawrence's warbler, which is rarely encountered.

The golden-winged warbler seems to prefer "middle-aged" fields for its breeding habitat, while blue-winged warblers use the earliest shrubby habitats right through to the latest. Thus, the golden-winged warbler may be more specialized than the blue-winged, and so is vulnerable as the blue-winged continues to increase its range northward.

Some good sites for golden-winged warbler in the southern Lower Peninsula include the Gratiot-Saginaw State Game Area and the Port Huron State Game Area. Farther north, look in appropriate habitat in areas such as the Huron-Manistee National Forest, especially in the western portions (Manistee section).

# Great Gray Owl
*Strix nebulosa*

The great gray owl is very large, all-gray owl, about 27 inches in length, with a very large head, large facial disks and piercing yellow eyes. They are frequently active in daylight and are nearly unmistakable once sighted.

About every three to five years, populations of mice and voles in the far North crash, forcing their predators farther south in winter than normal. These forced migrations are called irruptions. The great gray owl is mainly an irruptive winter visitor to Michigan, occurring from December through March. Occasionally, after large irruptions, some birds may be seen into late spring or even early summer. During some winters they are completely absent.

When present, great gray owls are usually easy to find because they perch in the open on the edges of open fields, where they hunt their rodent prey. Few of these birds have encountered human beings before, and some are probably near starving, so they are typically quite tame and approachable. Most irruptions do not take these birds farther south than the Upper Peninsula, and the best areas to search for this species includes the open fields south of Sault Ste. Marie, as well as Neebish Island and Sugar Island in the St. Mary's River.

# Kirtland's Warbler
*Dendroica kirtlandii*

The Kirtland's warbler is one of our largest warblers, at slightly less than 6 inches in length. Its upperparts are blue-gray with black streaks on the back, white wing bars, and a broken white eye ring. The underparts are yellow from the chin to the belly, and white under the tail. The song is one of the loudest and most cheery of any warbler, a richly warbled "chur chur CHEE CHEE wee wee."

The Kirtland's warbler is Michigan's most unique bird because it breeds nowhere else in the world and is listed as threatened on the federal endangered lists. Breeding is restricted to jack pine forests between about six and twenty years of age in the north central Lower Peninsula, largely within the Huron-Manistee National Forest. The bulk of the population breeds in Crawford, Oscoda, Alcona, and Ogemaw counties. Jack pine cones do not open to allow the seeds to drop to the ground unless they have been exposed to fire, and the warbler's requirement of younger trees has earned it the nickname "bird of fire."

In 1974, a survey turned up only 167 singing males. The declines were due to habitat loss due to fire suppression, and nest parasitism by brown-headed cowbirds. Habitat management, through controlled burns, has increased the available habitat, and cowbird control through capture and removal has reduced parasitism levels. In recent years, the number of singing males has increased, reaching a high of 1,341 in 2004. The best way to see Kirtland's warblers is to go on a National Forest Service tour out of Mio, or on a U.S. Fish & Wildlife Service tour out of Grayling between May 15 and July 4.

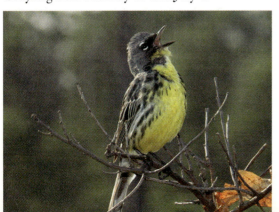

# Pileated Woodpecker
*Dryocopus pileatus*

Our largest woodpecker, at 17 inches, the pileated is about the size as a crow. The body is all black with a black-and-white striped neck. The underwings are white, and the upsides of the wings have a small white patch. The males have a red crest, pointed at the rear, and a red whisker mark. Females have crests that are red toward the rear and dark at the front, and have a black whisker mark. Pileated woodpeckers, as do all woodpeckers, fly with a bounding flight and perch vertically on tree trunks where they hammer at the bark hunting for insect prey.

The pileated woodpecker is an uncommon to fairly common permanent resident in Michigan, inhabiting mature forested areas that have larger trees. It is scarce in much of the southern Lower Peninsula, but as suburban areas are becoming reforested this species is reclaiming portions of its former range.

Any large forested area throughout the state will hold at least one breeding pair of this magnificent woodpecker. Despite their size, they can be difficult to locate as they range quite widely, and often feed rather quietly. Large, rectangular excavations in tree trunks are evidence of the presence of these birds. Sometimes they can be located by their loud, somewhat maniacal calls, sounding something like a northern flicker on steroids.

# Piping Plover
*Charadrius melodus*

This small shorebird, about 7 inches in length, is often described as the color of dry sand above and white below. Adults have a narrow black band running around the breast and back of the neck, a white forehead, a small black band across the crown, dark eyes, a short orange bill with a black tip, and yellowish-orange legs. In flight, they show a white rump, a white tail with a broad black tip, and black flight feathers with a prominent white band. Juveniles lack the black breast and crown bands, and have all-black bills.

The piping plover, a species listed as threatened on federal lists, is a rare summer resident in Michigan. Nest sites and numbers vary from year to year, but are currently at about forty to fifty pairs statewide. Piping plovers arrive on their breeding beaches in late April or early May, breed during the summer months, and depart the state for their wintering grounds in August and September.

In the Great Lakes, piping plovers nest on undisturbed sandy beaches, of which precious few remain. They are most easily found during the breeding season where such beaches have been preserved and are protected from human disturbance. Sites where they have nested include Sleeping Bear Dunes National Lakeshore, Wilderness State Park, near Munising, and near Whitefish Point. Nesting sites are closely monitored, and will usually be posted as closed to entry. These signs should be obeyed, as they protect the bird's from being disturbed, and their nests from being trampled. At most sites, the birds can be viewed from outside the closed areas.

# Prairie Warbler
*Dendroica discolor*

This small warbler, slightly less than 5 inches in length, is largely olive-yellow on the upperparts with a bright-yellow eyebrow and yellow crescent below the eye, and black markings through the eye and below the yellow eye crescent. The back shows reddish streaks with exceptionally close views, while the tail shows large white tail spots. The underparts are bright yellow, whitish under the tail, and with prominent black streaks on the sides. The song is a rapid, slightly buzzy, rising series of whistles, "zoo zoo zoo zee zee zee ziii zii."

The prairie warbler is widely distributed throughout the eastern United States, but is at the northern limit of its occurrence in Michigan, where it is a rare migrant and summer resident, arriving in May and departing by early September. Listed as threatened in Michigan, there are probably fewer than 200 breeding pairs statewide. Despite its name, the prairie warbler does not breed in prairie anywhere in its range. In the southeastern United States, where it is perhaps most common, it nests in coastal scrub and even in mangroves. Elsewhere, it nests in open or semi-open shrubby habitats. In Michigan, the species nests almost exclusively in pine woodlands covering sand dunes with a shrubby understory.

The largest breeding population is at Sleeping Bear Dunes National Lakeshore, with birds also breeding at Nordhouse Dunes, Oval Beach near Saugatuck, Grand Mere State Park, and Warren Dunes State Park. Prairie warblers have occasionally been found at the Allegan State Game Area and the Island Lake State Recreation Area.

## Sandhill Crane
*Grus canadensis*

This tall, stately bird, standing nearly 5 feet tall, has long legs, all-gray plumage with a red patch on the forecrown, and can be confused with nothing else. The sexes are similar. Sandhill cranes fly with their long necks and legs extended and flap with a distinctive upward flick of the wings. Their loud, bugling calls are among the most stirring sounds of Michigan's wetlands in summer and during fall migration.

The sandhill crane is a fairly common summer resident and a locally common migrant. They breed nearly throughout the state, but with two main population centers: one in the central southern Lower Peninsula between Jackson and Battle Creek, and the other in the eastern Upper Peninsula in the Rudyard area. The birds arrive in February or March, and depart in late November or early December. In recent years, a few individuals have overwintered in the southern part of the state.

During fall migration, sandhill cranes stage in wetlands, sometimes in large numbers. Two of the best places to see this spectacle are the Phyllis Haehnle Sanctuary northeast of Jackson, and the Bernard W. Baker Sanctuary northeast of Battle Creek. From mid-October through November, counts of several thousand birds are typical at these locations. Watching them come flying in to roost in the late afternoon in increasingly larger groups is a stirring sight, not soon forgotten.

## Spruce Grouse
*Falcipennis canadensis*

The spruce grouse, at about 16 inches in length, is similar in size to the more familiar ruffed grouse, but is a bit chunkier. Males are brown with a black neck and throat, white spots on the belly, white markings on the throat, and a bright red wattle over the eye that enlarges during the mating display.

The spruce grouse is an uncommon to rare permanent resident, found primarily in boreal forest. Boreal forest is patchy in Michigan, and is most prevalent in the Upper Peninsula.

They are surprisingly quiet and difficult to see for such large birds, spending most of their time on the ground. They rarely flush unless almost stepped upon. Walking slowly and quietly through suitable habitat until one is seen is usually the best strategy; once found the bird will often reward the bird watcher by staying put, or even walking out into the open, seeming to ignore the observer. In April, spruce grouse are at their peak of courtship activity, and at that time are perhaps easier to find, though they can be chanced upon throughout the year. Some have said that wearing red laces in your shoes might actually attract a male spruce grouse; apparently the hormonally charged males will investigate any bright red object, presumably mistaking the laces for the enlarged red wattle above the eye of a rival male! The Vermillion Road near Whitefish Point has traditionally been a reliable spot for finding spruce grouse. Other areas of boreal forest that could be productive include the Yellow Dog Plains near Marquette, the boreal forest near Trout Lake, and the Kingston Plains in the western Upper Peninsula.

# Michigan's Ten Best Bird-Watching Spots

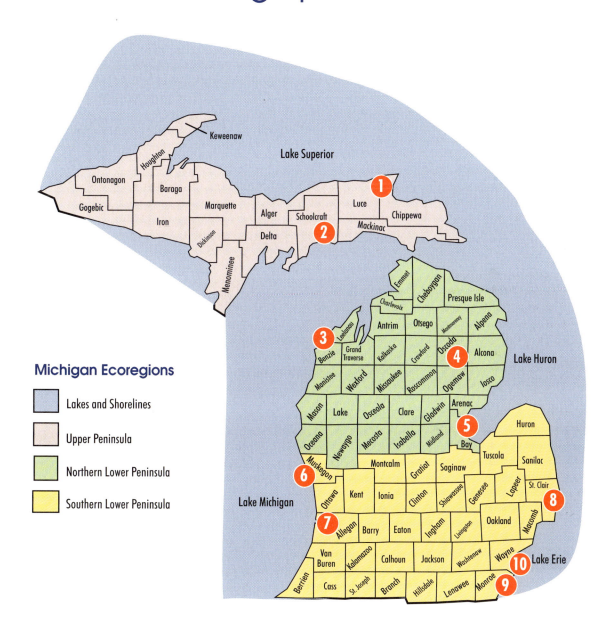

**Michigan Ecoregions**
- Lakes and Shorelines
- Upper Peninsula
- Northern Lower Peninsula
- Southern Lower Peninsula

## Key Code

1. Whitefish Point Bird Observatory
2. Seney National Wildlife Refuge
3. Sleeping Bear Dunes National Lakeshore
4. Huron-Manistee National Forest
5. Nayanquing Point State Wildlife Area
6. Muskegon County Wastewater Treatment System
7. Allegan State Game Area
8. Port Huron State Game Area
9. Pte. Mouillee State Game Area
10. Lake Erie Metropark

## Allegan State Game Area

Allegan Field Office
4590 118th Avenue, Route 3
Allegan, MI 49010
(269) 673-2430
www.michigan.gov/DNR

Covering more than 50,000 acres of deciduous woodland, farmland, marshes, swamp, and riparian woodland along the Kalamazoo River, the Allegan State Game Area provides a great diversity of birding opportunities. Numbers of waterfowl, including Canada geese and snow geese, use the open fields from fall through spring. In winter, raptors use the area, including bald and (occasionally) golden eagles, northern harrier, and red-tailed and rough-legged hawks. At these times birding is done mainly from the roads, though there are a number of hiking trails that permit access to the woodlands. Some areas are posted as closed to protect wildlife, and these signs should be strictly obeyed. In summer, an interesting diversity of breeding species can be found. Of particular note is the Kalamazoo River, which can be birded by canoe. Perhaps the state's healthiest population of prothonotary warbler is found along the river, in addition to good numbers of yellow-billed cuckoo, Acadian flycatcher, red-eyed vireo, blue-gray gnatcatcher, cerulean warbler, American redstart, and many others.

## Huron-Manistee National Forest

U.S. Forest Service   U.S. Fish & Wildlife Service
Mio Ranger District   East Lansing Field Office
401 North Court Street   2651 Coolidge Road
Mio, MI 48647-9314   East Lansing, MI 48823
(989) 826-3252   (517) 351-2555
www.fs.fed.us/r9/hmnf/kw   www.midwest.fws.gov/EastLansing/tour.html

The Kirtland's warbler breeds mainly in a few counties in north-central Michigan, primarily in the Huron-Manistee National Forest. The easiest way to see a Kirtland's warbler is to go on a tour. The U.S. Forest Service runs tours (for a nominal fee) out of Mio, and the U.S. Fish & Wildlife Service runs tours out of Grayling. In addition to being taken to an area where up-close sightings are virtually guaranteed, both tours provide interesting introductory programs on the natural history and conservation of this most unique of Michigan's birds. Other species likely to be seen on these tours include upland sandpiper, black-billed cuckoo, eastern bluebird, brown thrasher, Nashville and black-and-white warblers, clay-colored, field, vesper, and Lincoln's sparrows, and Brewer's blackbird. Finding a Kirtland's warbler on your own is possible by driving the numerous forest service roads in the area. Do not enter any areas posted as being closed and stay on the road. Do not play tapes of the bird's song or let pets wander into the breeding area. Do not disturb these endangered birds in any way.

## Lake Erie Metropark

32481 West Jefferson
P.O. Box 120
Brownstown, MI 48173
(734) 379-5020
www.metroparks.com/parks/pk_lake_erie.php

Lake Erie Metropark is one of the premier fall hawk-watching sites in all of North America. Each fall, more than 100,000 broad-winged hawks (occasionally 500,000-plus) pass over the park as they cross the Detroit River from Ontario, Canada, to the east. An additional fifteen raptor species are counted here annually, including more than 25,000 turkey vultures, several hundred northern harriers, several thousand sharp-shinned and red-tailed hawks, and more than one thousand American kestrels. Smaller numbers of other species, ranging from tens to hundreds, are tallied for osprey, bald eagle, Cooper's, red-shouldered, and rough-legged hawks, merlin, and peregrine falcon. This is perhaps the best site in eastern North America to see golden eagles in late October through November, when more than hundred are counted annually. Swainson's hawk, a rarity anywhere in the East, is recorded here annually in small numbers (fewer than twelve) each fall. The best weather conditions for hawk migrations are on days when north or northwest winds follow a cold front. The main site for watching this spectacle is the boat launch, though if winds are strong out of the north the count site is moved about two miles south to the headquarters of Pte. Mouillee State Game Area. Additional details about the hawk migration can be found at the Website of Southeastern Michigan Raptor Research (**www.smrr.net**). Other attractions here include migrant songbirds in the woodlands and along trails behind the Marshlands Museum, and migrant and wintering waterfowl; twenty-four species of waterfowl are typically reported annually. More than 20,000 canvasbacks have been found in late fall, and more than one thousand tundra swans have overwintered on Lake Erie offshore from the park in recent years.

## ⑥

## Muskegon County Wastewater Treatment System

8301 White Road
Muskegon, MI 49442
(231) 724-3440
www.co.muskegon.mi.us/wwtf.htm

Wastewater treatment facilities, sometimes called sewage ponds, may seem to be an unusual bird-watching destination. But waterbirds, including ducks, shorebirds, herons, and gulls are often found here in considerable numbers. It may be fair to say that if you haven't visited a sewage pond, you haven't been birding! The Muskegon Wastewater System is Michigan's largest, and is perhaps one of the largest in the United States, with 11,000 acres of settling ponds, surrounded by open fields. In migration, large numbers of waterfowl, especially northern shovelers and ruddy ducks, can be found in the ponds. The muddy edges along the diked roads running between ponds attract migrant shorebirds. Rarities are found annually. In summer, this area has been the most reliable spot for finding eared grebes, rare in the state, and in late fall and winter the diked roads have attracted snowy owls and snow buntings, and, rarely, a gyrfalcon. The adjacent fields are a good place to look for rough-legged hawk, American golden-plover, black-bellied plover, horned larks, American pipits, Lapland longspurs, and snow buntings. During some years a golden eagle may join one or two bald eagles, which feed on the abundant waterfowl. A permit, available at the administration building Monday through Friday, is necessary to drive on the diked roads here. Permits can be obtained in advance by telephoning.

##

## Nayanquing Point State Wildlife Area

Nayanquing Point Field Office
1570 Tower Beach Road
Pinconning, MI 48650
(989) 697-5101
www.michigan.gov/DNR

More than 1,400 acres of wetlands and flooded cropland along the shoreline of Saginaw Bay on Lake Huron is encompassed within the Nayanquing Point State Wildlife Area. Interesting marsh-nesting species can be found here including least bitterns, American bitterns, black-crowned night-herons, sora and Virginia rails, common moorhen, and Caspian and Forster's terns. Michigan's most reliable breeding colony of yellow-headed blackbirds, a species typically found farther west, can be found here in spring and summer. A pair of bald eagles has nested in the area. Songbirds that can be found nesting in the marshes and adjacent areas include marsh and sedge wrens, yellow warbler, common yellowthroat, and song and swamp sparrows. With the varying lake levels, emergent marsh vegetation, and mudflats, migrant shorebirds and waterfowl can often be found from spring through fall. The area has also attracted its fair share of rarities.

### ⑧

## Port Huron State Game Area
Port Huron Field Office
6181 Lapeer Road
Kimball, MI 48074
(810) 664-8355
**www.michigan.gov/DNR**

After the migrant warblers have passed through southeastern Michigan, many local birders head to the Port Huron State Game Area in early June. The reason is the interesting mix of breeding warblers, with both northern and southern affinities, that include sixteen regularly occurring and nine less-than-annually occurring species. Blue-winged, yellow, and chestnut-sided warblers, American redstart, ovenbird, and common yellowthroat are common and widespread. Golden-winged, magnolia, cerulean, Blackburnian, black-throated green, pine, and black-and-white warblers, northern waterthrush, and mourning and hooded warblers are more locally distributed. Less-than-annual warblers include northern parula (2002), Nashville, yellow-rumped, yellow-throated (nested in 1982), worm-eating (2002), Louisiana waterthrush, Kentucky, Canada, and yellow-breasted chat (formerly regular and local). Four species of vireos and four *Empidonax* flycatchers are regularly seen in summer, and this is also a regular area for both black-billed and yellow-billed cuckoos. Recently, sandhill cranes have summered, along with the more regular sora and Virginia rails.

### ⑨

## Pte. Mouillee State Game Area
Pte. Mouillee Field Office
37205 Mouillee Road, Route 2
Rockwood, MI 48173
(734) 379-9692
**www.michigan.gov/DNR**

This is one of the top bird-watching sites in Michigan, consisting of more than six square miles of marsh and diked ponds managed for breeding waterfowl. Abundant waterfowl and shorebird migrations are the main attraction here, and rarities are found annually. The area's attraction to shorebirds varies from year to year, as water levels are dependent on those of adjacent Lake Erie. Large stands of cattail marsh provide breeding habitat for American and least bitterns, sora and Virginia rails, American coot, common moorhen, marsh wren, common yellowthroat, and swamp sparrow. Great blue herons and great egrets breed on islands in the area, and black-crowned night-herons and green herons are seen regularly. The extensive wetlands provide habitat for a number of waterfowl to linger into summer, some of which breed here far from their normal ranges farther north. Northern shoveler, redhead, greater scaup, lesser scaup, common goldeneye, and ruddy duck can be found in summer in most years. The area is closed to all entry, except for waterfowl hunting, from September through November.

### ②

## Seney National Wildlife Refuge
HCR #2, Box 1
Seney, MI 49883
(906) 586-9851
**http://midwest.fws.gov/Seney/VisInfo.htm**

With approximately 5,000 acres of bogs, marshes, swamps, grasslands, and forest, the Seney National Wildlife Refuge provides excellent bird watching opportunities from spring through fall. Breeding Le Conte's sparrows (rare) and yellow rails (listed as threatened on state lists) can be found in the area's sedge marshes. This is the primary site where trumpeter swans were introduced into Michigan, and the state's largest breeding population is found here. Boreal habitats are home to black-backed woodpeckers, gray jays, and boreal chickadees, and recently the state's first confirmed nesting great gray owl was found. In the grassland areas sharp-tailed grouse can be found in early May. The main vehicle access is from the seven-mile Marshland Drive, where many migrant and breeding waterbirds can be seen, including common loons, American bitterns, and sandhill cranes. The 1.4 mile Pine Ridge Nature Trail passes through wetland and forested habitats where a variety of breeding warblers, vireos, thrushes, and sparrows may be found. Evening tours are operated to see the elusive yellow rail in May.

## ❸

## Sleeping Bear Dunes National Lakeshore

9922 Front Street
Empire, MI 49630
(231) 326-5134
www.nps.gov/slbe

Part of the National Park system since 1970, Sleeping Bear Dunes protects 35 miles of Lake Michigan shoreline and both North Manitou and South Manitou Islands, including more than 70,000 acres of dunes, forests, and rare beach vegetation. Sleeping Bear Dunes National Lakeshore is home to Michigan's largest breeding population of prairie warbler (considered endangered in the state) and accessible nesting pairs of piping plover (listed as an endangered species by the federal government). The warblers nest in low vegetation among the large white pines in the dune areas, especially near Good Harbor Bay. The plovers nest along the protected, uninhabited beaches (a scarce commodity in this well-populated state), particularly near the mouth of the Platte River. Other areas of mixed deciduous and coniferous woodlands are breeding areas for warblers, tanagers, and flycatchers, and in migration nearly any patch of vegetation can support migrants refueling to continue their migrations northward or southward. Bald eagles and common loons also nest in some areas of the park.

## ❶

## Whitefish Point Bird Observatory

16914 North Whitefish Point Road
Paradise, MI 49768
(906) 492-3596
www.wpbo.org

Located in Michigan's eastern Upper Peninsula, the Whitefish Point area is famous throughout the Upper Midwest for its impressive waterbird migrations, as well as its proven attraction as a vagrant trap. In spring and fall, significant flights of loons, grebes, and ducks including scoters and long-tailed ducks, can be observed from the beach at the tip of the point near the waterbird shack. Especially in fall, there may be no better place in the state for seeing migrant jaegers. In spring, hawks migrate along the point with a highlight in April being the numbers of rough-legged hawks. Owls also use this area during migration, and Whitefish Point is one of the better sites in the state for migrating northern saw-whet and long-eared owls, and for rare irruptives including boreal, great gray, and northern hawk owls. Numerous songbirds also migrate along the point, and the bird checklist for the area exceeds 300 species. Nearby patches of boreal forest hold other resident species of interest, including spruce grouse, black-backed woodpecker, gray jay, and boreal chickadee. In many winters pine grosbeaks, red and white-winged crossbills, common redpolls, pine siskins, and evening grosbeaks can be found in the area.

# Resources for Michigan Bird Watchers

## National and State Parks, Forests, Lakeshores, and Wildlife Refuges

**Hiawatha National Forest**
2727 North Lincoln Road
Escanaba, MI 49829
(906) 786-4062
www.fs.fed.us/r9/forests/hiawatha

**Huron-Manistee National Forests**
1755 South Mitchell Street
Cadillac, MI 49601
(800) 821-6263
www.fs.fed.us/r9/hmnf

**Michigan Department of Natural Resources**
Mason Building, Third Floor, P.O. Box 30257
Lansing, MI 48909
(517) 373-9900
www.michigan.gov/DNR

**Ottawa National Forest**
E6248 US-2
Ironwood, MI 49938
(906) 932-1330
www.fs.fed.us/r9/ottawa

## Hotlines and Chat Groups

**BBCList**
To subscribe, email: listserv@ andrews.edu with a blank subject line, and in the body of the message note "subscribe bbclist".

**Birders**
www-personal.umich.edu/~bbowman/birds/birders_FAQ.html

**Birding Sites in Southeastern Michigan**
www.umich.edu/~bbowman/birds/locations.html

**Detroit Rare Bird Alert**
(248) 473-0484. Reports are posted to Mich-Listers and to BIRDCNTR.

**Kirtland's Warbler Information**
www.'fs.fed.us/r9/hmnf/pages/kirtland.htm

**Michigan Statewide Rare Bird Alert**
(269) 471-4919

**Mich-Listers**
www.jlesser.com/mich-listers.htm
An Internet forum for reporting accidental, casual, and rare species throughout the state.

**Northern Michigan Birding**
www.northbirding.com

**Rouge River Bird Observatory**
www.umd.umich.edu/dept/rouge_river

**Saginaw Bay Birding**
www.saginawbaybirding.com

**Southeastern Michigan Raptor Research**
www.smrr.net

**Whitefish Point Bird Observatory**
www.wpbo.org

## Conservation Organizations

**Detroit Audubon Society**
1320 North Campbell Road
Royal Oak, MI 48067
(248) 545-2929
www.detroitaudubon.org

**Michigan Audubon Society**
6011 West St. Joseph Highway, Suite 403
P.O. Box 80527
Lansing, MI 48908-0527
(517) 886-9144
www.michiganaudubon.org

**Michigan Nature Association**
326 East Grand River Avenue
Williamston, MI 48895
(517) 655-5655
www.michigannature.org

**The Nature Conservancy of Michigan**
101 East Grand River Avenue
Lansing, MI 48906
(517) 316-0300
www.nature.org/wherewework/northamerica/states/michigan

## Publications

*Michigan Birds and Natural History* is Michigan's ornithological journal of record. Contact the Michigan Audubon Society.

Brewer, R., G. McPeek, and R. Adams, eds. *The Atlas of Breeding Birds of Michigan*. 1991. East Lansing, MI: Michigan State University Press.

McPeek, G., and R. Adams, eds. *The Birds of Michigan*. 1994. Bloomington, IN: Indiana University Press.

Chartier, A., and G. Ziarno, eds. *A Birder's Guide to Michigan*. 2004. Colorado Springs, CO: American Birding Association.

# Getting Started in Bird Watching

Bird watching, or birding, is one of North America's fastest-growing and most popular hobbies. According to a recent survey by the U.S. Fish & Wildlife Service, there are as many as 44 million bird watchers in the United States. Back in 1978, when my family began publishing Bird Watcher's Digest in our living room, bird watching was still considered a bit odd. The image many people associated with bird watching was Miss Jane Hathaway of The Beverly Hillbillies. Fortunately, that stereotype is long gone now, and our culture has come to embrace bird watching as an enriching, exciting pursuit—one that can be done with little expense and enjoyed almost anywhere at any time.

## Why Do We Watch Birds?

Birds have inspired humans for thousands of years. Birds can fly—something we humans have mastered only in the past 100 years. Birds have brilliant plumage, and some even change their colors seasonally. Birds are master musicians, singing beautiful and complex songs. They possess impressive physical abilities—hovering, flying at high speeds, and withstanding extreme weather conditions, as well as the rigors of long migration flights. Birds also have behaviors to which we can relate, such as intense courtship displays, devotion to their mates, and the enormous investment of effort spent in raising their young. Sound familiar? In short, birds are a vivid expression of life, and we admire them because they inspire us. This makes us want to know them better and to bring them closer to us. We accomplish this by attracting them to our backyards and gardens, and by using optics to see them more clearly in an "up close and personal" way.

## Early Bird Study

Before the advent of modern optics that help us view birds more closely, humans used a shotgun approach to bird watching. Literally. Famed ornithologist and bird artist John James Audubon was the first European to document many of the North American bird species in the early 1800s. He did so by shooting every unfamiliar bird he encountered. Having a bird in the hand allowed him to study it closely and draw it accurately. This was an excellent method of learning a lot about birds quickly, but it was rather hard on the birds. This method of bird study continued largely unchecked until the

*Millions of Americans enjoy bird watching.*

early 1900s, when the effects of market hunting on birds became unhappily apparent. In 1934, a young bird enthusiast and artist named Roger Tory Peterson published *A Field Guide to the Birds*, with a system of arrows showing key field marks on the plumage of each species. This enabled a person to identify a bird from a distance, with or without the aid of magnifying optics. Modern bird watching was born, and it was no longer necessary to shoot birds in order to positively identify them. The era of shotgun ornithology was over.

## Modern Bird Watching

Bird watching today is about seeing or hearing birds and then using these clues to identify them. To reach this identification, we use two important tools of the bird-watching trade: binoculars and a field guide. The binoculars (or perhaps a *spotting scope*, which is a telescope especially designed for nature watching) help you to get a closer, clearer look at the bird. The field guide helps you interpret what you see so that you can identify the bird species.

I like to say that we live in the golden era of bird watching. When I started birding more than 35 years ago, feeders, seed, birdhouses, and other supplies were hard to come by—we had to make our own. Now they are available in almost any store. We can buy a field guide or a book like the one you're holding in any bookstore. We can try out optics at camera stores, outdoor suppliers, and at birding festivals. We can learn about birds in special bird courses, on the Internet, in magazines, or from CD-ROMs, DVDs, and videos. We can join a local or state bird club and meet new bird-watching friends. We can take birding tours to far-off places.

*Select binoculars that feel good in your hands and are easy to use.*

There's never been a better time to become a bird watcher. So let's get started!

## Basic Gear

If you're just starting out as a birder, you may need to acquire the basic tools—binoculars and a field guide.

### Binoculars

You may be able to borrow optics from a friend or family member, but if your interest takes off, you'll certainly want to have your own binoculars to use anytime you wish. Fortunately, a decent pair of binoculars can be purchased for less than $100, and some really nice binoculars can be found used on the Internet or through a local bird club for just a bit more. The magnification powers that are commonly used for bird watching are 7x, 8x, and 10x. This is always the first number listed in the binoculars' description, as in 8x40. The second number refers to the size of the objective lens (the big end) of the binocular. The bigger the second number, the brighter the view presented to your eye. In general, for bird-watching binoculars the first number should be between 7x and 10x, and the second number should be between 30 and 45.

Try to find binoculars that are easy and comfortable to use. Make sure they focus easily, giving you a clear image, and that they are comfortable to hold (not too large or heavy) and fit your eye spacing. Every set of eyes is different, so don't settle for binoculars that just don't feel right. The perfect pair of binoculars for you should feel like a natural extension of your hands and eyes. Over time you will become adept at using your optics and, with a little practice, you'll be operating them like a pro.

### Field Guide

When choosing a field guide, you'll need to decide what type of birding you'll be doing and where you plan to do it. If nearly all of your bird watching will be done at home, you might want to get a basic field guide to the backyard birds of your region, or at least a field guide that limits its scope to your half of the continent. Many field guides are offered in eastern (east of the Rocky Mountains) and western (from the

*A field guide is one of birding's essential tools.*

Rockies west) versions. These geographically limited formats include only those birds that are commonly found in that part of the continent, rather than continent-wide guides that include more than 800 North American bird species. Choose a field guide that is appropriate for you, and you'll save a lot of searching time—time that can be better spent looking at birds!

## It Starts at Home

Most bird watchers like to start out at home, and this usually means getting to know the birds in your backyard. A great way to enhance the diversity of birds in your yard is to set up a simple feeding station. Even a single feeder with the proper food can bring half a dozen or more unfamiliar bird species into your yard. And it's these encounters with new and interesting birds that make bird watching so enjoyable.

Start your feeding station with a feeder geared to the birds that are already in your backyard or garden. For most of us this will mean a tube or hopper feeder filled with sunflower seeds. Place the feeder in a location that offers you a clear view of bird activity, but also offers the birds some nearby cover in the form of a hedge, shrubs, or brush pile into which the birds can fly when a predator approaches. I always set our feeding stations up opposite our kitchen or living room windows because these are the rooms in which we spend most of our daylight hours, and because these rooms have the best windows for bird watching. We'll discuss bird feeding and attracting in greater detail in the next section.

Once you've got a basic feeder set up outside, you'll need to get yourself set up inside your house. You've probably already selected the best location for viewing your feeder. Next you should select a safe place to store your binoculars and field guide—somewhere that is easily accessible to you when you suddenly spot a new bird in your backyard. At our house we keep binoculars hanging on pegs right next to our kitchen windows. This keeps them handy for use in checking the feeders or for heading out for a walk around our farm.

## Keeping Your Bird List

Most bird watchers enjoy keeping a list of their sightings. This can take the form of a written list, notations inside your field guide next to each species' account, or in a special journal meant for just such a purpose. There are even software programs available to help you keep your list on your computer. In birding, the most common list is the *life list*. A life list is a list of all the birds you've seen at least once in your life. Let's say you noticed a bright, black-and-orange bird in your backyard willow tree one morning, then keyed it out in your field guide to be a male Baltimore oriole. This is a species you'd never seen before, and now you can put it on your life list. List keeping can be done at any level of involvement, so keep the list or lists that you enjoy. I like to keep a property list of all the species we've seen at least once on our 80-acre farm. Currently, that list is at 181 species, but I'm always watching for something new to show up. I also update my North American life list a couple of times a year, after I've seen a new bird species.

## Bird Watching Afield

Sooner or later you may want to expand your bird-watching horizons beyond your backyard bird feeders. Birding afield—away from your own home—can be a wonderfully exhilarating experience. Many beginning bird watchers are shy about venturing forth, afraid that their inexperience will prove embarrassing, but there's really no reason to feel this way. The best way to begin

# Ten Tips for Beginning Bird Watchers

1. Get a decent pair of binoculars, ones that are easy for you to use and hold steady.
2. Find a field guide to the birds of your region (many guides are divided into eastern and western editions). Guides that cover all the birds of North America contain many birds species uncommon or entirely absent from your area. You can always upgrade to a continent-wide guide later.
3. Set up a basic feeding station in your yard or garden.
4. Start with your backyard birds. They are the easiest to see, and you can become familiar with them fairly quickly.
5. Practice your identification skills. Starting with a common bird species, note the most obvious visual features of the bird (color, size, shape, and patterns in the plumage). These features are known as field marks and will be helpful clues to the bird's identity.
6. Notice the bird's behavior. Many birds can be identified by their behavior—woodpeckers peck on wood, kingfishers dive for small fish, and swallows are known for their graceful flight.
7. Listen to the bird's sounds. Bird song is a vital component to birding. Learning bird songs and sounds takes a bit of practice, but many birds make it pretty easy for us. For example, chickadees and whip-poor-wills (among others) call out their names. The Resources section of this book contains a listing of tools to help you to learn bird songs.
8. Look at the bird, not at the book. When you see an unfamiliar bird, avoid the temptation to put down your binoculars and begin searching for the bird in your field guide. Instead, watch the bird carefully for as long as it is present—or until you feel certain that you have noted its most important field marks. Then look at your field guide. Birds have wings, and they tend to use them. Your field guide will still be with you long after the bird has gone, so take advantage of every moment to watch an unfamiliar bird while it is present.
9. Take notes. No one can be expected to remember every field mark and description of a bird. But you can help your memory and accelerate your learning by taking notes on the birds you see. These notes can be written in a small pocket notebook, in the margins of your field guide, or even in the back of this book.
10. Venture beyond the backyard and find other bird watchers in your area. The bird watching you'll experience beyond your backyard will be enriching, especially if it leads not only to new birds, but also to new birding friends. Ask a local nature center or wildlife refuge about bird clubs in your region. Your state ornithological organization or natural resources division may also be helpful. Bird watching with other birders can be the most enjoyable of all.

birding away from the backyard is to connect with other local bird watchers via your local bird club. Most parts of North America have local or regional bird clubs, and most of these clubs offer regular field trips. Bird watchers are among the friendliest people on the planet, and every bird club is happy to welcome new prospective members. If you don't know how to find a local bird club, ask your friends and neighbors if they know any bird watchers, check the telephone directory, search the Internet, or ask at your area parks, nature centers, and wild bird stores.

Getting out in the field with more experienced bird watchers is the fastest way to improve your skills. Don't be afraid to ask questions ("How did you know that was an indigo bunting?"). Don't worry if you begin to feel overwhelmed by the volume of new information—all new bird watchers experience this. When it happens, relax and take some time to simply watch. In time you'll be identifying birds and looking forward to new challenges and new birds.

# Feeding and Housing

**B**irds need four basic things to live: food, water for drinking and bathing, a safe place to roost, and a safe place to nest. These vital elements are actually quite easy for you to offer to birds, even if your backyard is small.

## Food

Bird feeding is a good place to start your bird-attracting efforts. It's wise to begin with a single feeder, such as a hopper feeder or tube feeder filled with black-oil sunflower seeds. The black-oil sunflower seed is the most common type of sunflower seed available, because it's the seed type that most of our feeder birds can readily eat. Think of it as the hamburger of the bird world. The black-oil sunflower seed has a thin shell (easy for seed-eating birds to crack) and a large, meaty seed kernel inside. As you can see from the seed preference chart on page 147, many backyard bird species eat sunflower seeds.

Other excellent foods for birds include: mixed seed (a blend that normally includes millet, milo, cracked corn, and other seeds), sunflower bits (shells removed), peanuts (best offered unsalted and without the shell), suet or suet cakes, cracked corn, thistle seed (also known as Niger or nyjer seed), safflower seed, nectar (for hummingbirds), mealworms, fruits, and berries. Bird feeding varies from region to region—don't be afraid to experiment with new feeders or food. Birds will vote with their bills and stomachs and will let you know their preferences

Eating the food at feeders is not the only way birds find sustenance. A backyard or garden that includes natural food sources for birds—such as seed-producing flowering plants and fruit-bearing trees and shrubs—will further enhance its attractiveness to birds. In fact, it's often the natural features of a backyard habitat that attract the birds' attention rather than the bird feeders. Read the Bird-Friendly Plants section on page 162 for more specific suggestions.

## Feeder Types

It's important to match the foods and feeders to each other, as well as to the birds you wish to attract. Sunflower seed works in a wide variety of feeders, including tube, hopper, platform, and satellite or excluder feeders (that permit small birds to feed, but exclude larger birds), as well as for ground feeding. Mixed seed does not work as well in tube or hopper feeders for a couple of reasons. First of all, the birds that prefer mixed seed tend to be ground feeders, so it's less natural for them to go to an elevated feeder for food. Secondly, elevated feeder designs (such as tubes or hoppers) are built to dole out seed as it is eaten and the smaller size of most mixed seed kernels causes excess spillage. Mixed seed works best when offered on a platform feeder or when scattered on the ground.

*Pictured from the top down: Black-oil sunflower seed, peanuts, mixed seed, and cracked corn.*

*A fruit feeder will attract orioles, tanagers, and other fruit feeders.*

When purchasing your feeders and foods, make sure they will work effectively with each other. Specialty foods such as suet, peanuts, thistle (Niger), mealworms, fruit, and nectar require specific feeders for the best results for you and the birds. The Food and Feeder Chart on page 147 is a great place to start.

## Your Feeding Station

Place your feeding station in a spot that is useful and attractive to you and the birds. When we moved into our farmhouse, we looked out all the windows before choosing a spot for our feeding station. You may want to do the same thing. After all, the whole point of bird feeding is to be able to see and enjoy the birds. From the birds' perspective, your feeders should be placed adjacent to cover—a place they can leave from and retreat to safely and quickly if a predator appears. This cover can be a woodland edge, brushy area or brush pile, hedges or shrubs, or even a weedy fencerow. If your yard is mostly lawn, consider creating a small island of cover near your feeding station. This will greatly enhance the feeders' appeal to birds.

Be patient. You've spent the money and effort to put up feeders, but don't expect immediate dividends. Birds are creatures of habit, and it may take a few days or even a few weeks before they recognize your offering as a source of food. Sooner or later, a curious chickadee, finch, or sparrow will key into the food source, and the word will spread along the local bird "grapevine."

## Housing for Birds

Almost every bird species builds or uses some type of nest to produce and rear its young. However, only a small fraction of our birds use nest boxes provided by humans. Birds that use next boxes or birdhouses are called *cavity nesters*, because they prefer to nest inside an enclosed space, such as hole excavated in a tree, as many woodpeckers do. Nest boxes simulate a natural cavity, but they have the added advantage (for humans) of our being able to place them in a convenient spot. To the birds' advantage, we can protect the nest box from predators, bad weather, and other problems.

Being a landlord to the birds is a thrilling experience. You are treated to an intimate peek inside the lives of your "tenants" and rewarded with the presence of their offspring, if nesting is successful. To help ensure the nesting success of your birds you need to provide the proper housing in an appropriate setting, and you should monitor the housing during the nesting season.

## The Right Housing

Two factors are key to providing the right nest box for your birds: the size of the housing and

*Male northern cardinals eat sunflower seed from a hopper-style feeder.*

*Exterior latex stain helps prolong the life of a birdhouse and protects the birds inside from the weather.*

the size of the entry hole. Not all cavity nesters are picky about the interior dimensions of the cavity, except when it is excessively big or small. But the size of the entry hole is important because it can effectively limit the entrance of large, aggressive nest competitors, predators, and inclement weather. For example, an entry hole with a diameter of $1^{1}/_{2}$ inches on a bluebird nest box will permit entry by bluebirds and many smaller birds, including chickadees, titmice, nuthatches, wrens, and tree swallows. But this same size keeps European starlings out and prevents them from usurping the box.

Use the Nest Box Chart (page 148) to help you determine the appropriate nest box details for your backyard birds. Whether you build your own birdhouses or buy them at your local wild bird products supplier, see page 40 for a few tips for "landlords" that you will want to consider.

## An Appropriate Setting

Place your nest boxes where they will be most likely to be found and used by birds. Bluebirds and swallows prefer nest sites in the middle of large, open, grassy areas. Wrens, chickadees, nuthatches, flycatchers, woodpeckers, and other woodland birds prefer sites that are in or adjacent to woodlands. Robins, phoebes, Carolina wrens, barn swallows, and purple martins prefer to nest near human dwellings, perhaps for the protection from predators that we provide.

## Monitoring Your Nest Boxes

By taking a weekly peek inside your nest boxes, you will stay abreast of your tenants' activities, and you'll be able to help them raise their families successfully. During most of the year, your birdhouses will appear to be empty. This does not mean that the boxes are going unused. In fact, many birds use nest boxes during the win-

*An example of a pole-mounted predator baffle below a bluebird nest box.*

## Nest Box Tips for Landlords

- Do build or buy sturdily constructed nest boxes that are built from untreated wood (or another weatherproof material) with walls that are at least 3/4 inch thick. See page 157 for a simple bird house plan.
- Do not stain or paint the interior of the box. Stain or paint on the box exterior will help the box last longer. Light colors reflect sunlight and keep box interiors from getting too hot.
- Perches by the entry hole are unnecessary and may actually encourage competitors and predators.
- The box roof should be slanted and extend out several inches over the entry hole to keep out the weather.
- Nest boxes should have an access door for monitoring. Access doors that swing upward to open on the side or front of the box are easiest to use and safest for birds.
- The box should have holes for ventilation at the top of the vertical walls. Drainage holes in the floor will permit excess moisture to escape.
- Mount boxes on poles away from nearby trees and structures.
- Place a pole-mounted predator baffle beneath the nest box to keep snakes and mammals from gaining access to the nest.

ter months as nighttime roosts. A loose feather, insect parts, berry seeds, or a few droppings are classic evidence of roosting activity.

During breeding season, your regular visits will help you know when nest building begins and when eggs are laid, and will give you an idea about how soon the eggs will hatch and the babies leave the nest. Bird nests are vulnerable to a variety of dangers, including harsh weather and predators such as cats, raccoons, snakes, and even birds, as well as nest-site competitors. These dangers are greatly reduced when nest boxes are monitored because the birds' landlord (you) can take steps to protect the nest.

On my trips to check each of our 10 nest boxes, I keep a small notebook with me to record my observations. Each nest box has its own name and number in my notebook, along with the date of each visit and a note about what I've found. When nesting starts in a box I note the date, what materials are used to construct the nest, and the date that the first egg was laid. Once the clutch is complete and the female begins incubating the eggs, I can estimate the hatching date. This usually takes about 14 days. Another 14 to 21 days later, I know the young birds will be ready to leave the nest.

### Peeking Inside

When checking a nest box, approach quietly. During the breeding season, you may scare the female off the nest temporarily when you open the box. Don't worry. If you keep your visit brief, she'll be back to the nest soon. I visit nest boxes

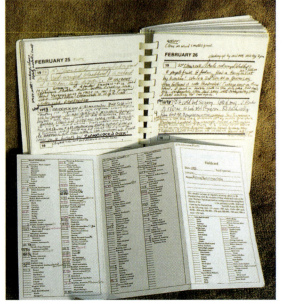

*Top: A daily bird notes diary. Bottom: A checklist for sightings.*

*Checking the nest box.*

in the late morning on sunny days, when the adult birds are likely to be away finding food. I open the box, quickly count the eggs or young, close the box and move away before pausing to record my notes. It's a myth that opening a nest box or checking the young will cause the adults to abandon the nest. In fact, over time many cavity-nesting birds that use nest boxes grow quite accustomed to regular visits.

One final note on nest monitoring. As fledging time approaches for the young birds—normally about two weeks after the eggs hatch—you should curtail your box visits to avoid causing a premature nest departure.

### When Things Go Wrong
You open your nest box, and you find broken or missing eggs and the nest in disarray. What happened? The bad news is: A predator has raided your nest, and, in the natural order of things, the eggs or nestlings have been eaten. The good news: There are steps that you can take to avoid such an event in the future.

It's important to protect your nest boxes so predators cannot easily access them. For many landlords the best option is to mount the housing on galvanized metal poles with pole-mounted predator baffles installed beneath the boxes. An added advantage to pole-mounting (as opposed to mounting on a fencepost or tree) is that the housing can be moved to a new location fairly easily.

Follow the steps outlined on page 148 for nest box placement, mounting, and baffling. You may also wish to consult one of the publications listed in the Resources section for specific strategies for dealing with nest box predators and pests.

### Creating Bird Habitat
To make your backyard or garden a haven for birds, all you need to do is think like a bird. Look around your yard. Where is the food, the water? Where are the places to hide from predators or to shelter in bad weather? Is nesting habitat available?

An ideal bird habitat can be created in a tiny, urban garden just as it can be created in a large, rural setting. Birds love varied habitats; so when you are planning your yard, landscape, or gardens, resist the urge to plant matching plants in straight lines. Instead, let your imagination go wild—literally. Give the edges of beds or gardens natural curves. Scatter trees, shrubs, and vines in clumps or islands around the area you are designing. On the edges of your property, try to create natural transitions from the grass of your yard to the tops of your trees with short- and medium-height plants that provide food and shelter for birds.

### Edible Habitat
Birds have evolved over millions of years right alongside the native plants with which they share the planet. These same native plants can work for you in your bird-friendly habitat plan. Your local nursery, nature center, or native plant society should be able to recommend plant species that are native to your region. Native plants not only provide food in the form of fruits and nuts, but birds may also eat the plants' buds, leaves, nectar, and sap, as well as the insects that live on the plants. When choosing your native plants, select a wide variety of species, sizes, shapes, and seasonality. Planting only one or two plant species will minimize the number of birds your habitat will attract. Consult the Bird-Friendly Plants chart on page 162 for suggested plant families.

## Water

Birds need water all year long for drinking and bathing. The best way to offer water to birds is in a shallow birdbath with about 2 inches of water in it. I've always had good luck attracting birds to water in my yard when the bath was on or near the ground and when the water had some motion to it.

The sight and sound of moving water are highly attractive to birds. You can add motion to any birdbath or water feature with a mister, dripper, or a recirculating pump. Misters and drippers attach to your garden hose and let out a small amount of water that disturbs the surface of the bath; these ripples are eye-catchingly attractive to birds. Recirculating pumps, which require electricity, recycle the water from the main bath through a pump and filter, and then back to the bath. In winter, add a small, electric birdbath heater to keep the water open and available to birds.

If you already have a water garden or water feature, consider making part of it accessible to birds. This can be accomplished by placing a flat rock shelf on or near the water's surface, or by allowing recirculating water to trickle over an exposed flat rock. Our backyard water garden is ringed with American goldfinches almost every day all year-round. They use a large, flat piece of slate that gets splashed by our small waterfall as a place to grab a quick drink.

*A male scarlet tanager bathes in a water feature.*

Water is a universal attractant for birds—species that might otherwise never visit your yard, feeders, or birdhouses will visit a clean and alluring birdbath or water feature.

## Shelter

When they need to rest, hide from danger, or get out of the weather, birds seek deep cover in the form of thick vegetation, vine tangles, dense evergreens, or brushy areas. These bits of habitat may not be first on a landscaper's list of backyard beautifying accents, but to a bird they are vital havens. Even a brush pile in a corner of your property can offer enough shelter during a storm to help sparrows, cardinals, and other backyard birds survive.

Look at your bird habitat, and observe where the birds go just before a storm or at dusk. These are the places in which they shelter themselves. Consider adding more such habitat, and your yard will be even more attractive to birds.

## Places to Nest

The majority of North American birds do not use nest boxes. Most build their nests in places that are hidden from view—in trees, bushes, or in secluded spots on or near the ground. Birds—such as phoebes, barn swallows, and Carolina wrens—are bold enough to build nests on porch ledges, in garages, and in barns. House finches and mourning doves are known for building their nests in hanging flower baskets, but these sites won't satisfy most of our birds.

The places where birds choose to nest are similar to the places they choose to roost and shelter—in thick vegetation and deep cover out of view of passing predators. In providing a nesting habitat for birds, the key is diversity. As you read through the species profiles in this book, notice the habitat features that each species prefers. Then factor this information into your habitat plans.

## Helping Other Nesting Birds

There are many things you can do to help non-cavity nesters—all those birds that build

*Allow lawn edges to grow wild; bird species thrive in transition or edge habitat.*

open-cup nests and will never use one of our nest boxes. The most important thing is to offer variety in your landscaping or backyard habitat. A backyard that is mostly lawn with a tree or two staked out in the middle will not be nearly as appealing as a yard featuring a variety of plant types, including grasses, perennial plants, shrubs, bushes, trees, and other natural elements. The more your landscape looks like nature, the more attractive it will be for birds.

## Places for You

As you plan for your bird-friendly habitat, you'll also want to incorporate elements that you can use and enjoy, such as a water garden, benches, shady relaxation spots, and perhaps a location for your feeding station. Remember, the whole point of attracting birds to your property is so that you can enjoy them while they enjoy your offerings. Plan with your favorite viewing spots in mind, and you'll be rewarded with year-round free (and natural) entertainment.

### Tips for Helping Nesting Birds

- Consider letting a portion of your yard grow up into a weedy patch for sparrows, finches, and towhees to enjoy.
- Offer a basket of nesting material, such as 2- to 3-inch pieces of natural fibers (yarn, pet or human hair, stiff dry grasses, and the like).
- Keep pets, especially cats, from roaming freely in your yard during nesting season.
- Try to limit or eliminate the use of lawn and garden chemicals in and around the parts of your property being used by nesting birds.
- Trim hedges, shrubs, and trees in early spring before nesting season, or in late fall, after nesting season. This way you'll avoid disturbing nesting birds, which are often so secretive that you are unaware of the nest until you stumble onto it.

# How to Use This Book

Hello! *and welcome to the fun, friendly, and exciting word of bird watching. Birding is America's fastest-growing hobby and requires little more than some basic tools—binoculars and a field guide—and an interest in the fascinating world of birds. The primary purpose of this book is to start you down the path to a greater understanding and enjoyment of this engaging pastime. To that end, we've chosen the content carefully to provide you, the reader, with the ideal blend of information and detail on many of the most commonly encountered birds of your state. If we've done our job right, this will* not *be the last bird book you buy.*

At the heart of this book is a set of profiles of your state's 100 most commonly encountered birds. These are the birds that you're most likely to see and hear regularly. *But remember*—birds have wings and they tend to use them, so you'll certainly see and hear many other species as your bird-watching experience grows. For this reason we suggest that you augment this book with a good field guide to help you identify those unfamiliar species you encounter.

Each species profile features a beautiful photograph of the bird, typically an adult male in breeding plumage since this is the most identifiable version of many birds. Please note that adult females, winter-plumage adults, and young birds can look very different. We describe these plumage differences in the profile, but space constraints prevent us from showing images of all these variations. Once again, a good field guide (see the Resources section on page 166 for suggestions) will be useful in identifying any mystery birds you encounter.

We cover all the interesting and useful natural history information about each of the 100 birds—appearance, sounds, behavior, nesting, feeding, range, and migration—and we even tell you where to go and what to do in order to encounter a particular bird in the "Backyard and Beyond" section.

The profiles in the main body of the book are organized *taxonomically*—this means that related species are grouped by bird family using the same general order that ornithologists use to list and classify birds. See the facing page to find a convenient alphabetic listing. In the 100 species profiles, we've used a series of symbols to provide instant insight into the lives of these birds. Here is a key to what each of these icons represents:

 Will use a birdhouse for nesting or roosting.

 Can be attracted to bird feeders.

 Will visit birdbaths or water features for bathing and drinking.

 Has a song or call and can be identified by its vocalizations or sounds.

 A migrant species, seen primarily during spring or fall migration.

Also, turn to pages 7 through 32 to read more about the natural history and ecology of your state and its bird life. We focus on bird watching by season—the specific birds you're likely to encounter and how to attract them—by feeding and by offering the appropriate bird-friendly habitat. This section also describes the many migrants that pass through in spring and fall. As an extra bonus, we briefly describe the "Ten Must-See Birds" for your state. We also include a summary of the "Ten Best Bird-Watching Spots."

At the end of this book you will find a resources list for bird watching (feeding and planting charts, answers to frequently asked questions, birdhouse plans, bird books, field and audio guides, and more) to help you enjoy this hobby more.

Happy bird watching!

—*Bill Thompson, III*

# 100 Most Commonly Encountered Birds

American Coot ..................................................67
American Crow ..................................................99
American Goldfinch .........................................144
American Kestrel ..............................................65
American Redstart ..........................................120
American Robin ...............................................111
American Woodcock ........................................71
Bald Eagle .........................................................63
Baltimore Oriole .............................................140
Barn Swallow .................................................103
Barred Owl .......................................................79
Belted Kingfisher .............................................85
Black-capped Chickadee ..............................105
Black-throated Green Warbler .....................123
Blue-gray Gnatcatcher ..................................109
Blue Jay ............................................................98
Blue-winged Teal .............................................54
Bonaparte's Gull ..............................................72
Brown-headed Cowbird ................................137
Brown Thrasher .............................................115
Canada Goose .................................................51
Cedar Waxwing .............................................117
Chimney Swift .................................................83
Chipping Sparrow ..........................................131
Common Grackle ...........................................139
Common Loon .................................................48
Common Merganser .......................................58
Common Nighthawk .......................................82
Common Yellowthroat ..................................122
Cooper's Hawk .................................................60
Dark-eyed Junco ...........................................135
Double-crested Cormorant .............................47
Downy Woodpecker ........................................88
Eastern Bluebird ............................................110
Eastern Kingbird ..............................................95
Eastern Meadowlark .....................................136
Eastern Phoebe ...............................................93
Eastern Screech-Owl ......................................80
Eastern Towhee .............................................129
Eastern Wood-Pewee ......................................92
European Starling ..........................................116
Field Sparrow .................................................130
Gray Catbird ...................................................114
Great Blue Heron .............................................49
Great Crested Flycatcher ................................94
Great Horned Owl ............................................78
Green Heron .....................................................50
Hairy Woodpecker ...........................................89
Herring Gull ......................................................74
Horned Lark ...................................................100

House Finch ...................................................141
House Sparrow ..............................................145
House Wren ...................................................107
Indigo Bunting ...............................................128
Killdeer .............................................................68
Lesser Scaup ...................................................56
Lesser Yellowlegs ............................................69
Magnolia Warbler ..........................................118
Mallard .............................................................53
Mourning Dove ................................................75
Northern Cardinal ..........................................127
Northern Flicker ...............................................91
Northern Harrier ..............................................62
Osprey .............................................................64
Ovenbird ........................................................121
Pied-billed Grebe .............................................46
Pine Siskin .....................................................143
Purple Finch ..................................................142
Purple Martin .................................................101
Red-bellied Woodpecker ................................87
Red-eyed Vireo ................................................96
Red-headed Woodpecker ...............................86
Red-tailed Hawk ..............................................61
Red-winged Blackbird ...................................138
Ring-billed Gull ................................................73
Ring-necked Duck ...........................................55
Rock Pigeon ....................................................76
Rose-breasted Grosbeak ..............................125
Ruby-crowned Kinglet ..................................108
Ruby-throated Hummingbird .........................84
Ruddy Duck .....................................................57
Scarlet Tanager .............................................126
Song Sparrow ................................................134
Spotted Sandpiper ..........................................70
Tree Swallow .................................................102
Tufted Titmouse ............................................104
Turkey Vulture .................................................59
Veery ..............................................................113
Warbling Vireo .................................................97
Whip-poor-will .................................................81
White-breasted Nuthatch .............................106
White-crowned Sparrow ...............................133
White-throated Sparrow ...............................132
Wild Turkey ......................................................66
Wood Duck ......................................................52
Wood Thrush .................................................112
Yellow-bellied Sapsucker ................................90
Yellow-billed Cuckoo .......................................77
Yellow-rumped Warbler ................................119
Yellow Warbler ...............................................124

# Pied-billed Grebe
*Podilymbus podiceps*

Most North American grebes either breed far to the north or in the West, but the stocky little pied-billed grebe also breeds through much of the eastern United States. You can find this frequent diver in varied wetlands, including ponds, lakes, and marshes that have a thick cover of cattails or other vegetation. Pied-billed grebes most often are seen singly or in twos or threes. They don't often vocalize, except during breeding season when they call out a series of penetrating, barking notes.

## All About
In general, pied-billed grebes occur in sheltered, lush wetlands. This bird is smallish but has a big head, stocky neck, and a thick bill that differs from the more pointed bills of horned and eared grebes. During breeding season, the bill (which is pale in winter) becomes distinctively adorned with a thick, black band that wraps around an otherwise horn-colored bill. Breeding pied-billed grebes also have black throats, but at other times their soft-brown necks and bodies contrast with whitish throats and puffy, whitish undertails.

## Habitat & Range
Pied-billed grebes nest in well-vegetated lakes, ponds, and pockets of marsh. You may find them in brackish water in winter, but they prefer freshwater habitats. The numbers of pied-billed grebes dwindle in the North and swell in the South during winter and migration, when many northern nesters abandon their frigid habitats for warmer, more productive wintering areas.

## Feeding
Pied-billed grebes are frequently seen diving for food or diving to evade predators or observers. Their wide-lobed feet push them beneath the water's surface in search of small fish, amphibians, and a wide variety of aquatic invertebrates, including crayfish and insects. They also eat some plant matter.

## Nesting
Mates call to each other as part of their courtship. Together, they build a nest that is basically a mound of matted vegetation. This mound is fastened to nearby plants and may float or rise from the shallows. The female lays four to six eggs, with the pair sharing the three-week incubation period. Both parents feed the young, which can fly by two months of age.

## Backyard & Beyond
Scan marsh edges and ponds to find pied-billed grebes; they are rarely spotted in flight. They have a tendency to appear as if by magic and to disappear just as fast, often leaving a ring of ripples on the water's surface as the only evidence of their presence.

# Double-crested Cormorant
*Phalacrocorax auritus*

- Spring/Summer
- Year-Round
- Winter

Often, the somewhat snakelike black neck and head is all that betrays the presence of a swimming double-crested cormorant. They are most numerous during the breeding season in spring and summer. In fall, long lines of cormorants can be seen migrating southward. A few may linger all winter in ice-free waters. Double-crested cormorants declined earlier in the twentieth century due to disturbance and hunting at nesting grounds, followed by DDT and other pesticide contamination. Protection, wetland conservation, and the DDT ban have helped these birds recover.

## All About
With practice, birders can easily distinguish a distant, flying double-crested cormorant from a pelican, goose, heron, or other large bird by its all-dark form, thick and somewhat wavy neck, longish tail, and slow wingbeats. The cormorant's bright orange throat, bill, and lores stand out on its otherwise black body. Even its heavy webbed feet are blackish. Immatures are dull brown with whitish necks and chests. The double-crested cormorant is named for its pair of head crest plumes that are most visible during breeding season and rarely seen otherwise.

## Habitat & Range
Most double-crested cormorant populations are migratory, and these birds turn up at rivers, marshes, swamps, large lakes, bays, and along the coast. Because they travel widely during the day, don't be surprised to see cormorants flying over inland habitats in loose formation. Double-crested cormorants breed in western Alaska, central Canada, and down both coasts of the United States; they winter along the coast and well inland throughout the eastern United States.

## Feeding
Double-crested cormorants are very adaptable, seeking a wide variety of fish, and also crustaceans, amphibians, and other aquatic animals. Their webbed feet propel them under water after their aquatic prey, and much of their feeding is done not far beneath the surface.

## Nesting
Double-crested cormorants nest in colonies in trees, on cliffs, and on islands. Females build much of the platform nest, while males provide the many sticks and other materials. Females usually lay three or four eggs, which both parents incubate for about a month. Young leave the nest 21 to 30 days after hatching, but are not fully on their own until after two months.

## Backyard & Beyond
Watch for the "periscope" heads of partially submerged cormorants and try not to confuse them with those of the more dagger-billed loons, which have slimmer, straighter bills and at least some light coloration on the head. After long swims, cormorants often sun themselves on dead trees and shorelines, holding out their wings to dry.

# Common Loon
## *Gavia immer*

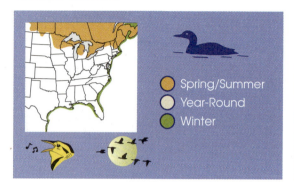

The common loon is one of the best-known North American water birds. Its high yodeling cry echoes across large, remote northern lakes evoking unspoiled wilderness to the listener. Once heard, the loon's wailing tremolo is hard to forget.

## All About
The common loon is a large, long diving bird that rides low in the water. In profile the loon's massive head and bill help to separate it visually from other waterfowl. In breeding plumage it has a black head, bill, and neck band. Its throat and breast are white and its back is checkered in black and white; this nondescript plumage may render the loon unfamiliar to some bird watchers. In winter plumage the common loon is a dull gray-and-white. In flight the common loon appears dark above, white below.

## Habitat & Range
Common loons breed on remote lakes as far north as the treeless tundra and as far south as New England and northern Michigan, Wisconsin, and Minnesota. In recent decades, the species has declined due to human disturbance, pollution, and habitat loss. Though most common loons spend winter on the ocean, some linger on large inland rivers, lakes, and reservoirs. They can be encountered on large bodies of water during spring or fall migration; huge concentrations occur on protected bays in the Great Lakes.

## Feeding
A foraging common loon swims along with its head underwater scanning for schools of small fish, its primary food. It catches fish by diving in pursuit, powered by strong webbed feet. Once caught in the loon's bill a fish cannot escape. The loon's tongue and the roof of its mouth have small, inward-pointing barbules that enhance its grip. Fish are swallowed headfirst. Other foods include small crustaceans and aquatic plant matter.

## Nesting
Common loons nest on remote lakes where both mates build a mound of aquatic plant matter for their one or two eggs on land but near the water. Both birds share the incubation duties, which can last a month. After hatching, young loons may leave the nest within a day and are able to swim and dive immediately, but they may hitch a ride on a parent's back. They are able to fly after about 10 weeks, at which point they become independent from the parents.

## Backyard & Beyond
Loons are partial to large bodies of water because they need the "runway" space for take-off and landing. They are heavy-bodied birds that must run across the water's surface to build up speed for flight. Loons spend much of the non-breeding season alone, so scanning the surface of a lake or reservoir is a good way to spot a distant swimming loon.

# Great Blue Heron
*Ardea herodias*

North America's largest and most widespread heron is found, at one time or another, virtually wherever water and small aquatic creatures are found. Although the best known of our dozen heron species, the great blue heron is not always called by its correct name. Many non-birders call it a crane or a stork, but the heron can be instantly distinguished from these other large, long-legged birds by its folded-back neck in flight and the S-shaped curvature of its neck at rest.

## All About
Adult great blue herons have a black stripe running from the eye to the back of the neck; immature birds have a blackish cap. During the breeding season the heron's plumage is enhanced by long plume feathers on the head, neck, and back. The great blue heron's croaking *ccrraaaaaaaank* call is often heard as it takes flight.

## Habitat & Range
Found across the United States, southern Canada, and up the Pacific coast to Alaska, the great blue heron ventures where few other herons dare. Many eastern birds migrate to the South or to the tropics—as far south as northwestern South America—in winter. However, many great blues spend the winter in the Midwest, wherever there is ice-free water.

## Feeding
Great blue herons seek a variety of prey in a range of wet habitats. Fish are a mainstay, but amphibians, reptiles, birds, small mammals, and invertebrates feature on the menu, as well. Feeding strategy varies: They may hunt alongside each other, wading slowly up to their bellies in water, or may stand alone for long periods, waiting to thrust their bills at unsuspecting prey. Great blue herons sometimes stalk rodents in dry fields or haunt beaches and docks in search of live or discarded sea life.

## Nesting
Great blue herons nest in large colonies, often in tall trees away from human disturbance. They will nest in the company of other water birds, in areas with water beneath nesting trees, probably to thwart predators. Each year, great blue heron pairs form bonds through a series of posing displays, including stretching, preening, crest raising, circling in flight, and twig shaking. Males provide sticks, which females place in the large platform nest. Females usually lay three to five eggs, which they incubate for almost a month. Both parents feed the young, which take flight 2 to 2 1/2 months after hatching.

## Backyard & Beyond
Despite their large size, great blue herons sometimes turn up at small backyard ponds seeking fish and frogs. They are far more frequent in marshes, swamps, rivers, lakes, and reservoirs.

# Green Heron
*Butorides virescens*

The green heron isn't exactly green, but it's the most greenish of the North American herons. Perhaps a better name would have been "squat heron" or "little heron" or "common pond heron." The bird was known until recently as the "green-backed heron," and this is an apt moniker since the adults have blackish green backs.

## All About
The least bittern is our smallest heron, but the green heron is the smallest *easily seen* heron. While a green heron will sometimes stretch its neck out to peer at approaching birders or predators, its head is usually held close to the body, giving the bird a squat look. Identification of adults is straightforward: The back and crown are blackish with a green tinge, the neck and face are dark chestnut, and the belly is gray. Yellow legs flush to bright orange during breeding season. Young birds are brown streaked, and care should be taken not to mistake them for bitterns. Subadults are a mixture of brown and streaky and rusty necked. The piercing *KEEE-OWK* call will draw attention to birds flushed out to the open that might otherwise be missed.

## Habitat & Range
In spring and summer, look for green herons along wooded streams and ponds, around lakes, at drainage ditches, and in marshes, often near woody cover. In winter, green herons move south from northern nesting areas, spending the winter in Florida and the Gulf States and southward into the tropics. Green herons also nest throughout the West Indies and in Central America south to Panama.

## Feeding
Like stock-still balls of rust and greenish feathers, green herons wait patiently by the water's edge for fish, frogs, crayfish, various insects, and other small prey. They also slowly walk through the water and wait for prey to show. They have even been known to drop small baits, such as fish food pellets, bits of bread (from people feeding park ducks), or flower petals into the water to attract curious fish and other potential prey.

## Nesting
Green herons nest in pairs or small clusters, but avoid large colonies. They nest in trees or shrubs that may either be near or fairly far from water and feeding areas. Three to seven eggs are laid in a stick platform nest primarily built by the female. Both parents incubate the eggs for about three weeks; both then feed their young, which can fly by three weeks of age.

## Backyard & Beyond
Green herons may visit backyard ponds to investigate the goldfish or frogs. They also frequently fly over neighborhoods en route to golf course ponds, streams, lakes, or drainage ditches. Green herons are frequently overlooked until startled into flight.

# Canada Goose
*Branta canadensis*

The Canada goose enjoys an almost iconic status with human observers (though large, nonmigratory flocks can wear out their welcome). Their huge, V-shaped flights mark the passing of seasons, their honking is reminiscent of wilderness itself, and their strong family bonds (they mate for life) endear them to us. Many non-bird watchers mistakenly call this bird the Canadian *goose*.

## All About
The Canada goose's black neck and white cheek strap are unmistakable. In flight, Canadas beat their wings deeply and slowly and show a black-and-white tail. Their familiar call is a deep, two-syllable *ha-ronk* and is given by mated pairs as well as flocking birds. Canadas also give a variety of softer cackling calls to each other, especially when they are on the ground. More than a dozen different subspecies exist in North America, and their sizes vary from 25 to 45 inches in length.

## Habitat & Range
The Canada goose is a habitat generalist when it comes to water, settling in lakes, bays, rivers, and city parks and ponds. The species has enjoyed unprecedented success in living with or near humans, and today it nests all across the upper two-thirds of North America. Some re-established populations of Canada goose are year-round, nonmigratory residents, though many birds nesting in northern North America migrate to the southern United States in winter. Spring migration begins early, and many females are incubating by mid-March.

## Feeding
Aquatic plants, grasses, grains, and seeds are the Canada's primary foods. To reach submerged food, it will tip its tail in the air and extend its neck below the water's surface. Flocks leave roosting areas in the morning to forage in nearby fields, meadows, and marshes. Urban populations often live on handouts of cracked corn near city park lakes and golf course ponds.

## Nesting
Located on a high spot near water, the nest is a small mound made of surrounding sticks and vegetation and lined with down plucked from the female. Half a dozen or more eggs are laid and incubated by the female for nearly a month while the male stands guard and brings her food. Within two days of hatching, young goslings are herded by their parents to the nearest water. Families stay together until the following breeding season, though young birds become self-sufficient in about two months.

## Backyard & Beyond
Some housing developments and golf courses find them (and their droppings) a nuisance. To best see Canadas, visit a wildlife refuge where large flocks congregate during winter and during spring and fall migration. Watching hundreds of loudly honking Canadas is quite a spectacle.

# Wood Duck
## *Aix sponsa*

The up-slurred WHEEEP of the wood duck is a familiar sound to anyone frequenting areas where woodland and fresh water mix. Patience and a bit of stealth will reward the birder seeking a good look at these cagey, dazzling ducks. Across much of the Midwest, wood ducks abound, finding ample habitat and welcoming nest boxes.

### All About
The male wood duck takes its colorful plumage to an extreme. In breeding plumage, it has a green crown and black face offset by white slashes reaching up from its white throat. The bill looks painted, a bright red-orange with black and white touches. Breast and undertail are chestnut, while the sides are adorned with vertical white and blackish slashes followed by a panel of butterscotch yellow. The male's back is metallic green. These colors fade during summer, as the birds molt into *eclipse*, or nonbreeding, plumage, but the bright bill and eye and face pattern remain. Both male and female have backward-facing crests that give them a helmeted look. The female wood duck is easy to identify, not only because of her head shape, but also because of her white, tear-shaped eye rings. Otherwise, females are grayish brown and generously flecked with whitish spots on their sides.

### Habitat & Range
The perfect setting for wood ducks combines tranquil fresh water with plenty of trees—bottomland swamps, riverside forests, and tree-lined ponds and lakes. Wood ducks are permanent residents in much of the Midwest and South, except in the Appalachians, where populations withdraw during the cold months. Northern populations, from southern Canada through the Northeast, retreat south in winter.

### Feeding
Wood ducks eat a variety of seeds and some fruits from aquatic and forest plants, including acorns. Sometimes, they eat grain. Insects and other small animals supplement their diet; though, for recently fledged birds, these are a mainstay.

### Nesting
Wood ducks are cavity nesters, setting up house in holes high in mature or dead trees. They also nest down low in nest boxes. The nest is simply an accumulation of down placed on the cavity floor, where the female incubates her 8 to 15 pale eggs between $3^{1}/_{2}$ and 5 weeks. Chicks usually tumble out of their nest the day after hatching. Females accompany them for about six weeks, and they can fly at about two months of age.

### Backyard & Beyond
If you live near fresh water, you may see wood ducks fly over your property. If your property includes a pond or wetland, you may attract wood ducks with a nesting box, which ideally would be set in the water on a pole fitted with a pole-mounted, predator baffle.

# Mallard
*Anas platyrhynchos*

- Spring/Summer
- Year-Round
- Winter

Of all the North American duck species, there's one that nearly everyone knows—the mallard. Abundant all across the continent, the mallard is known to interbreed commonly with black ducks and other wild duck species, as well as with domesticated ducks. Large numbers of semi-tame mallards exist on city park ponds, golf courses, and reservoirs, getting by on handouts from humans.

## All About
The male mallard's green head and yellow bill are easily recognizable, but female mallards—with their overall dark brown coloration—can be confused with black ducks, mottled ducks, and other female ducks. Look for her orange and black bill and listen for the loud, raucous *quack, quack-quack, quack-quack* call, given only by female mallards. Mallards are fairly large ducks with a 23-inch body length.

## Habitat & Range
Like other dabbling ducks, mallards prefer shallow bodies of fresh water at all times of year, including marshes, flooded woodlots, ponds, and swamps. They can be found year-round across most of the United States, but a large number of mallards breed in the far North and spend the winter in the Southeast.

## Feeding
Mallards feed by scooping up seeds and plant material from the water's surface, by tipping up—tails in the air—to reach submerged plants, and by grazing for waste grain in agricultural fields. They eat everything from seeds and vegetation to insects, small fish, crawfish, and frogs.

## Nesting
Mallards pair up well before the spring breeding season. The hen mallard chooses the nest site, usually in or near thick vegetation on the ground. She then builds a small bowl out of nearby plant material and lines it with her own down. Between 7 and 12 eggs are laid and incubated by the hen for a month. Like other ducks, mallard ducklings leave the nest within hours after hatching and follow their mother to the nearest water. Though ducklings feed themselves right away, it's nearly two months before they are able to fly. Predators take a heavy toll on nests and young, especially in parks where natural predators are augmented by domestic pets.

## Backyard & Beyond
If you want to feed the mallards in your local park, don't bother with stale bread, which holds little nutritional value for birds. Instead, offer some cracked corn. This inexpensive food is available at most stores selling birdseed and is relished by mallards. When you've got a hungry flock of panhandling mallards nearby, take time to look at the birds' fine plumage. Look, too, for wild ducks of other species that may be "hanging out" with the local flock of tame mallards, as well as for the many interesting hybrids that result from the mallard's promiscuous nature.

# Blue-winged Teal
## *Anas discors*

A fast-flying, small (14 inches long) duck, the blue-winged teal shows the blue shoulder patch for which it is named only when the wings are extended. Blue-wingeds fly in tight flocks and seem to be wary as they pass repeatedly over a body of water before landing. However, they are not as skittish as other ducks when approached by humans, perhaps because they know they can explode off the water and straight into the air in seconds.

## All About
Males have a blue-gray head and a distinctive white face crescent and hip patch, making them easy to identify even from a distance. Females are a warm, gray-brown overall with a slight echo of the males' white face crescent. Identifying them is made somewhat easier by the fact that blue-winged teal pairs form in early winter and stay together through spring migration.

## Habitat & Range
Blue-winged teal breed throughout the northeastern, central, and western United States. Most blue-winged teal spend the winter south of the United States, as far as South America. They are considered fair-weather ducks by many bird watchers because they stay far to the south until spring is in full force. Perhaps it is their later spring arrival and their earlier fall departure that has earned them the nicknames "summer teal" and "August teal." Their preferred habitats—at all seasons—are shallow, freshwater marshes and ponds.

## Feeding
Teal feed on seeds and plant matter gleaned from the water's surface or by swimming with their heads submerged to find snails, aquatic insects, and crustaceans. Unlike other dabbling ducks, blue-wingeds do not "tip up" to feed on submerged vegetation.

## Nesting
Like many other ducks, blue-winged teal nest on the ground in a spot concealed by thick vegetation. The female builds a shallow, basket-shaped nest out of dried grasses lined with her down. A clutch of nine or more eggs is laid and incubated by the hen for slightly more than three weeks. Teal ducklings leave the nest almost immediately and are able to feed themselves right away, but it will be six weeks before they are fully flighted.

## Backyard & Beyond
The blue-winged's preference for shallow water means that it can show up almost anywhere—from farm or city ponds to marshes, mudflats, and sewage settling pools. If you see a flock of small ducks flying pell-mell, twisting and turning as one, chances are they are blue-winged teal. You can clinch the identification by looking for the male teal's white face crescent, or for the flash of blue, white, and green in the wings.

# Ring-necked Duck
## *Aythya collaris*

The ring-necked duck is fairly common all across the United States and Canada and a common migrant through the Midwest. Flocks of ringnecks frequent marshes, swamps, and sheltered and wooded corners of lakes. These birds are often found in areas where the only other regularly sighted ducks are wood ducks and mallards (in interior areas). Ringnecks are also found on open water and areas with a wider diversity of ducks.

## All About

Closely related and superficially similar to the greater and lesser scaups, this diving bird has a few embellishments that easily set it apart from the scaup. Like the scaup, the male ringneck is blackish—in most light—on its head, chest, and back. However, even at a distance, the adult male ring-necked duck has a vertical white comma that edges its gray sides. Its bill is three-toned: The tip is black, followed by a white band, then much gray, then a white border where the bill meets the head. Like the scaup, the female ringneck is more somber in coloration and markings, but she has a noticeably dark crown compared with the rest of her head. She sports a white eye ring, and usually has a clearly three-toned bill. As with the red-bellied woodpecker, the ring-necked duck's name was poorly chosen by "dead-bird-in-the-hand" early ornithologists: Only in rare circumstances will you see its namesake rusty collar.

## Habitat & Range

Most ring-necked ducks winter in the United States, below the northern tier of states, and south into central Mexico. Others winter in the West Indies, and a few are found as far south as Panama. Unlike scaup, ring-necked ducks frequent small or smallish bodies of water, and they rarely enter salt water. Summer finds them nesting in Canada, Alaska, and a good number of northern U.S. states in freshwater wetlands, usually surrounded by forest.

## Feeding

Ring-necked ducks dive for their supper, snipping roots and stems of plants, eating seeds, insects, and mollusks. Like other waterfowl, their recently hatched young eat mostly insects.

## Nesting

The female ring-necked duck usually lays between 8 and 10 eggs in a nest of grasses or other plants clipped from nearby. She incubates the eggs for almost a month. After they hatch, she accompanies her chicks until they can fly, shortly before two months of age.

## Backyard & Beyond

Early in the morning or in well-protected areas, you may catch close-up looks at ring-necked ducks on small ponds or lakes. Even at a distance, though, the gray, white, and black markings on the male's sides help identify these birds as they dive underwater and pop back up to the surface.

# Lesser Scaup
## *Aythya affinis*

We have two scaup species in North America—greater and lesser scaup—both are medium-sized, black-and-white ducks, and they can be difficult to tell apart. The lesser scaup is by far the more commonly encountered of the two, especially on inland bodies of water. Both species are named for their characteristic *skawwp!* call, but the similarities don't end there. Both scaup species are excellent swimmers and divers, both have drab brownish mates, and both show lots of white in the wing in flight.

## All About
Older field guides suggest that greater and lesser scaup can be identified based upon head color, but this is very unreliable in poor light. Separating scaup species in the field is most accurately done based on head shape—lessers have a thinner head with more of a peak on top, while greaters have a rounder head and larger bill. Female scaup are brownish gray overall with a white ring around the base of the bill. Hens can be identified based on the males with which they associate because the two scaup species are rarely seen in mixed flocks. All scaup show a blue-gray bill with a black tip—an important clue to separate the scaup from the superficially similar ring-necked duck, which has a white ring on its bill.

## Habitat & Range
Lesser scaup are one of most common wintering ducks on inland bodies of water, with flocks sometimes numbering in the thousands. They are very late migrants in both spring and fall migration, arriving on the breeding grounds as late as mid-May and not leaving until just before the winter freeze-up.

## Feeding
Specialists in diving for their food, lesser scaup eat snails, mussels, small clams, fish, and aquatic insects. They also rely on plant matter and seeds for food, especially in fall and winter.

## Nesting
Preferring to nest in thick vegetation on dry ground or islands near water, the female lesser scaup does nearly all of the hard work. The nest is a scrape lined with dry grass and lots of the hen's down into which 8 to 10 eggs are laid. Hen scaup incubate their eggs for longer than three weeks before hatching. Hatchlings leave the nest within a day of emerging and are able to feed themselves immediately. Within two weeks they are diving for food, and two months later they are fully flighted.

## Backyard & Beyond
Lesser scaup can be found on almost any open (ice-free) body of water in the continental United States in winter, but they are especially abundant along the Gulf and southern Atlantic coasts. Look for flocks of black-and-white ducks actively diving and bobbing to the surface of a pond, lake, or reservoir.

# Ruddy Duck
## *Oxyura jamaicensis*

This little dark duck is a familiar sight on marshes, bays, and ponds across North America where it often gathers in sizeable flocks in winter. Perhaps because they are rarely hunted they are among our least "spooky" ducks and thus can often be viewed from close range.

### All About
Named for the ruddy-orange color of the breeding male, the ruddy duck is a compact-bodied bird with a big head. The long spiky tail is often held up at an angle, hence its alternate name, "stiff-tailed duck." Breeding males are a lovely blend of colors with rusty body, black head, white cheeks, and blue bill. Females and juveniles are drab gray-brown overall with a contrasting white face stripe. Males retain their white cheeks in winter plumage. In all plumages ruddy ducks are dark-capped and pale-cheeked. Ruddies are swift flyers with rapid wingbeats.

### Habitat & Range
During the nesting season, most ruddy ducks are on small marshy lakes and wetlands of the western prairies and the interior West. They winter along the entire U.S. coast and across the eastern U.S., as far north as there is ice-free water. Ruddies migrate at night in small flocks and spend daylight hours during migration resting or sleeping on the water. Because many of North America's ruddy ducks use the prairie pothole region of the western Great Plains, drought years can have a devastating effect on this species.

### Feeding
A diving feeder, the ruddy duck uses its large bill stir up food items from the bottom of a pond or lake. Aquatic insect larvae, invertebrates, seeds and plant matter make up the diet, nearly all captured as the ruddy strains the stirred-up mud through its bill. In summer the diet is primarily insect larvae while the winter diet may rely more heavily on seeds.

### Nesting
The female weaves a platform nest out of cattails and grasses in thick vegetation suspended just inches above the water. She may also weave a partial roof overhead. She lays between five and ten eggs and incubates them for nearly about 25 days, during which time the male takes his leave and the female assumes all parental duties. Ducklings leave the nest a day after hatching and are able to swim and feed themselves immediately, though the female still cares for them. Young attain flight after seven weeks.

### Backyard & Beyond
Look for ruddy ducks on marshy ponds and shallow lakes, along large rivers, and on reservoirs during their prolonged spring and fall migration. In spring, males perform amusing courtship displays with lots of head bobbing, tail spreading, and unusual posturing.

# Common Merganser
*Mergus merganser*

Mergansers are the only North American ducks that are primarily fish eaters; the common merganser is our largest, most boldly marked one. Like our two other mergansers, the common has a serrated bill enabling it to catch and grasp the fish it captures on underwater dives. This adaptation is why the mergansers are often called "saw-bills."

## All About
The clean white body, dark green head, and bright-orange bill of the male common merganser are unmistakable identification clues, even at a great distance. The common merganser has the least obvious crest of any of the mergansers, but its large size and bold coloration separate it from the hooded and red-breasted mergansers. Female commons have a dark-brown head and a gray body with a white belly, but share the same bright orange bill color as the male. In flight, common mergansers appear slender and cleanly marked, showing lots of white.

## Habitat & Range
Common mergansers breed near northern lakes and rivers that are surrounded by mature forests. Their breeding range covers much of Canada and tiny bits of northern Minnesota, Wisconsin, Michigan, and northern New England. Wintering birds will remain as far north as possible wherever clear, ice-free water is available. During most winters, this bird is the most-common merganser found across the Midwest on deep lakes, rivers, and reservoirs.

## Feeding
Doing most of its feeding at morning and dusk, a common merganser will swim along with its head submerged (much like a loon), looking for fish. It pursues fish by diving and swimming after them; common mergansers have been observed swallowing foot-long fish head-first! They also consume mussels, crayfish, shrimp, and salamanders. When dive-feeding in deep water, they may stay under for 30 seconds or more.

## Nesting
Common mergansers are cavity nesters, usually choosing a hole in a large tree near water. They will use nest boxes in proper habitat and successful adult females return to nest at the same site in successive years. A lining of wood chips and down is the only improvement made to a cavity and into this nest the female lays between six to twelve eggs. She incubates the eggs for a month or more before they hatch. Young mergansers leap from the cavity a day or so after hatching and follow their mother to the water. They can feed themselves immediately but do not attain flight for at least two months.

## Backyard & Beyond
Look for common mergansers on lakes, rivers, and reservoirs from the onset of fall migration in September through spring migration ending in early April. In Europe common mergansers (called "goosanders" there) have increased significantly thanks to the availability of nest boxes.

# Turkey Vulture
## *Cathartes aura*

- Spring/Summer
- Year-Round
- Winter

*C*atharsis—a cleansing or purification—is the root of the turkey vulture's Latin name. It refers to this bird's invaluable service in ridding the landscape of animal carcasses—a necessity in the age of superhighways. The highway system, with its continual supply of shoulder fare, may have contributed to the turkey vulture's northward breeding range expansion.

## All About
The tilting flight, with wings held in a shallow "V", immediately distinguishes a turkey vulture from most other large, dark birds in flight. At close range, the underwings appear two-toned, with the flight feathers having a reflective, pewter sheen. The small, naked head is red; the bill bone-white. On the ground, a turkey vulture appears to be all wing—a long blackish trapezoid, topped by a tiny red head. Hoarse hisses are their only sounds. Nestlings produce a continuous breathy roar when cornered in the nest.

## Habitat & Range
Ranging widely as they search for food, turkey vultures prefer farmland pastures where carcasses might be found, and with nearby forests where they find nesting and roosting spots. Communal roosters, they may be seen warming themselves with wings spread open to the sun. Turkey vultures are migratory in the northern parts of their range, mingling with resident birds in the southern United States, some traveling as far south as Amazonia before returning in early spring.

## Feeding
Powerful olfactory senses help the turkey vulture locate carcasses, and they may circle in groups, narrowing down the scent source, before spotting it. This allows them to find carrion in deep woods. One circling vulture brings sharp-eyed companions from miles around, and they share their plunder, rising with heavy flaps from roadsides when disturbed. Its bare head allows the vulture to reach into larger carcasses without fouling its feathers.

## Nesting
Turkey vultures hide their nests on rock ledges, in hollow logs, under boulders, or in unused animal burrows. The female lays two eggs, which she and her mate incubate for around 28 days. The young are in the nest cavity and its vicinity for about 12 weeks, making first flights as early as 60 days of age. After a few weeks of exercising and being fed in the nest vicinity, they appear to be independent upon their first extended flight.

## Backyard & Beyond
Turkey vultures have learned to exploit factory farms, especially chicken farms, for the inevitable carcasses they produce. They are closely attuned to spring calving and lambing times. Rather than being seen as harbingers of death, turkey vultures might be considered for their great beauty in flight and as a vital cleanup crew.

# Cooper's Hawk
*Accipiter cooperii*

Cooper's hawks often perch in inconspicuous places, shooting through the branches or dropping from trees to nab unsuspecting prey. A flurry of fearful birds and a gray flash may mark the arrival of a Cooper's hawk to your backyard. Cooper's hawks are medium-sized hawks and formidable hunters that are usually seen singly except during migration, when they pass by in varying numbers at hawk-watching spots.

## All About
Care must be taken to differentiate the Cooper's hawk from the similar sharp-shinned hawk. Adults of both species have similar markings, as do their brown-backed immatures and that of the northern goshawk (larger birds rarely seen south of Virginia, Indiana, and Missouri). Size is often not a trustworthy identification tool in the field—proportions and tail edges are more telling. Compared with the sharp-shinned hawk, the Cooper's has a proportionately larger head and neck and a rounded (not notched) or square-tipped tail (as does the sharp-shinned). Perched, adult Cooper's hawks often show a contrast between a blackish crown and gray nape and back. In flight, its head protrudes well beyond its often straight-held wings, and its tail usually looks rounded. Sharp-shinned hawks look like a capital "T" in flight, their shorter heads almost even with the leading edge of their wings.

## Habitat & Range
In many areas, Cooper's hawks are uncommon nesters. Far-northern birds generally winter to the south. You can look for Cooper's hawks in any type of forest, along forest edges, and in woods near watercourses. But don't be surprised if you find one elsewhere, particularly in winter and fall. They seem to be adapting to suburban life, nesting near backyards or in city parks. During spring and fall, migrating Cooper's hawks gravitate toward ridges and coasts.

## Feeding
These midsized hawks generally feed on midsized birds, including robins, flickers, and pigeons, but they also eat small mammals, including chipmunks and squirrels. Insects and reptiles sometimes feature on the menu.

## Nesting
Cooper's hawks place their bulky stick nests high on horizontal branches in large trees, sometimes building them atop another large bird or squirrel nest. The female lays three to five eggs and incubates them for about five weeks. The male brings food, but the female feeds it to the young, which usually take flight about four or five weeks after hatching.

## Backyard & Beyond
Cooper's hawks are attracted to what bird feeders attract—keeping intact natural predator and prey interactions, even in the suburbs. They will not scare birds from your feeders for long and, when successful, Cooper's hawks are usually weeding out the less-fit birds.

# Red-tailed Hawk
## *Buteo jamaicensis*

*This bird is the large raptor people most often see doing "lazy circles in the sky." The red-tailed hawk inhabits open terrain across the continent and south to Central America. It thrives in habitats opened up by human activities, such as farming or forest clearing. They are also the large raptor most commonly seen perched along roadways and power lines.*

## All About
Red-tailed hawks occur across the continent in quite a variety of plumage colorations. In the East, however, count on a few easy field marks to help identify adult birds: the reddish-orange tail, a dark-streaked belly band, and a white chest. This hat trick of field marks can easily be seen in many soaring redtails, as well as in perched birds. Additionally, two chocolate-colored bars adorn the leading edge of the underwing. Overall, soaring red-tailed hawks are bulkier and more formidable in general appearance than slimmer red-shouldered hawks and broad-winged hawks, which have shorter tails. Red-tailed hawks younger than two years old lack the telltale reddish tail, but they still exhibit the belly band and white chest.

## Habitat & Range
Look for red-tailed hawks along highway edges, over farm fields and forest clearings, and in almost any other open habitat with at least some telephone poles or trees on which they can perch and scan for prey. From tundra to tropical forests, the red-tailed hawk is a formidable predator. They breed as far south as Panama and on various Caribbean islands, thus the species name *jamaicensis*. For nesting, they usually avoid areas with a lot of human activity, even though they nest near New York City's Central Park and pass through suburbs during migration.

## Feeding
Many farmers appreciate seeing red-tailed hawks flap over their acreage, as they eat many voles, mice, rats, rabbits, squirrels, and other small mammals. Other prey can include a variety of birds and reptiles. Red-tailed hawks may glide down from a perch to grab prey, dive down, or hover and then drop on prey.

## Nesting
Nests are usually found in tall trees, although these birds will nest on cliffs and sometimes even buildings. Both mates build the large stick nest, which they line with softer materials. The female usually lays two or three eggs, which both parents incubate for about a month. The male hunts for food, passing it to his mate, who feeds their young. Nestlings fly after about 10 weeks.

## Backyard & Beyond
You may hear the red-tailed hawk's blood-curdling cry around its nesting grounds. Because they range widely and some populations migrate short or long distances, you may see red-tailed hawks soaring or gliding over your home.

# Northern Harrier
*Circus cyaneus*

- Spring/Summer
- Year-Round
- Winter

The slender, low-flying form of the northern harrier is associated with grasslands and marshes across most of North America during one season or another. Young birds, adult females, and adult males are very different in appearance and size—an unusual trait among raptors.

## All About
The northern harrier's key field mark is a large white rump patch, but its shape—long slender wings and long tail—is also distinctive. First-year juveniles sport a rich chocolate brown on their back and wings accompanied by an unstreaked, rust-colored breast. Adult females, which can be twice as large as males, are the same colors as juveniles but have a heavily streaked breast and belly. Adult males are pale gray below and slate gray above, and are sometimes referred to by bird watchers as "gray ghosts." A ring of feathers surrounding the face form a facial disc, an owl-like adaptation that channels sound to the ears.

## Habitat & Range
Present year-round in grassland habitat across the northern two-thirds of North America, the northern harrier is considered a locally common species. Their winter range includes most of the U.S. with the exception of high-mountain habitat in the East. Prairies, marshy grass-lands, wetlands, and old hayfields are home to the harrier. Unlike many other raptors, harriers will migrate and forage in rainy or snowy weather.

## Feeding
Voles, mice, rats, shrews, rabbits, and other small mammals are the primary prey of the northern harrier, but small birds, snakes, other reptiles, and insects are also eaten. Harriers glide very low over grassy habitat, watching and listening for movement below them, and then wheeling to turn, hover, and pounce when prey is located.

## Nesting
Harrier nests are built out of grasses, weed stems, and sticks placed on the ground, or on top of a platform built in cattails or other vegetation and suspended over water. The nests are always in dense vegetation and built primarily by the female. She lays a clutch of three to seven eggs and incubates them for about 30 days. The male delivers food to the female during incubation and after hatching, but she takes over when the chicks are about two weeks old. Five weeks after hatching the young harriers can fly.

## Backyard & Beyond
Harriers prefer grasslands, rough meadows, and grassy marshes (the harrier was formerly called the marsh hawk) for foraging, though they can also be seen along grassy dunes, old strip mines, and airport fields. Look for a large bird with a small head flying low over the ground, wheeling and teetering like a vulture. When the white rump patch flashes, you'll know you've got your harrier.

# Bald Eagle
## *Haliaeetus leucocephalus*

- Spring/Summer
- Year-Round
- Winter

The bald eagle barely edged out the wild turkey when our founding fathers were voting on a national symbol. Skilled fishing bird, scavenger, and pirate, the bald eagle is an opportunistic raptor that's been given a second chance thanks to improved conservation and bans on DDT, which dramatically impaired the birds' breeding and sent their population into steep decline in the decades following World War II.

## All About
There is no confusing the adult bald eagle, with its huge size and gleaming white head and tail. Adult plumage is not attained until after the third year. Until then, immature birds are dark brown with varying degrees of white mottling on their backs, wings, bellies, and, in older birds, heads. Depending upon age, the large bill is blackish or accented in the bright yellow seen in adults. Immatures and adults have strong, bright yellow talons.

## Habitat & Range
Water plays a strong role where bald eagles hunt and nest. In the process of rebounding in many areas, bald eagles now nest in most states, where they are often local nesters tied to specific sites. They are particularly common from Florida to coastal South Carolina and around the Great Lakes, but the largest breeding populations are in Alaska and western Canada. During winter, bald eagles often congregate at wetland areas, rivers, and dams, where fishing or carrion feeding is particularly productive.

## Feeding
Bald eagles hunt from perches or swoop down after sighting prey while soaring. Although fish are preferred prey (frequently grappled from the water in the eagle's mighty talons), eagles also eat a wide variety of other foods, depending upon individual, time of year, and location. Carrion—particularly dead fish, birds, and mammals—plays an important dietary role. Many live animals are also caught: muskrats, reptiles, amphibians, crustaceans, and birds—as large as great blue herons—have been documented. Bald eagles also steal fish from ospreys and other birds.

## Nesting
Bald eagles nest high in large trees in huge, bulky stick nests that are often used again over the years. Both mates collect sticks, and nest building may take several months. The female usually lays two eggs, which she and her mate incubate for just over a month. Once the first chick hatches, both parents incubate and *brood*, or cover, the eggs and hatchlings. Both parents feed their young, which leave the nest between 8 to 14 weeks after hatching.

## Backyard & Beyond
Recently, bald eagles have started nesting in closer proximity to human development, thanks to protection from disturbance. If you see a large, dark raptor soaring slowly in the sky, with flat wings, look for the other clues to the bald eagle's identity.

# Osprey
*Pandion haliaetus*

The bold chocolate and white "fish hawk," so familiar to boaters and fishermen, is happy to exploit artificial nesting platforms, from power poles to those built specifically for it. Though osprey populations declined by 90 percent from the 1950s to the 1970s (poisoned by persistent organochlorides), they have made a heartening rebound in recent decades.

## All About
Chocolate-brown above and pure white below, the osprey is armed with long, pale green legs and grappling-hook talons for seizing fish. Fierce yellow eyes are ringed in black, making the bird look as though it is wearing aviator's goggles. A banded gray tail and ragged crest complete this gangly bird's unusual look. Females have streaked upper breasts and are larger than males. When disturbed, ospreys give a series of high, piercing, chicklike peeps and thin screams.

## Habitat & Range
One of the most widespread species, the osprey inhabits rivers, lakes, and coastlines throughout much of the United States. It is still reclaiming territory in the interior United States, helped by osprey reintroduction programs. Lacking body down, ospreys must migrate to stay warm and to find sufficient food in unfrozen waters, traveling down both coasts of Mexico and Central America.

## Feeding
The only North American raptor to feed exclusively on fish, the osprey soars and hovers over shallow, clear waters of estuaries, marshes, lakes, and rivers, searching for fish. Spotting prey, it folds its wings and plunges, feet first, often completely beneath the surface. Unique cylindrical, recurved talons and horny spikes on the soles of its feet hold the fish securely until the osprey reaches a "carving block," usually a dead snag, where it can eat. Fish are always carried with the head facing into the wind, and are sometimes eaten as a snack on migration, far from water.

## Nesting
The huge stick nests ospreys build are a familiar site on channel markers, dead trees, and artificial nesting platforms along shorelines. Nesting pairs add sticks yearly until the nests assume enormous proportions. In the soft, grass-lined center the female lays two to three eggs, which she and her mate incubate for around 37 days. The male provides all the female's food during this time. Chicks stay in the nest for about 55 days, taking short flights, and are fed on or near the nest for around two weeks after first attaining flight.

## Backyard & Beyond
Though artificial nesting platforms have had a positive influence on osprey populations, they are by no means out of danger. Overfishing, pesticide contamination, and persecution on Latin American wintering grounds (where they are shot by the hundreds at fish farms) continue to limit populations.

# American Kestrel
## *Falco sparverius*

**N**orth America's smallest falcon is also the most familiar to many, hovering over farm fields and air strips, perching on telephone poles and wires, and nesting in boxes put out by concerned landowners, who welcome these insect and rodent eaters. In some regions, kestrel numbers have fallen in recent decades, probably due to large-scale landscape changes, as farm areas have reverted to forest and as cities and suburbs have stretched out to once-rural areas.

### All About
In flight, the kestrel has sharp-looking, pointed wings and a slender, long tail. In comparison to the merlin and peregrine falcons, it is slim. Sharp-shinned and Cooper's hawks also have long tails, but their wings are broad, not pointed. While soaring, the kestrel's wings look more rounded and the tail fans. Adult males are brightly colored, with blue-gray wings and crown, rufous tail, and a rusty back embellished with black barring. Black spots speckle the underparts. Both sexes have two vertical stripes on the face and a black spot on the back of the neck. Adult females lack the male's blue-gray wings, have barred tails, and—instead of black spots—sport rusty lines of spots on their underparts.

### Habitat & Range
The American kestrel is not strictly a farm bird, although many farms provide the ideal habitat for them. They also nest and hunt in open urban areas, open forest, clearings, and even deserts. They are truly American in the New World sense, nesting from Alaska to southern Argentina. In the North, numbers dwindle in winter, when northern birds move south *en masse* to winter in warmer areas.

### Feeding
Grasshoppers and other large insects are important prey to kestrels, but voles, mice, and other rodents also play a part in their diet, as do small birds, reptiles, and other small animals.

### Nesting
American kestrels are cavity nesters. Females usually lay their four to six eggs in a tree hole or other cavity, sometimes in a crevice in a building or cliff, or in a nest box. Both parents share the month-long incubation duties. Young fly about a month after hatching, and parents feed them until about two weeks after they leave the nest.

### Backyard & Beyond
Provision of nest boxes in rural areas has helped American kestrel populations, and this is one potential way to attract kestrels to your property if you live in an open area. Kestrels also pass through suburban areas during migration. They may frequent open suburbs rich in grasshoppers and such prey as small birds and lizards. They will use snags placed in the middle of grassy meadows as hunting and eating perches.

# Wild Turkey
## *Meleagris gallopavo*

When restocking programs abandoned using farm-raised birds and turned to releasing wild-caught birds in the 1940s, the repopulation of wild turkeys into their former haunts took off. Today, the large dark forms of wild turkeys are a familiar sight along many highways, and the birds even come to backyard feeders.

### All About
A tall, strong-legged bird, the wild turkey's feathers are iridescent with dark bronze, shot with hints of copper and acid green. Displaying in spring, the male erects its plumage in the strut posture, its enormous tail fanned, wings drooping, and wattles ablaze. A "beard" of wiry, barbless feathers sprouts from the center of his breast. Hens are visibly smaller and paler than gobblers, with a brown cast to their plumage and without distensible wattles. Along with the male's explosive gobble, turkeys employ a great variety of calls, including yelps and hollow *putt* sounds, in their intraflock communication.

### Habitat & Range
Dense deciduous forests—either uplands or bottomlands—with some clearings are ideal turkey habitats. The nuts from oaks and other nut trees make up an important component of their diet. Some exploit agricultural fields for spilled grain. Wild turkeys are nonmigratory and may fast for more than a week in severe weather.

### Feeding
The wild turkey's strong legs and feet help it scratch its way across the forest floor, raking away debris to uncover acorns, tree seeds, and invertebrates. Turkeys pluck buds and fruits as they walk or clamber through branches, and they strip grasses of their seeds by running stems through their bills. Young poults take a number of insects and invertebrates.

### Nesting
Gobblers display—gobbling and strutting—in early spring to attract visiting hens. After mating, the hen lays about a dozen eggs in a feather-lined bowl in the ground at the foot of a tree or under brush. She incubates them alone for about 26 days. When all chicks have hatched and imprinted on the hen (from one to three days later), they leave the nest, following her every move. She feeds them for the first few days; after that they pick up their own food. She broods them on the ground until they are able to join her in a roost tree at night; she still shelters them with spread wings on the roost.

### Backyard & Beyond
Wild turkeys may, in some rural and suburban situations, be attracted into yards with cracked corn spread on the ground. A small flock can consume as much as 50 pounds per week. Watching their fascinating social behavior and courtship behavior is a rich reward. Rotate feeding areas to prevent the spread of disease.

# American Coot

*Fulica americana*

- Spring/Summer
- Year-Round
- Winter

What looks like a duck and acts like a duck, but is not a duck? It's the American coot, of course. Coots are duck-like in many ways, but they are actually members of the rail family and are the most common (and most commonly seen) of all the rails. Like ducks, coots are excellent swimmers and use this ability to find and eat aquatic vegetation. However, coots are reluctant and awkward fliers—they must run, pattering across the water's surface and flapping madly to lift their heavy bodies into the air.

## All About
Chunky and almost all black with a contrasting white bill and red eyes and forehead patch, the coot is hard to mistake for anything else. The common moorhen and purple gallinule are similar in shape, but both are more colorful (the gallinule much more so) and less common than coots. Coots swim using the lobed toes on their powerful feet, and when swimming they bob their heads back and forth with a "funky chicken" motion. Coots are raucous, loud birds that utter a variety of grunts, cackles, and croaks.

## Habitat & Range
American coots are widespread across North America, especially in winter when they can be found in huge flocks on large bodies of water. They breed throughout the central and western portions of the continent, and they are year-round residents in parts of the Midwest and South. During the breeding season, coots prefer ponds, lakes, and marshes of almost any size, provided that they have large stands of tall reeds, such as cattails.

## Feeding
Finding most of their food on or below the surface of the water, coots dabble, swim, and dive when foraging. They are equally at home on land, grazing on the grass of city parks and golf courses. Their diet is largely vegetarian with the main menu items being duckweed, algae, and various pondweeds and sedges.

## Nesting
The female coot builds a floating, basket-shaped platform of vegetation with a lined cup to hold the eggs. She lays up to a dozen eggs and incubates them for about 23 days. Young coots have shiny, bald, red heads and golden down, an adaptation that is thought to trigger feeding by the parents. Babies leave the nest after a day or so and are able to find food on their own shortly thereafter.

## Backyard & Beyond
Though they may not be a backyard bird, coots should be easy to find in nearby parks and on golf course water hazards. In winter, look for flocks of coots on almost any body of water, from reservoirs to sewage ponds.

# Killdeer
*Charadrius vociferus*

The killdeer is a large, double-banded plover that screams its name across farm fields and other grass- and dirt-covered habitats. If you see an orange-tailed, stripe-winged bird calling KILL-DEEE, KILL-DEEE, you can rest assured that it's this plover. Despite their lousy-tasting flesh, many killdeer were shot during the late 1800s, along with a wide range of other shorebirds. These species are now protected from harm by federal and state laws.

## All About
On its white breast, two black bands stand out. Other plovers—such as the smaller but similar semipalmated plover—have only one band or none at all. Otherwise, killdeer are wet-sand brown above and clear white below, with white around the front of the face and eye. The killdeer is one of our largest and longest-tailed plovers, so even mixed with a few other species on a mudflat, they stand out, especially when you spot those two breast bands. Much of the tail is orange, except the tip, which is black punctuated with white dabs.

## Habitat & Range
Unlike most other plovers, killdeer often forage or nest far from water. You may find them on ball fields and airport runways, on turf, in pastures, and in farm fields, as well as on mudflats. They are found throughout North America, but northern birds head south for the winter.

## Feeding
A farmer's friend, the killdeer spends its foraging time searching for beetles, grasshoppers, caterpillars, and other insects. Crayfish, centipedes, spiders, and other invertebrates are also eaten, as well as some seeds.

## Nesting
A simple scrape in the dirt or gravel (including gravel-covered roofs) will do for a killdeer pair, although they sometimes add embellishments, such as a lining of pebbles, grass, or other small materials. Females lay three to five blotched eggs, which both parents incubate for just less than a month. Nesting in exposed habitats, killdeer rely on camouflage and deception to keep their eggs and chicks safe. If an intruder approaches the nest, an adult killdeer may feign injury—dragging a wing as if it is broken and exposing its bright tail—then lure the person or predator away from the nest. Adults watch over their hatchlings, little puffballs that can run around and find food by themselves shortly after hatching. They can fly before they reach one month old.

## Backyard & Beyond
Killdeer are attracted to large areas of grass as well as to short-cropped fields, so you may see them on your property if it's relatively treeless and large. Their cries carry long distances, so you may also hear killdeer passing by or calling from nearby nesting grounds.

# Lesser Yellowlegs
## *Tringa flavipes*

Lesser yellowlegs is a tall shorebird commonly seen in a variety of saltwater and freshwater situations. It winters in the Gulf States and along southern seacoasts, both east and west, so wherever you live in North America you stand a chance of seeing this species at some time during the year. Lessers often travel in large flocks and may be found together with greater yellowlegs.

### All About
True to its name, this bird has bright yellow legs, which really stand out against its dark back and speckled underparts. The sexes are alike. When alarmed, it will take flight with a loud *tu* or *tu-tu* call, trailing its long yellow legs behind. The only species the lesser yellowlegs is likely to be confused with is the equally common greater yellowlegs, a nearly identical, but larger, close relative. In flight, both show white on the rump. The smaller lesser yellowlegs has a shorter, straighter bill than the greater, and overall it has a much more delicate appearance.

### Habitat & Range
During migrations, the lesser yellowlegs is more likely than the greater yellowlegs to visit fresh water. It occurs widely and may stop at small ponds or wetlands, temporary rainwater puddles, marshes and mudflats, and flooded fields.

### Feeding
Lesser yellowlegs feed in shallow water where they find their prey—aquatic insects, snails, small fish, and crustaceans—on or just beneath the water's surface. They sometimes swing their heads back and forth underwater in an effort to stir up food. On land, the lesser yellowlegs may snatch up terrestrial insects and worms from the ground, or pick flying insects out of the air.

### Nesting
Breeding at the edge of the northern tundra, lesser yellowlegs nest in natural clearings with small clusters of vegetation. The nest is merely a scrape in the ground, softened with a few fallen leaves and placed next to a fallen log or under a low shrub, usually within 200 yards of a water source. Nesting starts as early as May, with the male calling loudly from the top of a tree or other elevated perch. The female lays three to four eggs, and both parents share the 18- to 20-day incubation. Within hours of hatching, the young are able to leave the nest. As soon as the chicks are self-sufficient—as early as July—the adults leave for the south. The youngsters start south a few weeks later.

### Backyard & Beyond
Any marsh or wetland in your neighborhood might host lesser yellowlegs during migration. Look for lesser yellowlegs in spring from April through June, and in fall from July through September. You should be able to find it easily at mudflats and marshes, mingling with other shorebirds.

# Spotted Sandpiper
*Actitis macularia*

The spotted sandpiper is one of the easiest sandpipers to identify. Not only are its markings distinctive, but so are its mannerisms—the bird signals itself to birders by almost constantly bobbing its posterior. An inland nester across much of northern North America, the spotted sandpiper frequents waterways from creeks and streams to marshes, reservoirs, and mudflats during migration, and shoreline areas during winter.

## All About
The wood-thrushlike breast spotting of breeding adult spotted sandpipers sets them apart from other sandpipers, but you can also easily identify spotless immatures (as shown in the photo) and non-breeders. For one thing, the spotted sandpiper's tail and rear end constantly bob up and down as the bird walks or pauses; this is true even in birds that have just left the nest. Also, look for a white crescent on the sides, which curls around the bend of the bird's folded wing, inching toward the back. Spotted sandpipers are about the length of a wood thrush and smaller than a robin—in other words, they are not the tiniest sandpipers, but they are rather small. Breeding individuals have bright orange bills; otherwise, spotted sandpipers have pale pinkish or orangish bills and legs.

## Habitat & Range
Spotted sandpipers nest in freshwater habitats, both in forested and open settings across much of North America, except in the far South, where a good number winter. Find them at pools where rainwater collects, along lakeshores, and at streams, rivers, or marshes. Many winter far to the south, from Mexico and Central America to as far south as northern Chile and Argentina.

## Feeding
As would be expected of a bird that frequents a mixture of habitats, the spotted sandpiper captures a variety of prey in diverse ways. Insects, crabs, worms, small fish, and other creatures may be picked from the water or shore, caught in quick flights, or chased.

## Nesting
Parental care in spotted sandpipers differs from that in many other birds. Female spotted sandpipers often pair up with more than one male, laying two or more clutches of eggs. Both parents build the nest, a depression in the ground usually sheltered by some plant cover and lined with plants or moss. There the female usually lays four eggs, which may be incubated by the male or by both parents for about three weeks. The nestlings teeter as soon as they hatch and can almost immediately scamper from the nest. Usually the male watches over the young, which can fly when they are about 18 days old.

## Backyard & Beyond
Any park or backyard with a large pond, stream, or lake is likely to host a spotted sandpiper at one time or another.

# American Woodcock
## *Scolopax minor*

The male American woodcock's courtship display is one of Nature's most unusual and it may be performing it in or near your backyard on early spring evenings. Its nocturnal habits, amazing sky dancing, and camouflage coloration make it one of the most fascinating, weird, and mysterious North American birds.

### All About
The American woodcock is a short, stocky shorebird with a long, straight bill and large eyes set far back on the head. This eye position gives it rearward vision, allowing it to watch for danger even when it is probing the ground for earthworms. The woodcock's plumage is a mixture of dark earth tones that hide it perfectly in its preferred woodland habitat. Males find a small clearing from which they repeatedly give a loud, nasal *peent!* call to announce themselves prior to launching into their impressive courtship display. They spiral upward for twenty or more seconds, wings whistling with each flap, then plummet to earth uttering a whistling twitter. Males perform this display before dawn and after dusk, hoping to attract watching females to mate.

### Habitat & Range
During the spring and summer, woodcocks can be found in wet woodlands and swampy thickets all across the eastern half of the United States and southern Canada. At night they forage and display in open habitats such as old fields, meadows, and wetland edges.

### Feeding
The tip of the woodcock's bill is sensitive and flexible—ideally suited to probing for earthworms and subterranean insects. When it senses an earthworm, the woodcock opens the tip of the upper mandible like a flexible tweezer to grasp the worm and pull it out. Other foods taken include spiders, snails, and some grass seeds.

### Nesting
Several males may be displaying in one place while one or more females watch. A female will choose a male, mate with him, and leave. Males have no role in caring for the young. The nest is a simple scrape on the ground lined with and surrounded by dead leaves. Usual clutch size is four eggs and incubation lasts about three weeks. Downy hatchlings leave the nest almost immediately and are tended by the female for a few days until they can feed on their own. They are fully flighted and independent after five weeks.

### Backyard & Beyond
On an early spring night at dusk, visit an old meadow surrounded by woods and listen for the low nasal call of the male woodcock and the whistling wings as he ascends for his display flight. If you look toward the western horizon, you may see his silhouette as he dances in the night sky.

# Bonaparte's Gull
## *Larus philadelphia*

- Spring/Summer
- Year-Round
- Winter

Though it breeds in the coniferous forests of the far North, the Bonaparte's gull is a common winter visitor across much of the U.S. Its small size and lilting ternlike flight separate it visually from other common winter gulls. This species is not named for famed French general Napolean Bonaparte, but for his cousin, French zoologist Charles Lucien Bonaparte.

### All About
Between April and August, adult Bonaparte's gulls are in breeding plumage with a black hood and bill and a broken white eye ring. But it is the winter plumage (worn from September through March) that is most familiar to bird watchers. The only remnant of the dark hood is a dark ear spot behind the eye—giving the impressions that the bird is wearing earphones. The legs remain pink and the thin, straight bill remains black all year. In flight, the winter adult appears light overall with the wingtips outlined in black. First-winter birds show a faint black "M" pattern across the backs of their wings.

### Habitat & Range
Bonaparte's gulls nest far to the north from east-central Canada into Alaska. Though they spend winters primarily on the ocean coasts, including the Gulf of Mexico, many birds linger inland, moving southward only if a freeze closes all bodies of water. They congregate in huge flocks at dam spillways, reservoirs, sewage lagoons, coastal estuaries, and along rivers, especially where food is abundant.

### Feeding
Insects are a primary food during the breeding season, but Bonaparte's gulls also eat small fish, crustaceans, and grasshoppers. They forage while flying and can plunge into the water for a fish, pluck a morsel from the water's surface, or hawk insects in flight with equal skill. In winter you may often seen Bonies foraging among flocks of mergansers, grebes, or cormorants, seizing small fish and other items stirred up by these diving birds.

### Nesting
Unlike any other North American gull, the Bonaparte's gull frequently builds its nest in trees, usually in a conifer adjacent to water. They may nest in small, loose colonies. The pair builds the nest of sticks lined with lichen or moss. Three or four eggs are laid and the shared incubation duties last about 24 days. Both parents care for the young until they are ready to undertake fall migration with the adults as early as late July.

### Backyard & Beyond
Almost any large, ice-free body of water in winter can host a flock of Bonaparte's gulls. Bonies are usually found in single-species flocks—they rarely associate with other, larger gull species. Though they may be found hawking insects at sewage ponds, don't look for them at garbage dumps with other gulls.

# Ring-billed Gull

## *Larus delawarensis*

This gull might almost be called the inland gull. Though found in coastal areas like most gulls, it is also the most numerous and widespread gull away from the seacoasts, sometimes found in huge flocks. At first glance it looks like a slightly smaller version of the herring gull, but it has a personality all its own.

## All About
The ring-billed gull is a medium-sized (19 inches long) gull, and in adult plumage it has a light gray back and wings on a pure white body. Its wing tips are black with white spots, and it has a black ring near the end of its yellow bill. Males and females look alike. Young ring-billed gulls take three years to mature, during which time their bodies and wings are varying shades of mottled brown and gray, with a white tail that has a prominent, black terminal band. These gulls are smaller, lighter, and more graceful-looking than similarly patterned herring gulls, and they have a more buoyant appearance in flight.

## Habitat and Range
In addition to the beaches and bays of the seacoasts, ring-billed gulls may be found at large inland lakes and rivers, in newly plowed fields and pastures, and at sod farms, garbage dumps, and parking lots throughout their range.

## Feeding
Ring-billed gulls are omnivorous, thriving on whatever food is on hand. Fish are a favorite item, but insects and earthworms are high on the list, along with grains, refuse, and even small rodents. They will eat the eggs of other species, and they are not averse to taking handouts from humans at parking lots and picnic grounds. (French fries, caught in midair, are popular. Ketchup is optional.)

## Nesting
After a courtship routine by the male (which includes bowing, throat-puffing, and a ceremonial walk around the female, enlivened by many odd gesticulations), the mated pair will build its nest on the ground in a fairly open area near water. The ring-billed is colonial, so there are usually lots of similar nests nearby. Both sexes build the flimsy nest of grasses, sticks, and moss; and both take turns incubating the two to four eggs for up to four weeks until hatching. The downy young are tended by their parents in the general vicinity of the nest until they attain flight at about five weeks of age.

## Backyard & Beyond
Look for ring-billed gulls in large, open fields after spring or autumn rainstorms, or watch for them anywhere there is an infestation of large insects, such as grasshoppers or locusts. If there is a landfill or dam nearby, it may attract gulls from a wide surrounding area and can make for productive gull watching.

# Herring Gull
## *Larus argentatus*

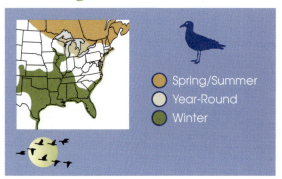

This is the bird that most people think of when they hear the term seagull. Large, abundant, and widespread, the herring gull is an imposing bird—and, in its adult plumage, it is certainly beautiful. Picture a dozen or more sitting on a pier with ocean waves lapping below, and you have a perfect coastal postcard scene.

## All About
Measuring up to 26 inches in length, the adult herring gull has silver-gray wings tipped in black and white, a dazzling white body, bold yellow bill, and pink legs. Males and females are alike, and they are considerably larger than similar-looking ring-billed gulls. Immature herring gulls wear varying shades of brown or gray-brown and are not fully mature until their fourth year. All ages join in making the yelping or trumpeting calls, which are a constant fact of life throughout the herring gull's entire range.

## Habitat & Range
Herring gulls are birds of shorelines, major lakes and rivers, garbage dumps, and, occasionally, farmlands—especially recently tilled fields. Their population, once confined to the northern states, has been spreading southward for decades. They nest across Canada and are found year-round throughout the Great Lakes. Winter flocks may be found along major rivers.

## Feeding
Herring gulls eat almost anything, which is one reason for their success. Fish, along with all manner of other seafood, are a staple of the herring gull diet, but they also eat the eggs and chicks of other bird species (they can decimate a tern colony if given the opportunity), all kinds of garbage, large insects and grubs, and even carrion. They are smart and have learned to drop clams onto rocks or pavement to open them. They are quite willing to steal food from other birds. In the gull world, there is no such thing as a guilty conscience.

## Nesting
Herring gulls nest on the ground, preferably in the lee of a rock or some other natural feature. Both sexes help scrape out a site and line it with grass, weeds, and feathers. Many nests contain a ball of some kind—whiffle ball, tennis ball—which may be a courtship gift from the male. The usual clutch is three eggs, and both parents share the month-long incubation. The young, downy and active from the start, depend on their parents at least until they fly at about 50 days of age.

## Backyard & Beyond
Check the range map above to see when herring gulls might be expected in your area, and then visit the nearest beach! These birds also hang out at sewage outlets, dams, or anywhere that human activity may generate a reliable food supply.

# Mourning Dove
## *Zenaida macroura*

Whether you regard them as songbirds or living skeet targets, if you feed birds, you probably have mourning doves as constant companions. These tapered, graceful brown and pinkish birds wholeheartedly embrace human alterations of the natural landscape, finding their greatest abundance in agricultural and suburban areas. Doves love water, but may foul birdbaths by sitting around the rim, tails in.

### All About
The mournful *oooahh*, *oooh*, *ooh*, *ooh* song of the mourning dove echos from power lines and treetops in early spring. Mourning doves travel in flocks, breaking rank only to nest and raise young. Males defend their mates as a kind of mobile territory, defending her and the immediate nest site—but not much else—from other birds.

### Habitat & Range
The only habitat shunned by mourning doves is deep, contiguous forest. They are most common in agricultural areas with hedgerows and shelterbelts. They are also abundant in suburban areas as well, where visits to feeding stations are an integral part of their daily routines. Mourning doves migrate, especially far northern populations, but some individuals are resident year-round.

### Feeding
Streamlined, fast, and powerful flyers, mourning doves travel in flocks, descending to feed on a great variety of grains and weed seeds that they peck from the ground. They are often seen in ranks on power lines over farm fields. A capacious crop allows mourning doves to gorge—sometimes to the point of being misshapen—and then digest their stored food later when resting.

### Nesting
Mourning doves may mate and nest in any month of the year, but males begin to tune up their songs in late winter. They have a production-line breeding mode, following one brood with another as often as six times in a season. The twig nest platform, placed in a wide variety of tree species, but frequently in a pine, is often flimsy enough so that eggs show through from beneath. Two eggs are incubated by both members of the pair, and they hatch in 14 days. Young doves are fed first on crop milk, a secretion unique to the pigeon family, and later on regurgitated seeds. Young remain in the nest for another 15 days but may fledge much earlier. The male feeds them until about day 30, while the female re-nests. Immature birds are visibly smaller and have fine, buff feather edges overall.

### Backyard & Beyond
Mourning doves take any seeds that might be offered at feeders, preferring sunflower seeds, cracked corn, millet, milo, and other grains found in seed mixes. They become adept at emptying hopper feeders into their ample crops, and then sitting for long periods afterward to digest their food.

# Rock Pigeon
## *Columba livia*

Originating in northern Europe, Africa, and India, rock pigeons—largely gone from their former wild haunts—have spread to cities and towns worldwide thanks to their domestication some five thousand years ago. Evidence of this domestication lies in their highly variable coloration; a flock may contain birds in every color from pure white to reddish to solid black.

## All About

A substantial bird with a small head, deep chest, powerful wings, and a square tail, the rock pigeon is built for flight. Wild-type birds are slate-blue with a white rump, black terminal tail band, and two black bars on the secondary wing feathers. Pinkish green iridescence adorns the neck. Pigeons have short, reddish legs and a short, straight bill. Their song is a series of soft, resonant coos—*ooh-ga-rooogh*—and a harsh *Woogh!* serves as an alarm call. Pigeons can be found in flocks except when tending young.

## Habitat & Range

It is rare to find rock pigeons in natural habitats, though there are still some cliff-nesting populations in North America. Most consider tall buildings, with their myriad ledges, to be ideal nesting grounds and are happy to take foods, such as bread and popcorn, from city sidewalks. Pigeons are nonmigratory, though their celebrated homing skills are exploited by pigeon racing clubs across the world.

## Feeding

Walking and pecking with rapidly bobbing heads, pigeons find their preferred food—grains, seeds, and some fruits—on the ground. Urban birds have highly developed scavenging skills, raiding trashcans and fast food litter for high-carbohydrate fare, such as bread.

## Nesting

It's easy to watch pigeons display and even mate; the male's spinning, bowing, and cooing may be conducted underfoot on city sidewalks. Pigeons mate for life, guarding females zealously. They may lay eggs and raise young anytime. Building ledges, highway overpasses, barns, bridges, and other structures may be selected as the site on which to build a stick-and-grass nest and lay two eggs. Both male and female incubate for about 18 days. The rubbery, black-skinned squabs stay in the nest for a variable period of 25 to 45 days. Fat at fledging, they may be forced to fend entirely for themselves upon leaving the nest.

## Backyard & Beyond

Thanks to the flocking habit of pigeons, most feeder operators are less than delighted when they descend. The most effective deterrents seem to be sturdy feeders enclosed by wire caging that excludes pigeons while admitting smaller birds. Some people opt to spread food at a distance to keep pigeons from overwhelming seed feeders. Pigeons will eat anything that might be offered, but millet and cracked corn are special favorites.

# Yellow-billed Cuckoo

*Coccyzus americanus*

The yellow-billed cuckoo is a furtive, skulking bird of thickets and brushy woodland edges and, though it is fairly large, its retiring habits make it far more easily heard than seen. It often hides deep within the foliage and, when perching in the open, it tends to remain very still. The yellow-billed cuckoo makes a unique repetitive clucking sound that is a sure clue to identification.

## All About
Slender and long-tailed, the yellow-billed cuckoo has a plain brown back and creamy white breast. The underside of the tail shows a pattern of bold white spots against a black background, and bright rufous wing patches are visible in flight. The lower part of the bill is yellow. Male and female yellow-billed cuckoos look alike. The only other species they are likely to be confused with is the related black-billed cuckoo, which lacks the rufous wing color and has a black bill, among other differences.

## Habitat & Range
Yellow-billed cuckoos inhabit deciduous woodland edges, thickets and tangles along watercourses or roadsides, willow groves, and overgrown orchards. Yellow-billed cuckoos are not generally found in deep interior woodlands, as they prefer some kind of "edge" to their habitat.

## Feeding
Yellow-billed cuckoos eat great numbers of hairy caterpillars and many large insects such as dragonflies, cicadas, grasshoppers, crickets, and beetles. Small fruits are a minor but regular part of their diet in summer. Most yellow-billed cuckoos forage by slowly and methodically exploring branches, twigs, and leaves for hidden insects, but they occasionally may act like flycatchers, darting into the air for a meal on the wing, or hovering to seize a caterpillar at the edge of a leaf.

## Nesting
Once paired, cuckoos survey the surrounding area for a leafy and secluded nest site, five to ten feet off the ground. Both help build a loose shell of twigs and stems, lining it with fine grasses. Three to five eggs are laid, and both parents share the incubation and feeding of the young. The entire process, from egg laying to fledging, takes only 17 days, one of the shortest such periods for any bird species.

## Backyard & Beyond
If you have mature trees rimming your backyard, you may have an occasional yellow-billed cuckoo stopping by on migration—listen for its patented clucking calls. An old folk name for the yellow-billed cuckoo is "raincrow," because these *kowp-kowp-kowp* calls are so often uttered on hot summer afternoons, when thunderstorms are likely to follow. Knowing the cuckoo's call will be helpful in finding this secretive bird; otherwise, check the thickets and edges of your local woodland or park for a chance to find this species.

# Great Horned Owl
*Bubo virginianus*

Huge, powerful, and widespread across North America, the great horned is the king of all of our owls. Armed with incredible vision, the great horned sees and pounces on prey, using its powerful talons and bill to dispatch its victim. The deep, hooting call of the great horned—whoo-who-o-o-o-who-who—a staple of movie and television soundtracks, is most often heard in nature just after sunset.

## All About
The great horned owl is named for its large size (up to 24 inches tall, with a wingspan of 44 inches) and its long feathered head tufts (horns). A deep rusty brown and buff overall, this owl has large, golden-yellow eyes. Its thick, soft feathers provide excellent insulation from either heat or cold, permitting the great horned to nest as soon as early to midwinter even in regions with harsh winter weather.

## Habitat & Range
A nonmigratory bird throughout the Americas, great horned owls can be found as far north as the tree line, and as far south as South America—and in nearly every conceivable habitat and setting. Great horned owls are equally at home in urban and suburban settings, as well as in deep woodlands, grasslands, and deserts.

## Feeding
Mammals (rabbits, hares, and large rodents) are the primary prey item of great horned owls. They also eat earthworms, fish, snakes, and even birds as large as great blue herons. They are one of the few predators that will readily kill and consume skunks. Within a great horned owl's territory, it's unusual to find other, smaller owls—they may have been eaten by the resident great horneds. Their primary hunting mode is to perch, watch, and pounce on prey.

## Nesting
Great horned owls most often take over an old stick nest built by a hawk, heron, or squirrel, but they will also nest on cliff ledges, in tree cavities, and even on the ground. Two to four eggs are laid and incubation by the female lasts slightly more than a month. The male brings food to his mate on the nest each night. Six weeks or so after hatching, the young owlets venture from the nest to nearby branches. They remain dependent on the adults for many months, but leave the nest area before the next breeding season.

## Backyard & Beyond
If you live in or near older woodlands, chances are good that great horned owls are your neighbors. Though there is little you can do to attract great horned owls to your property, listen just after dusk and before dawn for their deep hoots, which carry for great distances. Watch for the great horned's silhouette at dusk along woodland edges, especially in treetops and on power poles.

# Barred Owl
## *Strix varia*

**W**ho cooks for you? Who cooks for you all? The wild hoots of the barred owl echo through swampy, deciduous woodlands throughout the eastern United States. Its dark, liquid eyes give it a deceptively gentle look, but this owl is a top-of-the-line predator, taking everything from fish to rabbits. Though it does some daylight hunting, most of the barred owl's foraging takes place at night.

### All About
A rounded, earless outline, smoky gray-brown plumage that is heavily mottled and barred with white, broad brown streaks on a white belly, and dark eyes distinguish the barred owl. Its bill and feet are yellow. Its familiar eight-hoot call gives way to raucous and sometimes frightening caterwauling in breeding season. This species is more apt to call in daylight than any other; it may call all day during overcast conditions.

### Habitat & Range
Like its famous endangered cousin the spotted owl, the barred owl prefers old forest, probably in part because the large nesting cavities it requires occur in trees of ample girth. It is commonly associated with lowlands, but occupies upland sites as well. The barred owl does not migrate, but may wander in harsh winters.

### Feeding
Anything it can kill is fair game for this medium-large owl. Small mammals, as small as mice and up to the size of rabbits, make up at least half the barred owl's diet. It makes acrobatic strikes after squirrels, sometimes turning completely over in flight. Birds, amphibians, reptiles, insects, and other invertebrates compose the rest of its diet.

### Nesting
Most barred owls select large nest cavities, such as those formed when a large branch breaks off of a hollow tree. They will also use a hollow in a broken tree trunk, as well as the nests of other raptors or squirrels. Two to three eggs are incubated by the female alone. They hatch from 28 to 33 days later. The male feeds the family for the first two weeks of the chicks' life, after which the female leaves them and helps bring in food. Young owls, clothed in buff-colored down, begin venturing onto branches when they are around five weeks old, before they can fly. They give a hideous, rasping screech as a location call and may be found and observed discreetly from a safe distance. Fledglings are fed by their parents until early autumn, when they strike out to find new territory.

### Backyard & Beyond
Surprisingly enough, the barred owl will accept nest boxes, because tree cavities large enough to contain them are hard to find. Plans for a wood duck nest box with a seven-inch entrance hole should accommodate them. This should be mounted as high as possible in a large tree.

# Eastern Screech-Owl
## *Megascops asio*

Eastern screech-owls are very acclimated to humans, but their nocturnal habits and cryptic coloration keep us from seeing them regularly. Even when perched in full view in daylight, screech-owls have a remarkable ability to conceal themselves. Found commonly in cities and towns, the screech-owl's success may be due not only to its secretive nature, but also to its ability to take a wide variety of small prey.

## All About
A small bird (8$\frac{1}{2}$ inches long), the eastern screech-owl occurs in two color variations: reddish and gray, with gray being more common. The screech-owl's plumage appears very barklike. When a "screech" sits with its body elongated and ear tufts extended, it looks like a broken branch stub. This bird's name is misleading; a screech is rarely voiced. The call most bird watchers hear is a series of descending, whinnying whistles and tremolos on a single note.

## Habitat & Range
A nonmigratory, resident bird throughout the eastern United States, the screech-owl is found wherever woodlands are mature enough to have cavities. Unlike many other owl species, the screech-owl is commonly found in urban parks and suburban backyards.

## Feeding
Eastern screech-owls will eat almost anything—from mice and voles to moths, earthworms, crawfish, frogs, and fish. In spring and summer, they prey upon small and medium-sized songbirds, but during winter small mammals are more common prey. Screech-owls perch in a tree, waiting and watching for potential prey, most of which is captured with the owl's feet in flight or by pouncing on the ground.

## Nesting
Screech-owls nest in natural cavities and will readily use nest boxes. They begin nesting early, from mid-December in the South to late March in the North. Two to six eggs are laid and a month-long incubation period ensues. The female incubates the eggs and broods the young owlets, while the male delivers all the food. Owlets remain in the nest for a month before venturing into nearby trees. They remain dependent on their parents for two months.

## Backyard & Beyond
You may very well already have eastern screech-owls in or near your backyard. Spend some time outside at night—especially when the moon is full—listening for the screech-owl's wavering calls. Check natural tree cavities during the day for roosting or nesting owls—they may be peering out of the hole. You can attract screech-owls with an owl nest box. Boxes should be about 12 to 14 inches deep with an internal floor size of 7×7 inches and a 2$\frac{3}{4}$-inch diameter entry. Place the box above 10 feet high in a shady spot on a tree trunk wider than the box's width.

# Whip-poor-will
## *Caprimulgus vociferus*

Imagine sleeping all day and flying around the woods singing all night. That's the life of the whip-poor-will. Like its relatives the common nighthawk and chuck-will's widow, the "whip" is most active at night and is often heard calling out its name repeatedly—whip-poor-WILL! whip-poor-WILL! In fact, they have been known to give this call continuously, more than a thousand times in a row. Because of its nocturnal habits and coloration, many bird watchers never get a good look at a whip-poor-will.

## All About
The whip-poor-will's body is just under 10 inches in length, and its wingspan is 19 inches—nearly 7 inches shorter than that of the chuck-will's-widow. The whip-poor-will's plumage is a subtle mix of charcoal gray, buff, black, and white. In flight, it shows prominent white corners on the tail. The large, dark eyes of the whip-poor-will are designed to function in the low-light conditions of dawn and dusk.

## Habitat & Range
Whip-poor-wills prefer mixed woodlands with little underbrush, open farmlands, brushy fields, and rural roadways. These habitats all lend themselves to the pursuit of flying insects. Whips spend the winter in Florida, around the Gulf Coast, and into Mexico and Central America. They return each spring as early as March. In southern portions of the Midwest, the whip-poor-will is replaced by the closely related chuck-will's-widow.

## Feeding
The whip-poor-will is an insect specialist, perching and watching for passing prey, which it pursues in silent flight. Stiff bristle feathers line its wide-opening bill and funnel flying insects into its mouth as it flies along. Primary food items include mosquitoes, moths, beetles, and grasshoppers. Most foraging is done in the half-light of dusk and dawn, and on brightly moonlit nights.

## Nesting
A ground nester, the whip-poor-will builds no nest. As early as mid-April, two eggs are laid in a concealed spot on the ground and incubated by both sexes for about 20 days. After hatching, the young birds remain with the parents for two weeks, with both parents sharing the brooding. Young whips are able move around on the ground within a few days after hatching; they are able to fly at about 16 days old. This early mobility helps young whip-poor-wills avoid predators.

## Backyard & Beyond
Whip-poor-wills are declining in some parts of their range due to the effects of pesticides and the loss of breeding habitats. If you are close to a calling whip-poor-will, listen for the *cluck* sound that it makes just prior to the *whip*. Perhaps the best way to see whip-poor-wills is to watch for them at dusk as they make their silent, batlike forays after insects along woodland edges and over meadows.

# Common Nighthawk
*Chordeiles minor*

- Spring/Summer
- Year-Round
- Winter

*Peent!* *is the nasal flight call of the common nighthawk, a familiar sound in cities and towns, though it is usually mistaken for an insect call. This call accompanies the batlike flight of the nighthawk as it courses through the sky, hawking insects. Despite its name, the nighthawk is not a hawk and is active both day and night.*

## All About
The common nighthawk is a long-winged, dark bird with characteristic white wing slashes. Its distinctive bounding flight can be used to identify it from a distance as it forages over fields, towns, and woods. Nighthawks belong to the goatsucker family, a name based on the old myth that they drank milk from livestock at night.

## Habitat & Range
A common breeding bird throughout North America, nighthawks can be seen in flight over almost any habitat. In cities and towns, nighthawks are attracted to the insects around streetlamps. Beginning in late July, nighthawks can be seen at dusk in large migratory flocks, sometimes numbering dozens of birds. Nighthawks winter in South America, returning to the southern United States by early April.

## Feeding
A specialist in catching flying insects, the common nighthawk's mouth opens wide to capture its prey. The nighthawk sees its prey—most often flying ants, beetles, moths, and mayflies—and pursues and catches it. When a nighthawk needs water, it swoops low over a lake or river and skims a drink from the surface.

## Nesting
Historically, nighthawk nests were found on the ground in grasslands and in open patches of soil, gravel, or sand. The nest is a shallow depression near a log or stone that helps to shade and conceal it. Now, nighthawk nests are more commonly found on gravel roads or on flat, gravel-covered rooftops in urban areas. The female selects the nest site, lays two eggs, and handles the 18-day incubation. Young nighthawks are brooded by the female for 15 days, protecting them from sun and weather. The male feeds both his mate and the young in the nest. After 20 days, the young birds are able to fly, and the male then takes over their care while the female starts a second nest.

## Backyard & Beyond
Nighthawks have good success nesting on gravel roofs, but not so on roofs lined with rubber or foam, materials that pool water and retain heat. Watch and listen for nighthawks in the sky at dawn and dusk. You may hear their *peent!* before you see them. During courtship, male nighthawks perform a diving display near females, swooping swiftly toward the ground. As the male comes out of the dive, he flares his flight feathers, creating a booming sound much like a large truck shifting gears.

# Chimney Swift

*Chaetura pelagica*

Known by bird watchers as "the flying cigar," the chimney swift is a familiar sight in the sky over cities and towns during the spring, summer, and fall. Its nickname aptly describes the swift's elongated flight silhouette. The twittering calls of chimney swifts are one of the most common bird sounds of summer. The chimney swift is named for its preferred nesting and roosting site—the inside of chimneys. This species spends much of its life on the wing, stopping only to sleep and nest.

## All About

Chimney swifts are a dark charcoal-gray overall with a small black bill, eyes, and tiny feet. Indeed their feet are almost useless for walking, but are perfect for clinging to the inside of a chimney. The chimney swift is nearly all wing—with a 5-inch long body and a 14-inch wingspan. Four hundred years ago, all chimney swifts nested in hollow trees and caves, but the arrival of European settlers and their stone chimneys soon provided abundant nesting sites. Today most chimney swifts nest in chimneys and other human structures, such as unused smokestacks and abandoned buildings.

## Habitat & Range

Widespread and common across the eastern half of the United States and southern Canada, the chimney swift is found wherever there are suitable nest sites. Fall migratory flocks of swifts are a magnificent spectacle as they form a swirling, chattering cloud descending to roost in a large chimney at dusk. In winter, this tiny bird migrates to South America, returning again in March to the southern United States.

## Feeding

An all-insect diet is captured and consumed on the wing. Swifts often are seen flying high in the sky when foraging.

## Nesting

A pair of swifts chooses a nest site—usually a chimney. The nest is a half-saucer shape made of sticks held together and made to adhere to the wall of cavity by the birds' saliva. Swifts break small twigs off trees, grabbing them with their feet as they fly past a tree. Two to five eggs are laid, and both parents share incubation (15 days) and brooding duties until the young swifts fledge at about 19 days after hatching.

## Backyard & Beyond

Allowing chimney swifts to nest in your older, unused chimney is really easy—just let the swifts find it. They pose no danger and, if not for the sounds of hungry nestlings during a two-week period, you might not know they are there. If hosting swifts is not your cup of tea, check around your town or region for chimneys being used by swifts. Watch for them entering or leaving the large brick chimneys on schools and old factories. Modern chimneys with metal caps and flues are impossible for swifts to use.

# Ruby-throated Hummingbird
## *Archilochus colubris*

The only breeding hummingbird east of the Great Plains, the rubythroat enlivens many gardens and yards with its presence. Males are fiercely combative and will defend a single nectar source against all comers. Spectacular pendulum flights, constant chittering, the low hum of beating wings, and the occasional smack of tiny bodies colliding are familiar to anyone lucky enough to have rubythroats at their nectar feeders.

## All About

Seen in direct sunlight, the male's ruby throat patch dazzles. Both male and female are iridescent green above. The female's underparts are white, and she sports white spots on her rounded tail. Males appear smaller and darker overall, with grayish-olive underparts and a slightly forked, all dark tail. A squeaky *chip* is uttered constantly while feeding. Males sing a seldom heard, monotonous song from exposed perches at daybreak.

## Habitat & Range

Rubythroats prefer mixed deciduous woodlands with clearings, where wildflowers and abundant small insects can be found. They're fairly common in forested areas across the entire eastern United States, falling off abruptly at the Great Plains. Virtually all rubythroats leave for the winter, many making the arduous nonstop flight across the Gulf of Mexico on fat reserves alone. Rubythroats winter in Central America.

## Feeding

Though they are usually regarded as wholly nectivorous, rubythroats take a great number of small insects, which they catch by gleaning or in aerial pursuit. They may even rob spider webs of their catch. They are strongly attracted to red or orange flowers, but rubythroats will take nectar from flowers of any color. They hover and probe rapidly, often perching to feed.

## Nesting

Once a male rubythroat has mated, his investment in the offspring is over. The female constructs a walnut-sized, thick-walled cup of plant down and spider silk, bound tightly with elastic spider web and encrusted with lichens. This well-insulated nest protects the two lentil-sized eggs when she must leave to forage. The young hatch after about 13 days and remain in the nest for about 21 days. The female regurgitates small insects and nectar into their crops. They are fed for at least a week or longer after fledging.

## Backyard & Beyond

Attract rubythroats with a 1:4 solution of white table sugar (sucrose) and water. Wash feeders with hot soapy water every few days and replace the solution. Boiling the solution briefly helps it keep longer. Artificial coloring in the solution is unnecessary (feeders have ample red parts). To thwart a bullying male, hang several feeders within a few feet of each other. He'll be unable to defend them all.

# Belted Kingfisher
## *Ceryle alcyon*

The belted kingfisher is a bird many recognize but few know well. Kingfishers take wariness to new extremes, uttering a loud rattle of alarm and swooping off at the slightest disturbance. The belted kingfisher's piercing rattle call, usually given as it takes flight, is more often heard than this wary bird is seen. They are a thrilling presence on streams, rivers, lakes, and marshes—wherever clear water and small fish abound.

## All About
Almost comical in proportion, the belted kingfisher has an oversized crested head and a heavy spearlike bill, but diminutive feet. It cannot walk, but only shuffle, and it relies entirely on flight for most of its locomotion. Slate-blue upperparts, a stark-white collar and underparts, and a bluish breast band complete the ensemble. The female wears a "bra"—another rufous breast band below the blue one.

## Habitat & Range
Because it is a sight hunter, the belted kingfisher seeks out clear water. Most often found along clear running streams, lakes, and ponds, it will also hunt drainage ditches and marshes. Nesting requires an exposed earthen bank. Kingfishers are migratory in northern latitudes. Though they can survive winter temperatures, they require open water year-round; thus, southern birds may migrate only as far as they must to find open water.

## Feeding
Most of its hunting is done from a perch, but the belted kingfisher also hunts on the wing. Suspended in midair like an angel, it hovers, seemingly weightless, over a riffle. Spotting a minnow, it closes its wings and plunges bill-first into the water. It carries the fish in its bill to a sturdy perch (usually a dead snag or partially submerged branch), where it subdues its prey by whacking its head against the perch with sideways flips of its bill. The fish is then swallowed head first. Belted kingfishers also take crayfish and (to a much lesser extent) amphibians, reptiles, small mammals, and young birds.

## Nesting
Kingfishers occasionally are forced to commute, if they are unable to find a dry earthen bank near their chosen feeding territory. They may use sand and gravel pits, landfills, or road cuts. This species excavates, digging rapidly with tiny feet straight into the bank, creating a round entrance hole and an upward-sloping tunnel that may extend as much as six feet into the bank. A chamber at the end holds five to eight eggs, which both male and female incubate for about 22 days. Young stay in the burrow for up to 29 days and are fed by their parents for three more weeks.

## Backyard & Beyond
Any clear body of water, including backyard ponds with plump goldfish, can host a hunting kingfisher.

# Red-headed Woodpecker
## *Melanerpes erythrocephalus*

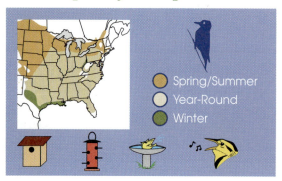

A striking combination of red, black, and white, the red-headed woodpecker is our most easily identifiable woodpecker and a favorite of many bird watchers. Though the species was first described in 1758, Native Americans had long used skins of the red-headed woodpecker as a battle ornament. Sadly, the red-headed has suffered population declines throughout its range, but it remains locally common in the proper habitat.

## All About
The red-headed woodpecker could be called the red-*hooded* woodpecker because the red on adult birds forms a complete hood. Some mistakenly refer to the red-bellied woodpecker (which has a Mohawk stripe of red) as a red-headed woodpecker. The red-head's black back and tail are set off by a bright white breast and belly and an all-white patch of secondary (inner) wing feathers. The effect of these contrasting colors is stunning in flight. Red-heads give a variety of *churr-churr* calls as well as a loud, throaty *Queeah!*

## Habitat & Range
Prior to the 1900s, red-headed woodpeckers were common in cities and towns. Today, red-heads are sparingly distributed across most of the eastern United States, usually in woods with mature oaks or beeches, in isolated woodlots along rivers, or in dead trees along flooded river bottoms and beaver ponds. Habitats affected by humans—strip mines, clear cuts, tree plantations, and farmlands—may attract red-headed woodpeckers as long as there are scattered, standing trees.

## Feeding
Red-heads have the most varied diet of all woodpeckers, but they seem especially attached to acorns and beechnuts. They are excellent flycatchers and are known to eat grasshoppers, fruits, corn, eggs, mice, and even bird nestlings. When nuts and insects are plentiful, red-heads will cache them for later consumption, hiding food items in bark crevices and knotholes. At bird feeders, red-heads eat sunflower seeds, peanuts, and suet, but they are particularly attracted to cracked corn.

## Nesting
Avid excavators of nesting and roosting holes, red-heads thus provide homes for many other cavity-nesting creatures. Nest holes are almost always in dead trees or dead portions of living trees, though wooden telephone poles are also used. Five eggs is the normal clutch, and both parents share in the two-week incubation duties. Young birds spend three weeks in the nest cavity before fledging, and they emerge with gray, not red, heads.

## Backyard & Beyond
Red-headed woodpeckers are very aggressive and can out-compete European starlings for nest cavities. Look for red-heads in large stands of trees (especially oaks) with little vegetation below them, as in a park or golf course. Reliable locations for seeing red-headed woodpeckers are becoming noteworthy as the species declines.

# Red-bellied Woodpecker
*Melanerpes carolinus*

The red-bellied woodpecker is so common, vocal, and eye-catching that it might be elected "most familiar woodpecker" in a vote of bird watchers in the eastern United States. Although occasionally misidentified as a red-headed woodpecker because of the male redbelly's bill-to-nape stripe of bright red, the red-bellied woodpecker actually is quite different in appearance—and much more common—than the real red-headed woodpecker, which sports an all-red head.

## All About

A medium-sized (9¼ inches long) woodpecker with a stout, chisel-shaped bill and a zebra pattern of black-and-white horizontal strips on the back, the red-bellied woodpecker is named for a feature we rarely see—a light wash of pink or red on its belly. Hitching up tree trunks with the aid of its strong feet and stiff tail, the bird's red belly is almost always obscured. Adult males have a solid strip of red from the top of the bill and head and down the back of the neck (the nape). Females have a red nape, but are brownish on the top of the head. The redbelly's loud, rich call sounds like *qurrrr*, and its longer version is more rattling and harsher—*chrr, chrr, chrchrchrchr*.

## Habitat & Range

A year-round resident across the eastern United States, the redbelly is an adaptable bird, found wherever there are mature trees. They do not migrate, though some northern birds may move southward in winter.

## Feeding

The redbelly is an expert at excavating insects from trees using its bill as a chisel and its long, barbed tongue to extract food items. It will also eat berries, fruits, nuts, tree sap, salamanders, mice, and even small nestling birds. At bird-feeding stations, redbellies relish peanuts, suet, sunflower seeds, and cracked corn.

## Nesting

The male redbelly begins courtship by drumming (a rapid pounding with the bill) on a tree trunk or branch to attract the female's attention. Both male and female excavate the nest cavity, which is usually located in a dead tree below an overhanging branch. The 8- to 12-inch deep cavity will accommodate four eggs. Incubation duties are shared and last about 12 days. Nestlings are fed in the nest cavity by both parents for almost a month before they fledge; afterward, they remain near the nest and are fed by the parents for several more weeks. Nest hole competition from European starlings can be fierce and usually results in the redbellies being evicted and forced to excavate a new nest elsewhere.

## Backyard & Beyond

Peanuts and suet are the redbelly's favored foods, but you can also offer apple halves stuck on a tree stub, sunflower bits, and grape jelly (in a small dish). Listen for the redbelly's loud, ringing calls and watch for its swooping flight.

# Downy Woodpecker
## *Picoides pubescens*

Downy woodpeckers are a favorite of backyard bird watchers because they are often the first woodpeckers to visit bird feeders. Common in any habitat with trees, downies are as equally at home in backyards as they are in remote woods. In all seasons, downy woodpeckers give a rattling whinny that descends in tone. They also utter a sharp pik! call regularly while foraging.

## All About
The downy is the smallest ($6^{3}/_{4}$ inches long), most common, and most widespread woodpecker. Its black-and-white plumage is similar to that of the larger ($9^{1}/_{4}$ inches long) hairy woodpecker. In both species, the males have a red patch at the back of the head. Downy woodpeckers have an all-white breast and belly and a white stripe down the middle of the back. The wings and tail are black with spots of white.

## Habitat & Range
A common resident of woodlands throughout North America, the downy is a habitat generalist—found anywhere there are trees or woody plants on which to find food. Though their population appears stable, downies suffer from nest site competition and from the removal of dead trees, which they need for nesting and feeding.

## Feeding
Downy woodpeckers use their stiff tails and strong, clawed feet to propel themselves along tree branches or trunks. As they move along, downies probe and chisel at the tree's bark, searching for insects, insect eggs, ants, and spiders. They also eat fruits, such as sumac and poison ivy. At bird feeders, sunflower seeds and bits, suet, peanuts, and peanut butter are favorite foods.

## Nesting
Like all woodpeckers, downies are cavity nesters. Each spring they excavate a new nest hole in the dead stub or trunk of a tree—usually one that is already rotting. The nest hole is placed underneath an overhanging branch higher than 12 feet above the ground. Excavation can take as long as two weeks—even with the male and female participating. Clutch size is usually four to five white eggs, with both sexes incubating. Hatching occurs at 12 days, and both parents feed the young for about three weeks until they fledge.

## Backyard & Beyond
Telling the downy and hairy woodpecker apart can be difficult. A way to remember which is which is: *Downy is dinky; hairy is huge.* Downies have a small body, small head, and a small, thin bill. Hairies have a big body, a big head, and a large, chisellike bill. Though downies rarely nest in nest boxes, they readily use them for nighttime roosting, especially in harsh weather. Leave a dead tree or large dead branch on a tree in your yard (in a safe location), and you will be much more likely to attract woodpeckers.

# Hairy Woodpecker
*Picoides villosus*

A familiar visitor to bird feeders, the hairy woodpecker is named for the long, hairlike white feathers on its back. The hairy looks like a super-sized version of a downy woodpecker, but the best way to tell these two similar species apart is to compare the length of the bill to the length (front-to-back) of the head. The hairy's bill is always longer than the width of its head, and the downy's bill is always shorter than the length of its head. An easier way to remember is: Downy is dinky; hairy is huge.

## All About
Hairy woodpeckers are medium-sized woodpeckers (9¼ inches long) with a long, sturdy, chisel-like bill that is used for finding food, for excavating nest holes, and for territorial drumming on hollow trees. Males and females look the same with white bellies, a white central back stripe, and distinctly patterned black and white on faces and wings. Adult males, however, have a red patch at the back of the head. Hairies utter a sharp *Peek!* call, as well as a loud ringing rattle on a single pitch.

## Habitat & Range
Hairy woodpeckers are year-round residents across North America in mature forests and wherever there are large trees, including suburban backyards, urban parks, and isolated woodlots. They are one of our most widespread woodpeckers with a range extending into Central America.

## Feeding
Using their bill, hairy woodpeckers can glean insects from tree bark or excavate them from beneath the bark's surface. Primary diet items include beetles, spiders, moth larvae, and ants, as well as fruits, seeds, and nuts. At bird feeders, hairies readily eat sunflower seeds, peanuts, suet, and cracked corn.

## Nesting
It can take up to three weeks for a pair of hairy woodpeckers to excavate their nest cavity in the trunk or dead branch of a living tree. When completed, the nest cavity will have a 2-inch entry hole and will be 4 inches wide and as deep as 16 inches. Into this cozy space, four eggs are laid, and both parents share the roughly two-week incubation period. Less than a month after hatching, young hairies are ready to fledge from the nest, though the parents tend them for several more weeks. A new nest is excavated each spring, but old cavities are used for roosting at night and in winter.

## Backyard & Beyond
If your neighborhood has large shade trees or mature woods, chances are good that you've got hairy woodpeckers nearby. Check large, dead snags and branches for woodpecker holes and listen for the birds' vocalizations and drumming in spring. Offer peanuts, sunflower seeds, or suet (in winter) in hanging feeders to attract hairy woodpeckers to your yard.

# Yellow-bellied Sapsucker
## *Sphyrapicus varius*

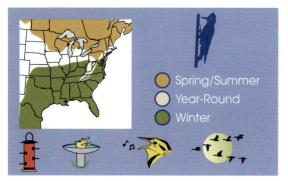

Even non-bird watchers know this bird's name, but few have ever seen this quiet member of the woodpecker family. Named for its habit of drinking sap running from the holes it drills in trees, the yellow-bellied sapsucker inadvertently provides sap to a host of other creatures, including hummingbirds, warblers, butterflies and other insects, squirrels, and chipmunks.

## All About
The yellow-bellied sapsucker is a medium-sized woodpecker with extensive black-and-white barring over much of its back, wings, and tail. Adults have a brilliant red crown patch and adult males have a red throat patch outlined in black. Females have a white throat. The lemon-yellow belly can be difficult to see on perched birds. Juveniles are very dull-brown versions of the black-and-white adults. Winter and migrant sapsuckers are usually silent, but may give a cat-like, nasal *queeaah* call. In breeding season, sapsuckers are very noisy with lots of calling and staccato drumming.

## Habitat & Range
Found in a variety of mixed-woodland habitats, but with a preference for aspen, maple, and fruit trees because of their sap production, the sapsucker will revisit and redrill sap holes from previous seasons and prior years. They breed across the entire breadth of Canada and across the northernmost tier of U.S. states from North Dakota to New England. They migrate to the southeastern quarter of the United States in winter, though some birds venture to Central America and to the Caribbean islands.

## Feeding
Sapsuckers drill a line of small holes in the bark of a tree trunk, causing it to ooze sap, which the sapsucker returns to drink later. Insects from sap wells, gleaned from trees or captured in flight, are another important food source, as are fruits, berries, and tree buds. Ruby-throated hummingbirds visit sap wells to drink the sweet sap and eat the insects attracted to it. Suet, suet dough, peanut butter, and fruit are among the foods sapsuckers eat at feeders.

## Nesting
Male sapsuckers excavate the nest cavity in a deciduous tree and the female lays up to six eggs on wood chips inside. Both parents share the two weeks of incubation as well as the month-long period of nestling care. After fledging, the adults teach the young for about ten days to forage and drill for sap on their own.

## Backyard & Beyond
Because they are mostly silent in winter, you might miss a sapsucker as it sits quietly drilling small sap holes in your backyard. Inspect trees for evidence that a sapsucker has visited: a line of uniform, small holes drilled midway up a tree trunk. If a sapsucker has visited recently you'll see the liquid sap oozing from the holes.

# Northern Flicker
## *Colaptes auratus*

A familiar and fairly large (13 inches long) woodpecker, the northern flicker is a distinctively marked bird that—unlike other woodpeckers—is often seen foraging on the ground. The eastern form of the flicker is known as the yellow-shafted flicker for its bright lemon-yellow underwing and tail color. A red-shafted form of the northern flicker occurs in the West. There are more than 130 different names by which the flicker is known, including high-hole, yellowhammer, and yawkerbird.

## All About
The northern flicker is all field marks with its bright yellow wing flashes, white rump, spotted breast, and barred back. It is not easily confused with any other bird. In the East, both sexes have a red crescent on the back of the head, but only males show a black "moustache" mark on the cheek. The flicker has several calls including a single note *kleer*, a short *wickawicka* series, and a monotonous *wickwickwickwick* song. It also communicates by drumming on the resonating surface of a tree, pole, or even metal downspouts and chimney flues.

## Habitat & Range
Widespread across North America, the northern flicker is found almost everywhere wooded habitats exist, though open woods and woodland edges are preferred. Flickers in the northern portion of the range migrate southward in winter, while southern birds are nonmigratory.

## Feeding
Flickers feed on the ground where they specialize in eating ants. A flicker pokes its long bill into an anthill and uses its long, sticky tongue to extract the ants. They also eat other insects, as well as fruits and seeds. At bird feeders, they will eat suet, peanuts, fruits, and sunflower bits.

## Nesting
Excavating a new nest cavity almost every year, flickers perform a much-needed service for many other hole-nesting birds—from chickadees to ducks—that use old flicker nests. Both sexes excavate the nest cavity in a dead tree or branch. The female lays between 5 and 10 eggs; both sexes share the 11-day incubation period. Young flickers leave the nest after about 25 days. Flickers will use nest boxes with an interior floor of 7×7 inches, an interior height of 16 to 24 inches, and a $2^1/_2$-inch entry hole. Because excavation is a vital part of courtship, boxes packed full of woodchips are more attractive. Competition for cavities from European starlings is fierce and may be causing a decline in flickers.

## Backyard & Beyond
Offering suet, corn, or peanuts and nest boxes in your wooded backyard is one way to attract flickers. Equally important is the presence of ground-dwelling insects (leave those non-threatening anthills alone!) and dead trees or dead branches. A large, dead tree branch placed vertically in your yard may entice a flicker to stop.

# Eastern Wood-Pewee

## *Contopus virens*

*PeeUWEEE? and PWEE-eehr are plaintive sounds familiar to many forest hikers, bikers, and birders. Eastern wood-pewees call their name time after time, but it often takes a little effort to see them—unless you happen to be standing under a branch from which one flaps out, snaps up an insect, and then returns to the same spot.*

### All About

Compared with smaller *Empidonax* flycatchers, the eastern wood-pewee is more sturdy, longer-tailed, and longer-winged. It is also generally grayer in appearance, with gray washed across its entire breast (the Acadian flycatcher is mostly whitish below). The wood-pewee lacks the prominent eye ring present in the Acadian and some other *Empidonax* species. Unlike the eastern phoebe, the eastern wood-pewee has two prominent wing bars and a two-toned black-and-orange (not all-black) bill, and it does not pump its tail. It usually feeds higher up than the phoebe, sallying forth from bare branches to grab its prey.

### Habitat & Range

Common nesters across the forested eastern United States and southeastern Canada, eastern wood-pewees reach their southern breeding limits from northern Florida west to central Texas. They nest in deciduous forests and mixed deciduous and coniferous forests; they are often active at the forest edge and in clearings.

### Feeding

Eastern wood-pewees pick their insect prey from leaves while hovering, but they are most noticeable when they sally forth from an exposed perch to capture flying insects (often the snap of bill meeting bug is audible). After the capture, they often return to the same perch to repeat the entire process—after ingesting their latest meal. They are most active and most vocal early and late in the day.

### Nesting

Eastern wood-pewee nests are shallow cups made of weeds, grasses, bark, and other materials; they are placed on tree branches above or well above head level. On the outside, the nest is often festooned with lichens; inside, it is lined with such soft materials as plant fluff, hair, and fine grasses. There, the female usually lays three eggs. She incubates the eggs for just under two weeks. Both the male and the female feed the young, which leave the nest about two weeks after hatching.

### Backyard & Beyond

In many areas, eastern wood-pewees are common migrants. It pays to learn this bird's field marks rather than just memorizing its song because wood-pewees don't usually sing while migrating to or from their South American wintering grounds. By "planting" snags—dead trees or large dead tree limbs—in your garden, you can provide hunting perches for migrating wood-pewees and other flycatchers.

# Eastern Phoebe
## *Sayornis phoebe*

A very adaptable flycatcher, the eastern phoebe often nests on human structures, such as on building ledges, inside barns, under bridges, and in culverts. Nesting in such proximity to humans, phoebes are used to our activity and this apparent tameness allows us to think of them as "our phoebes." Many bird watchers consider the early spring return of the phoebe (and not the American robin) to be the most reliable sign of spring's arrival.

### All About
The eastern phoebe, unlike most other flycatchers, is relatively easy to identify. A medium-sized bird that constantly wags its tail, the phoebe also gives a vocal clue to its identity by softly uttering its name—*fee-bee*. Phoebes are a dark, drab gray-brown on the back, with faint wing bars and a light breast and belly, often washed with yellow.

### Habitat & Range
Wherever there is a suitable nesting ledge (with abundant flying insects nearby), phoebes may be found. Natural habitats include woodland edges and small streams. Common throughout most of eastern North America during the spring and summer (eastern phoebes breed far into northern Canada), in winter many phoebes migrate to the southern Atlantic Coast and along the Gulf Coast into Mexico.

### Feeding
The eastern phoebe is a perch-and-wait hunter, watching for flying insects from an exposed perch and making short flying forays to nab its prey. Phoebes consume vast quantities of flying insects, but will also pluck food items from the ground or vegetation. Wasps, bees, flying ants, moths, and butterflies constitute much of their prey. In fall and winter, when insects are scarce, phoebes will eat small fruits and berries.

### Nesting
Phoebes are early nesters throughout the breeding range, and nest building often begins almost immediately after a male attracts a mate to a likely site. Favored natural nest sites include rock ledges and caves, but they also nest in barns or outbuildings, and on handy ledges or sills on house porches. The female builds the cup-shaped nest out of mud, moss, and grass. Four to six eggs are laid and incubated by the female alone, for just over two weeks. Young phoebes, unless disturbed earlier, fledge after about 16 days.

### Backyard & Beyond
Bird watchers love phoebes not only because they are common, but also because they are so full of energy and seem willing to make their nests in close proximity to humans. To attract phoebes to your property, place nesting shelves (about 6×8 inches in size) about a foot below the eaves of your house, garage, or outbuilding. Choose a site that is away from human activity and is as safe as possible from predators, such as snakes, raccoons, and cats.

# Great Crested Flycatcher
*Myiarchus crinitus*

Although one of the largest and most common eastern flycatchers, the great crested is raucous enough that it is usually heard before it is seen. A loud, enthusiastic wheeep! or whit-whit-whit-whit call is most often heard in woodland clearings during the summer months. The great crested is unusual among eastern flycatchers in that it is a cavity nester, relying on old woodpecker holes, hollow trees, and even birdhouses for nest sites. Adding to this bird's preference for the unusual is its habit of using shed snakeskin in its nest construction.

## All About
One of our larger flycatchers at $8^{1}/_{2}$ inches tall, the great crested is a pleasing blend of colors with a lemon belly and underwings and a rufous tail, set off by a gray head and olive back. Males and females are alike in appearance, and both will aggressively defend their nesting territory against trespassing birds of almost any species.

## Habitat & Range
Great crested flycatchers can be found in open woodlands, forest clearings, and even in wooded city parks throughout eastern North America during the summer months. Winter finds most of them in southern Mexico and southward to South America, though some spend the winter in south Florida. Fall migration starts in late August, with spring migrants returning to the United States as early as late March.

## Feeding
Capturing flying insects is the great crested's main foraging mode, but it will also glean insects from vegetation and supplement its diet with small berries and fruits. Butterflies, moths, beetles, and grasshoppers are its most common foods. Great cresteds usually forage high in the treetops or from a high, exposed perch.

## Nesting
A cavity nester that cannot excavate its own nest hole, it must rely on finding old woodpecker holes, naturally occurring hollows in trees, or human-supplied nest boxes. After inspecting possible nest sites with her mate, the female begins nest building using an incredible array of material, including animal hair, feathers, pine needles, string, cellophane, and shed snakeskin. Why great cresteds use such a variety of materials is a mystery. Five or more eggs are laid and incubated by the female for about two weeks. Two weeks after hatching, young flycatchers leave the nest.

## Backyard & Beyond
Any backyard with large shade trees and adjacent woodland in the eastern United States has the potential to attract nesting great crested flycatchers. To encourage them, leave standing any dead or hollow trees, especially ones with knotholes or existing woodpecker holes. Nest box dimensions should be: interior floor of 6×6 inches, inside height of 12 inches, entry hole of $1^{3}/_{4}$ to 2 inches. Mount at a height of 10 to 20 feet.

# Eastern Kingbird

*Tyrannus tyrannus*

- Spring/Summer
- Year-Round
- Winter

High in the treetops a medium-sized, black-and-white bird flutters out to catch flying insects and aggressively attacks other birds in flight, all the while emitting a sputtery series of sharp notes that sound like the zapping of an electric current. This is the eastern kingbird, whose Latin name translates into "tyrant of tyrants," the most common kingbird found in the East.

## All About

The eastern kingbird is an excellent flier, able to catch flying insects and aggressively defend its breeding territory with its aerial mastery. Both sexes are blackish above and white below. The female's chest is grayish. Male kingbirds have a small, red-orange patch of feathers on the crown, though this is rarely seen. A thin, white band on the tail margin clinches the identification.

## Habitat & Range

Spending the breeding season in open areas with scattered trees, eastern kingbirds prefer locations near water, probably for the bounty of insects. Fairly common in agricultural areas, pastures, city parks, and suburban neighborhoods with large trees and open understory during summer, most eastern kingbirds migrate to Central and South America in winter. In migration, the kingbird travels in loose flocks, and it is not uncommon to see a dozen or more birds in one tree in spring or fall.

## Feeding

The eastern kingbird, or beebird, is an insect eater, specializing in bees, wasps, moths, butterflies, and other large, flying insects. Sit-and-watch hunters, kingbirds find an exposed perch and wait for something edible to fly past. They then sally forth and grab the prey in their bill, returning to the perch to stun and eat the insect. Kingbirds also eat fruits at all seasons, including mulberries, cherries, and elderberries. Fruits make up the bulk of their winter diet in the tropics.

## Nesting

The kingbird's nest is placed high in a tree and is a large, loosely woven cup of bark, twigs, and weed stems. Females do all of the nest building and incubation. A typical clutch is two to five eggs with a 15-day incubation period. Hatchling kingbirds spend about 16 days in the nest before fledging, after which they are attended to by both parents for several more weeks.

## Backyard & Beyond

Kingbirds can often be seen perching high in a tree or along fences or power lines, hunting for insects. They are very active in their territories in summer, so watch for their fluttery flycatching flights and listen for their loud zapping calls. The old myth that eastern kingbirds prey primarily on honeybees resulted in many of these birds being shot. Studies have now shown that kingbirds eat relatively few honeybees, mostly drones.

# Red-eyed Vireo
## *Vireo olivaceus*

Easy to hear and hard to see, the red-eyed vireo is one of the most numerous summer birds of the eastern American woodlands. It arrives in April or early May from its South American wintering grounds, and its song rings out from every wooded tract. Foraging high in the emerging leaves, the vireo sings almost endlessly—one patient listener counted 22,197 songs from the same bird in one summer day!

## All About
The red-eyed vireo is about 6 inches long—an olive-backed, white-bellied bird with a gray cap and bold white stripe over its bright red eyes. Males and females are similar. They have sharp, slightly hooked bills designed to catch insect prey. Despite their small size, they are strong fliers; their twice-yearly migration carries them to the Amazon and back. Red-eyeds, like all vireos, are more deliberate in their movements than warblers.

## Habitat & Range
Red-eyeds are usually found in open deciduous or mixed woodlands with a strong understory of sapling trees. They sometimes occur in large city parks, orchards, or even wooded suburban backyards.

## Feeding
Like many small neotropical migrants, the red-eyed vireo feeds mostly on insects. It gleans its food from the upper branches of tall deciduous trees, singing as it moves slowly along the branches, peering under and around the leaves. Occasionally, it hovers to snatch a bug from an otherwise unreachable surface. In late summer, the red-eyed vireo will supplement its diet with berries of many kinds.

## Nesting
The female selects a suitable site, usually 5 to 10 feet off the ground on a horizontal forked twig. She builds a tightly woven nest of fine grasses and strips of grapevine, suspending it below the fork and decorating it with bits of lichen on its outer surfaces. Here she incubates her four eggs for 11 to 14 days. Both parents feed the nestlings for 10 to 12 days until they are ready to fledge. Red-eyed vireos are frequent victims of nest parasitism by cowbirds and only rarely do they fight back by building a floor over the cowbird egg and laying another clutch. Most of the time they simply accept the cowbird chick, to the detriment of their own.

## Backyard & Beyond
The best way to find a red-eyed vireo is to learn its song, then listen for it in the spring and summer woods. It is sometimes written as *Here I am, look at me, over here, here I am* sung over and over in a clear sweet voice, usually from high in a tree. Finding the singer will take some persistence and a good pair of binoculars. In fall, silent red-eyed vireos may be spotted in hedgerows and tangles, looking for berries.

# Warbling Vireo
## *Vireo gilvus*

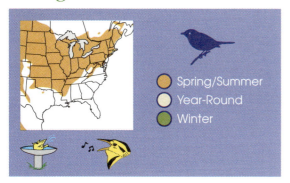

This persistent singer is much more impressive to the ear than to the eye. The warbling vireo is a dull greenish-gray overall, yet it has a vocal repertoire to match the most brilliant of warblers—it's as if the vireo wants to make up for its dull plumage by singing enthusiastically throughout spring and summer. This is one of the few vireos that has benefited from forest fragmentation, and it is far more common now than it was in Colonial times.

## All About
A plain little bird, stockier and duller than the equally common red-eyed vireo, the warbling vireo has few obvious field marks. It has a gray-brown back and light belly, offset by yellowish sides, a dark crown, and a white eyebrow line. The warbling vireo's song is described as *If I sees you, I will seize you, and I will squeeze you 'til you squirt!* It is sung repeatedly in a hoarse warble.

## Habitat & Range
The warbling vireo's breeding range covers much of the U.S. and western Canada, with the exception of the Southeast and arid regions in the Southwest. It occupies a variety of habitats from mature deciduous forests to urban parks and recovering clear-cuts. In the breeding season, the warbling vireo's habitats of choice are often associated with water; many bird watchers associate this bird's song with large shade trees along streams and rivers. Warbling vireos spend the winter along the western edge of Mexico and Central America.

## Feeding
An insect-eating specialist, the warbling vireo gleans moths, caterpillars, beetles, and other insects from foliage as it works its way along the outer branches of a tree. It also captures flying insects during short aerial forays. Large prey items are subdued by whacking them against a tree branch before they are eaten. During fall migration and in winter, warbling vireos eat fruit.

## Nesting
The female warbling vireo chooses a nest site, often high in a tall deciduous tree, such as a poplar, maple, or elm. A nest woven of grass, bark strips, and leaves is suspended from a forked branch. The female lays four eggs and both parents share the incubation duties, with the male often singing from the nest—an unusual behavior for a songbird. The young hatch within two weeks, are fed by both parents, and fledge about two weeks later.

## Backyard & Beyond
Warbling vireos can be most easily located by listening for their song during spring and summer. Listen for them along wooded waterways, around lakes, and in other places where large shade trees and water are present. Scan the treetops for this plain little songster with the bright, warbling song.

# Blue Jay
## *Cyanocitta cristata*

Blue jays are smart, adaptable, and noisy birds. They will often mimic the call of a red-tailed or red-shouldered hawk as they approach a bird feeder, in an apparent attempt to scare other birds away from the food. Sometimes persecuted by humans as nest robbers or bullies at the feeding station, blue jays are one of our most ornate and lovely birds. Bird watchers visiting the United States from abroad are astounded that such a beautiful bird is common in our suburban backyards.

## All About
No other eastern bird is blue and crested, making the blue jay almost unmistakable. Males and females are similar. Besides the standard *jay jay* or *jeer jeer* call often used as a scold, blue jays also emit a variety of squeaks, rattles, and croaks, in addition to mimicking other birds' calls. If you hear a sound in the woods that is loud and unmusical, chances are good that it's coming from a blue jay.

## Habitat & Range
Blue jays are common in wooded habitats, especially those with oaks. Indeed the blue jay has a special relationship with oaks, burying as many as 5,000 acorns in fall caches for future consumption. Many of these acorns are never retrieved, so jays are credited with helping with forest generation. Resident throughout their range, blue jays in northern latitudes migrate southward in early fall, traveling by daylight in flocks of 10 or more birds, many carrying acorns in their bills.

## Feeding
Blue jays will eat almost anything. Grasshoppers and other insects, and acorns and other nuts are their primary foods. Bird eggs or nestlings, mice, frogs, and a variety of human-supplied foods are also eaten. When storing acorns, blue jays will carry as many as five acorns in the throat and bill to the cache site, drop them in a pile, and bury them one at a time. They will return to recover only some of these acorns.

## Nesting
Males help gather nesting materials, but females do most of the building in a tree. The twig nest is woven into a cup and lined with wet leaves and rootlets. Suburban blue jays often incorporate string, plastics, and paper (human trash) into nests. The female lays four to six eggs and incubates them for 18 days, followed by about 20 days of nestling care before the young jays fledge.

## Backyard & Beyond
A common feeder visitor, blue jays are attracted to suet, peanuts, sunflower seeds, and even dog food. A source of water is highly attractive to blue jays, too. Look for blue jays along woodland edges and listen for their raucous cries, almost always the first clue to their presence.

# American Crow
## *Corvus brachyrhynchos*

Noisy, sly, opportunistic, and ubiquitous, the American crow lives among us; yet, comparatively little is known about it. Like other bold, brash corvids (the blue jay being a prime example), the crow is downright sneaky where its personal life is concerned. Few people know that crows may breed cooperatively in groups of up to a dozen birds, helping tend the dominant pair's nest.

## All About
An unrelieved glossy black from bill to toenail, crows are armed with a stout, strong bill that acts as a chisel, axe, shovel, or forceps, among other uses. Its distinctive wingbeats appear to row the bird through the sky. Crows are well known for their raucous *caw*. Evidence suggests that crows have different "words" for different situations (assembly, dispersal, mobbing); their language is complex, as is their social behavior. Few people are privileged to hear the crow's song, given by both sexes, which is a long recitation of rattles, coos, growls, and imitations of sounds.

## Habitat & Range
Though they are strongly associated with agricultural areas, crows find perfect conditions in cities and suburbs, where they raid pet dishes, bird feeders, and garbage cans. In the northern part of their range, crows are migratory, but all spend the winter within the continental United States. Throughout their range, crows use communal roosts when not breeding, and these can swell to massive proportions by late winter.

## Feeding
There's almost nothing edible an American crow will not eat. At roadkills, landfills, and compost piles, crows will load their distensible throat with food and fly heavily off, often caching it under leaves or sod for later enjoyment. Crows forage by walking slowly on the ground—hunting invertebrates and vertebrates alike—and are constantly scanning roadsides and fields as they fly, descending to investigate anything that might be edible.

## Nesting
Crows stay in family units composed of a pair and their young from the previous year. These yearlings may help build the nest, incubate, or feed the incubating female or her young. Four or five eggs are laid in the bulky twig nest, which is usually hidden high in a pine. The female incubates for around 17 days, and young fledge at around 36 days of age. Their strangled, nasal calls sometimes betray the nest location.

## Backyard & Beyond
Crows are always up to something, and feeding them gives us an opportunity to observe their always-intriguing behavior. To find something a crow might like, open the refrigerator. Freezer-burned meat is a favorite. Cracked or whole corn is irresistible as well. Neighbors may wonder, but crows are well worth watching.

# Horned Lark

*Eremophila alpestris*

The "horns" on the head of this small bird are not horns at all, but feather tufts that can be raised and lowered. In spite of this conspicuous field mark, horned larks can be surprisingly difficult to see when they are on the ground. Your first clue to their presence may be their high, tinkling call, or when a small flock is startled into flight.

## All About

Horned larks are sleek-looking birds of open ground where they are often found in flocks. Males show a yellow face and throat, and a bold black mask or moustache and breast band. The back and wings are a blend of tan and rust. The female's plumage is a paler version of the male's. Their flight style is light and undulating, providing glimpses of the black tail panels, and often accompanied by twittering call notes.

## Habitat & Range

Found in all types of wide-open, barren terrain from beaches and dunes to tundra, short-grass prairie, overgrazed fields, gravel roadways, recovering strip mines, and airport runways, the horned lark is widespread across North America. Its population and range have both expanded in the last half-century and the species is now found year-round in nearly every state. Breeding birds from the far North begin fall migration in September.

## Feeding

In winter, when horned larks commonly mingle in large flocks with longspurs and snow buntings, seeds are the primary food. During the breeding season and migration, insects are added to the larks' menu. Horned larks forage by walking over the ground, looking for food items. This type of foraging is especially productive in fields where manure has been spread or where the soil has recently been tilled or grain recently harvested.

## Nesting

Horned larks may nest very early in spring in the Midwest, but later in the far North. The female chooses the nest site on the ground and digs out a shallow scoop. Into this depression she weaves a nest from grass, rootlets, and other plant material. She lines it with soft materials such as fur or feathers and lays from two to five eggs into it. She alone incubates the eggs for 11 days. Young hatch with a warm down covering and stay in the nest until fledging about 10 days later

## Backyard & Beyond

Winter flocks of horned larks can be easier to find than breeding birds. Check in and around agricultural feedlots, in muddy farm fields, active pastures, and anywhere waste grain or seed might be scattered. Scan the ground carefully for the larks' movement—one or more birds may catch your eye as they flutter across the open ground.

# Purple Martin
*Progne subis*

No other North American bird has a closer association with humans than the purple martin. For more than four hundred years, martins in eastern North America have nested in human-supplied housing, at first in hollow gourds offered by Native Americans and today in a variety of specialized housing. Generations of people and martins have grown up together. Even non-bird watchers can appreciate this friendly and familiar bird.

## All About
Our largest swallow (at 8 inches), the purple martin is a graceful flyer with a bubbly, liquid song. The adult male has a deep blue body and black wings and tail. Females and youngsters are gray and black with some blue on the back. In flight, martins can be confused with European starlings, but martins have a notched tail and call out almost constantly.

## Habitat & Range
Purple martins breed across eastern North America, except for the extreme north. They spend winters in South America but return to the southern United States in mid-January, their arrival eagerly anticipated by their human landlords. Because of their reliance on human-supplied housing, most martins are found around cities, towns, and settlements.

## Feeding
Martins eat flying insects almost exclusively, but—contrary to popular opinion and marketing hype—martins do not eat many mosquitoes. Instead, their diet includes larger flying insects, such as beetles, flies, dragonflies, wasps, butterflies, and moths. In cold, rainy weather, martin landlords often resort to feeding them mealworms and bits of scrambled egg in an effort to keep their beloved birds alive. Some landlords even shoot mealworms into the air with a slingshot just so the martins can catch their food.

## Nesting
Martins are rather selective in choosing colony nest sites, but one thing is certain: They like to be with other martins. Research has revealed that they prefer white housing with a large (8×8×8-inch) interior and an 1 1/2-inch entry hole. The housing should be mounted near a human dwelling in an open area. Martins build a loose cup nest inside the cavity out of pine needles and grass, lined with green leaves (which limit parasites). The female lays four to six eggs and does most of the incubation, lasting about 16 days. Both parents feed the nestlings for the month-long period before fledging.

## Backyard & Beyond
The most successful martin landlords are those willing to put in the extra effort to care for their tenants with predator-proof housing, elimination of competing house sparrows and starlings, and regular monitoring. Your chances of attracting martins are greatly enhanced if there is an existing colony within a mile of you.

# Tree Swallow
## *Tachycineta bicolor*

The lovely tree swallow is making a breeding range expansion in many areas of the U.S. Once limited by the availability of the nesting cavities they require, tree swallows are benefiting greatly from artificial nest boxes erected to attract bluebirds. Their liquid twitters, sharp blue-and-white coloration, and trusting ways make tree swallows a welcome addition to our birdlife.

### All About
Long triangular wings, snow-white underparts, and glossy teal-blue upperparts make the tree swallow a beautiful signal of spring. Soaring kitelike, then rising with rapid flaps, they course and dive over meadows and ponds in search of flying insects. Their jingling calls have been likened to the sound of someone shaking paperclips in a glass tumbler. Females are somewhat browner above and a duller blue than males.

### Habitat & Range
Tree swallows prefer open fields, preferably near water, for nesting, though they will inhabit upland sites. Marshes also provide the flying insects they require. The tree swallow's breeding range extends across Canada and the northern tier of the U.S. and is expanding southward at a good clip. Tree swallows winter in coastal areas from South Carolina to Florida and along the Gulf Coast into Mexico and Central America. One of our heartiest swallows, the tree swallow often surprisingly shows up early in spring.

### Feeding
Eighty percent of a tree swallow's diet is insects; fruits make up the other portion, mainly bayberries that sustain them in adverse winter weather. "Myrtle swallow" would be a more apt name for these birds, as myrtle is another name for bayberry. This ability to eat fruit helps tree swallows survive cold snaps as they make their way northward to breed. During breeding season, insects are caught on the wing in spectacular zigzag flights and are stored in the throat to be fed to nestlings.

### Nesting
A foundation of coarse grass leaves and stems is lined with large body feathers, usually white. Tree swallows are mad for feathers in nesting season and can often be induced to take soft white feathers from the hand. The female incubates four to seven eggs for an average of 14 days. Young leave the nest 15 to 25 days later, flying strongly. Second broods are rare.

### Backyard & Beyond
Before the advent of artificial nest boxes, tree swallows were limited to old woodpecker holes—a hotly contested resource. A nest box with a $1^{9}/_{16}$-inch hole, mounted on a predator-proof pole in an open meadow near water, is the best bet for attracting tree swallows. Look for tree swallows hawking insects over ponds, lakes, and rivers during the summer months.

# Barn Swallow
*Hirundo rustica*

One early naturalist estimated that a barn swallow that lived 10 years would fly more than two million miles, enough to travel 87 times around the Earth. This species seems to define what it means to be at home in the air, and it has been compared to an albatross in its ability to stay effortlessly aloft. One of the most familiar and beloved birds in rural America, the barn swallow is welcomed everywhere as a sign of spring.

## All About
Glossy blue-black above and orange below, the barn swallow is the only American swallow that has a true "swallow tail," with an elongated outer pair of tail feathers. Males and females are similar, but females are not quite as glossy or highly colored, and the fork in their tails is not quite as pronounced. Like all swallows, they have short legs and rather weak feet used for perching, not walking.

## Habitat & Range
A bird of rural areas and farmlands, the barn swallow may be found over any open area, such as pastures, fields, and golf courses, as well as lakes, ponds, and rivers. It has adapted well to humans and is not shy of people, nesting close to settled areas as long as it has open space for feeding. Barn swallows travel in great flocks during migrations, often in company with other swallow species. They arrive in most of their U.S. range in April and leave in early to midfall.

## Feeding
Foraging almost entirely on the wing, the barn swallow takes a variety of insect prey, from flies and locusts to moths, grasshoppers, bees, and wasps. Occasionally small berries or seeds are added to the diet, but this is uncommon. Only in bad weather will barn swallows feed on the ground.

## Nesting
Nothing says "country" more than a pair of barn swallows zipping in and out of the open doors of a working barn, darting after insects and chattering incessantly. Sometimes two or three pairs will share a favored site. The nest itself is a cup of mud and grass, lined with feathers and placed on a rafter or glued under an eave. Besides barns, barn swallows may use other open buildings, covered porches, or the undersides of bridges or docks. During second nestings, immatures from the first brood help feed and care for their younger siblings.

## Backyard & Beyond
During breeding season, you may bring barn swallows into close range by throwing feathers into the air near a flock of soaring birds; the graceful fliers will swoop in to snatch them up for nest linings. Barn swallows also enjoy eating bits of baked eggshells (crumble them first) during breeding season.

# Tufted Titmouse
*Baeolophus bicolor*

From deep mixed woods to old orchards, from city parks to leafy suburban backyards, this friendly and active little bird makes itself at home throughout the year. It is noisy and sociable, quite tame in human company, and fearless among other small birds with which it associates. Its cheerful calls of peter, peter, peter ring out even in midwinter, chasing away the January blahs.

## All About
The tufted titmouse is 6½ inches long and dressed primly across its upperparts in gray, with a creamy breast and rusty flanks. A black-button eye stands out against its white cheek, and a crest adorns its head. Its small, sharp bill is black, as are its legs and feet. Titmice are very vocal and, besides their signature *peter* calls, they have a variety of whistled notes—similar to those of the cardinal and Carolina wren. Their harsh, raspy, scolding notes are similar to the chickadee's.

## Habitat & Range
The tufted titmouse was originally considered a southern woodland bird, but for the past 50 years it has been expanding its range northward. The species' affinity for bird feeders and nesting boxes has played a part in this expansion. Titmice are nonmigratory and able to survive harsh weather if sufficient food is available.

## Feeding
Tufted titmice eat mostly insects and seeds, depending on time of year. Caterpillars are a popular item in summer, but they also take wasps and bees, scale insects, beetles, the larvae of many species, and, in winter, insect eggs. Acorns are a mainstay in fall and winter. At feeders, titmice relish sunflower seeds, suet, suet dough, and peanuts.

## Nesting
The natural nesting choice of the tufted titmouse is a tree cavity—an abandoned woodpecker hole, or crack caused by a lightning strike. Other sites include rotted fenceposts, drainage pipes, and nest boxes. The female builds the nest of grass, moss, bark, and leaves, filling up whatever size hole they have adopted. When the main structure is completed, the birds line it with hair—often plucked from a living animal—woodchuck, rabbit, dog, or even a handy human. Five or six eggs are laid, incubated by the female for 12 to 14 days. Both parents feed the young, which fledge at about 15 days. The family group stays together, sometimes into the next year, and year-old birds may help their parents care for the nestlings of the newest brood.

## Backyard & Beyond
Tufted titmice sometimes breed in nest boxes, especially those with an entrance hole in the 1½-inch range. In winter they travel in mixed flocks with chickadees, sparrows, woodpeckers, and kinglets. Tufted titmice are easy to locate in woodlands by their noisy scolding calls.

# Black-capped Chickadee

*Poecile atricapillus*

In the southern portions of Ohio, Indiana, Illinois, and Missouri, the resident chickadee is actually the Carolina chickadee (Poecile carolinensis), *a slightly smaller but otherwise quite similar cousin of the black-capped chickadee of the northern half of the U.S. Chickadees travel in noisy little bands and draw attention to themselves with their frequent scolding chatter.*

## All About

Both chickadees have black caps and bibs as well as white cheek patches; gray backs, wings, and tails; and pale underparts with buff-colored flanks. The bill is tiny and dark, and the legs and feet are black. Males and females are alike, and there are no seasonal differences in plumage. In general, black-capped chickadees are larger (5 1/4 inches long), bigger-headed, with brighter white cheeks. Carolina chickadees are drabber gray overall, smaller (4 3/4 inches long), with less white in the wings. Vocal clues can be helpful. Black-cappeds sing *fee-bee* (two notes) while Carolinas sing *soo-fee, soo-fay* (four notes). The common *chick-a-dee-dee-dee* call is lower, hoarser, and slower from black-cappeds, and higher and more melodic from Carolinas.

## Habitat & Range

The Carolina chickadee is resident (nonmigratory) and through most of its range it is the only chickadee present. It is generally replaced by the black-capped chickadee in the northern half of the Midwestern states. Black-cappeds will occasionally move south in winter. Where the two species overlap they may occasionally interbreed, so identifying individual birds under such circumstances is tricky.

## Feeding

Both chickadees have a varied diet. Nearly half of the food taken in the wild consists of insects, such as aphids, ants, moths, and leafhoppers. They also eat spiders, weed seeds, and the seeds and small fruits of many trees and vines. At feeders they are partial to sunflower seeds, suet, and peanuts.

## Nesting

Cavity nesters, Carolina and black-capped chickadees seek out natural holes in woodland trees, often adapting old woodpecker holes. They readily accept nesting boxes. The nest (made by the female) is a thick mass of mosses, bark, and grasses, enclosing a cup of soft hair. One side is built up higher than the other and can be pulled down like a flap to cover the young when both parents are away. As many as eight eggs are laid and incubated by the female for 11 to 13 days; both parents then share the feeding of the young until they fledge after two weeks.

## Backyard & Beyond

To lure chickadees, offer black-oil sunflower seed in hanging tubes or hopper feeders, suet, or other fats such as "bird pudding." To induce a pair to stay and nest, install one or more nest boxes with entrance holes that are 1 1/4 to 1 1/2 inches in diameter.

# White-breasted Nuthatch
*Sitta carolinensis*

Nuthatches are universally referred to as "upside-down birds," because they forage by probing the bark of tree trunks with their heads downward. During their journeys down the trunk of a tree, they often pause, and then raise their head so that it is parallel to the ground—an absolutely unique posture among birds. The most well-known member of the family is the white-breasted nuthatch, a bird of deciduous woods and well-treed backyards.

## All About
At nearly 6 inches in length, the white-breasted nuthatch is the largest of its tribe. Males have gray backs with black caps, white underparts, and a beady black eye on a white face. Females are similar but wear gray, not black, on their heads. White-breasteds are thick-necked and short-tailed, with a stocky appearance. White-breasted nuthatch calls—uttered frequently in all seasons—are a nasal and repetitive *ank-ank*.

## Habitat & Range
White-breasted nuthatches prefer deciduous woods, but are also found in large parks and leafy backyards. In northern coniferous woods, and at high elevations along the Appalachian chain, they are replaced by the smaller red-breasted nuthatch, while the brown-headed nuthatch displaces them in the dry pine woods of the South.

## Feeding
The white-breasted nuthatch eats both insects and seeds, varying its fare with the seasons. Insects make up nearly 100 percent of their summer diet, with seeds being added in fall and winter. Autumn's extra seeds and nuts are sometimes stashed—or "hatched away"—in tree bark crevices, to be retrieved later—a habit that has given these birds their name. White-breasted nuthatches will come to feeders for sunflower and other seeds, or suet, but they tend to abandon backyard feeders almost entirely in spring and summer when insect prey is plentiful.

## Nesting
Nuthatches maintain their pair bond and territory all year long. The nest is placed in a natural cavity, old woodpecker hole, or more rarely a nest box. Built by the female, it is a cup of grasses, bark strips, and twigs and is lined with hair. When the nest is finished, the nuthatches "sweep" the entrance with their bills, rubbing a crushed insect against the wood—the chemicals released may aid in repelling predators. The female incubates a clutch of eight eggs for two weeks. Both parents feed the young for at least two weeks until fledging.

## Backyard & Beyond
Nuthatches are irregular feeder visitors, but they like black oil sunflower seeds and suet, peanuts, or peanut butter mix. In woodlands, listen for the nuthatch's nasal calls anytime. Male and female always forage near each other and, in winter, with other species in a mixed flock.

# House Wren
## *Troglodytes aedon*

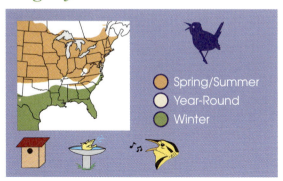

The rich and burbling song of the house wren is surprisingly loud for such a tiny (4 3/4 inches long) bird. House wrens are named for their preference for living in close proximity to humans, often in tiny houses we provide for them. This mostly plain brown bird makes up for its small size and drab coloration by being a fierce competitor for nesting sites.

### All About
House wrens are notable for their lack of field marks—the warm-brown upperparts and tail are matched by a grayish breast. Look closely at the house wren, and you'll see a variety of small white and black spots, the only variation in the bird's plumage. Males and females look alike and both have the wrenlike habit of cocking their tails up when perched. The thin, slightly curved bill is ideal for capturing and eating the house wren's insect prey.

### Habitat & Range
Spending the summers in thickets and brushy edge habitat adjacent to woodlands, the house wren is a familiar bird in parks, backyards, and gardens, often—but not always—near human settlements. Some house wrens winter in the southernmost states in the United States, but many travel beyond our borders farther south.

### Feeding
Insects make up the house wren's diet (grasshoppers, crickets, spiders, and moths are on the menu), but they will also eat snails and caterpillars. Most of their foraging is done in thick vegetation on or near the ground.

### Nesting
House wrens nest in a variety of cavities from woodpecker holes to natural cavities and nest boxes. Like Carolina wrens, house wrens will also nest in flowerpots, drainpipes, and other such sites. They are very competitive about nesting sites, often filling all or most available cavities with sticks. The male builds these "dummy" nests, and the female selects one in which to nest. The twig structures are lined with soft materials, such as grass or hair, and the female lays six to eight eggs. She performs the incubation duties, which last from 12 to 14 days. Fledglings leave the nest two or more weeks after hatching. House wrens are known to pierce the eggs of other cavity nesting birds in their territories.

### Backyard & Beyond
House wrens will readily accept nest boxes with interior dimensions of 4x4 inches and entry holes of 1 1/4 inches in diameter. Nest boxes placed adjacent to brushy habitat or a wood's edge seem to be most attractive. The house wren's song and scolding calls are heard often wherever they are present. Nest boxes for bluebirds and tree swallows should be placed far from edge habitat, in the open, to avoid conflict and competition from territorial house wrens.

# Ruby-crowned Kinglet
## *Regulus calendula*

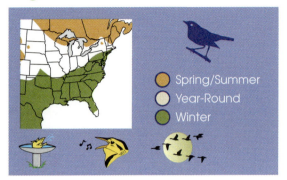

The appearance of this perky little bird within mixed songbird flocks is a sure sign that fall is on the way. Ruby-crowned kinglets nest in the north and northwest of the continent in mixed coniferous forests. They winter in abundance from the South into Mexico.

### All About
After hummingbirds, ruby-crowned and closely related golden-crowned kinglets rate as North America's smallest birds. Like the golden-crowned, the ruby-crowned kinglet is restless, briefly hovering by the tips of branches and constantly flicking its wings—a behavior that sets them apart from larger, longer-tailed warblers. Two other field marks are the bird's wide white eye ring and single, wide wing bar. Otherwise, the ruby-crowned kinglet is a study in olive-drab. Its namesake red crown patch is usually concealed.

### Habitat & Range
This bird abounds from northern Maine, New Hampshire, and Vermont west across the upper reaches of the Great Lakes, through central Canada, then south through the western mountain states. Some even nest in a few spots in Arizona and New Mexico. As cold months approach, ruby-crowned kinglets migrate south, spending the winter from southern New England south through the Southeast. In the West, the wintering range extends from the Pacific Northwest south and east across Oklahoma and Texas. Many ruby-crowned kinglets winter in Mexico, but rarely as far south as Guatemala. During migration and in winter, kinglets are found in a wide variety of habitats, feeding in trees from pines to oaks and in tall shrubs.

### Feeding
Much of a ruby-crowned kinglet's life is spent in the relentless pursuit of invertebrates, punctuated here and there in winter by the procurement of a seed or berry. In winter, these birds pick among branches and crags to find dormant spiders and insects and their eggs. In warm months, they feed exclusively on small invertebrates.

### Nesting
Surprisingly for such a small bird, the ruby-crowned kinglet may lay up to a dozen small white, brown-speckled eggs—the largest clutch of a North American bird its size. Seven to eight eggs is a more typical clutch, which a female lays and incubates for about two weeks in a tightly bound nest of lichen, moss, spider web, hair, and various plant materials. The nest is usually suspended from a branch close to the trunk and protected from above by overhanging branches. Both parents feed their young, which leave about 16 days after hatching.

### Backyard & Beyond
In many parts of the country, October and April are peak months for spotting migrating ruby-crowned kinglets. They may accompany chickadees and titmice that come to your feeders, or be seen with migrating warblers.

# Blue-gray Gnatcatcher
## *Polioptila caerulea*

- Spring/Summer
- Year-Round
- Winter

The blue-gray gnatcatcher is the birder's "mini-mockingbird," always in motion and usually talking about it. This graceful, delicate, miniscule bird seems to arrive too early in spring, sallying into swarms of midges from still-budding branches. Its slender, elongated form and flashy black-and-white paneled tail are hard to mistake, though the gnatcatcher often goes unnoticed. It's most likely to be spotted on its early spring migration, for it is a woodland denizen, often hidden by foliage after the trees leaf out.

### All About
It's often the gnatcatcher's twangy, whining call—like a miniature banjo being tuned—that alerts us to its presence. Its song is a sputtering, wheezy, petulant-sounding jumble, punctuated by *mews*. The blue-gray gnatcatcher has been recorded mimicking other species, a talent not widely appreciated, perhaps because its high, whispery voice is beyond the hearing register of many bird watchers. A white eye ring and neat black eyeline, blue-gray upperparts, and a long, slender tail edged in white distinguish this elegant bird. Females are similar, but lack the black eyeline.

### Habitat & Range
Blue-gray gnatcatchers are strongly associated with oaks in a wide range of habitats, sticking to woodlands dominated by broad-leaved species. They are more often seen along woodland edges than in yards and gardens, except during migration. Gnatcatchers winter in the western coastal scrub of Mexico and Central America.

### Feeding
Perching on the outer twigs in the mid- to high canopy, gnatcatchers go out after flying insects or glean the outer foliage for insects and spiders. As they forage, they flick their white outer tail feathers, which is thought to create bursts of light that startles UV-sensitive insects into flight. The bill is a fine black forcep, good for grasping tiny prey.

### Nesting
Gnatcatcher nests are often mistaken for those of hummingbirds, being neat, compact cups of silk (often gathered from tent caterpillar nests), plastered with lichens. They are usually saddled on a horizontal limb. It is often possible to witness construction because the male gnatcatcher escorts the nest-building female with much fanfare and conversation. Both male and female incubate four eggs for 13 days, and young birds leave the nest 13 days after hatching. They are still being fed by their parents three weeks after departing the nest but gain independence soon thereafter.

### Backyard & Beyond
This species has expanded its range explosively over the past three decades, pioneering into the Northeast and southeastern Canada. However, its range expansion cannot be attributed to feeding stations, as has been postulated for the northward movement of tufted titmice, northern cardinals, and red-bellied woodpeckers. The gnatcatcher relies solely on insects for sustenance.

# Eastern Bluebird

*Sialia sialis*

The eastern bluebird is our most famous thrush, even more popular than its cousin, the American robin. Its beauty, its song, and its willingness to live close to us has inspired many poets, songwriters, artists, and bird watchers. You can attract bluebirds to your property if you have a large open lawn, especially if you provide housing. Thanks to a concerted effort by bluebird lovers to provide nest boxes, the eastern bluebird has rebounded from its low population in the 1960s.

## All About

The sky-blue back and rusty breast of the male bluebird are echoed in the female's more muted tones. There are three bluebird species in North America, but only the eastern is commonly found in the eastern United States. Bluebirds are often seen perched along fence lines, on wires, or high in trees. They may appear all dark in bright sunlight, so many observers miss seeing them. During spring courtship, paired bluebirds can be seen fluttering their wings near a prospective nesting site, uttering their rich *turalee turalay* song.

## Habitat & Range

Bluebirds are resident (nonmigratory) throughout the eastern United States in open habitats, such as pastures, grasslands, parks, and large suburban lawns (especially where bluebird nest boxes are available). The two habitat requirements of bluebirds are large, open, grassy areas for foraging and cavities for roosting and nesting. In harsh winter weather, bluebirds may migrate short distances to find food or shelter.

## Feeding

From an elevated perch, bluebirds watch for moving insects and then drop to the ground to pounce on them or to capture flying insects in midair. They eat insects year-round and will shift to fruits and berries when insects are scarce. Bluebirds visit feeders for mealworms, berries, and suet or suet dough.

## Nesting

Bluebirds are cavity nesters and will use old woodpecker holes or natural cavities in trees where available. Human-supplied nest boxes are an important resource for the eastern bluebird. The female bluebird builds the nest inside the cavity using bark strips, grass, and hair. She lays four to six eggs and incubates them for 12 to 16 days. Both parents care for the nestlings until fledging occurs after 14 to 18 days.

## Backyard & Beyond

If you offer housing, it's important to monitor and manage it to keep non-native house sparrows and starlings from usurping it and to keep predators from accessing the eggs or young. Place the houses (with $1^{1}/_{2}$-inch entrance holes) on metal poles with a pole-mounted baffle beneath the house. House location should be in the middle of a large, open, grassy lawn or field. Bluebirds catch insects on the ground in grassy areas, so they are particularly vulnerable to lawn chemicals.

# American Robin
## *Turdus migratorius*

- Spring/Summer
- Year-Round
- Winter

Almost all North Americans have grown up having a fairly intimate acquaintance with a thrush. The American robin, the largest, most widespread, and most abundant North American thrush, has followed the watered lawn—with its plentiful earthworm prey base—westward across the continent. Only parts of Florida, Texas, and the Southwest, where the soil is too sandy to support the introduced common earthworm, lack robins.

## All About
The robin's simple yet evocative *cheerily-cheerio* song meshes well with the thunk of basketballs and the drone of lawnmowers in suburban neighborhoods all across North America; yet, they also hide their nests in mountaintop spruce and fir forests, where they are as wary as any hermit thrush. Males sport brick-red breasts and black heads with broken white spectacles and a streaked white throat and lower belly. Females are paler.

## Habitat & Range
The robin is primarily a bird of lawns with trees and shrubs, though it also breeds in high mountain forests near clear-cuts or openings. Few other species show its adaptability to diverse habitats, from landscaped parking lot islets to dense, secluded forests. Migration is marked in northern climes, but is less so in southern ones.

## Feeding
Running, then standing erect and motionless on a lawn, the robin watches and listens for earthworms and other invertebrates crawling in the grass. A quick stab captures them, sometimes resulting in a tug-of-war with a recalcitrant night crawler. Robins flock in fall to exploit fruiting trees and shrubs, fluttering and giggling as they reach for food.

## Nesting
Most bird watchers are familiar with the robin's sturdy mud-and-grass cup, often nestled in an evergreen, a climbing vine, on a horizontal branch, or even on a windowsill. The female incubates three to four eggs for 12 to 14 days. Adults can be seen foraging with bills full of earthworms as soon as the young hatch. Young leave the nest, barely able to flutter, on about the thirteenth day. They are distinguished by their spotted, whitish breasts and reedy, begging calls. The male feeds them for another three weeks, while the female usually starts a second brood.

## Backyard & Beyond
By mowing the lawn regularly and planting dense evergreens and fruit-bearing shrubs and trees, we unwittingly provide perfect conditions for robins. Robins seldom visit feeders, but will take bread, chopped raisins, and crumbled moistened dog chow in severe winter weather. Oddly enough, the American robin is the only member of its genus, *Turdus*, that breeds in any numbers in North America. The closely related clay-colored robin, which looks like a washed-out, American robin, breeds sparingly in south Texas.

# Wood Thrush

*Hylocichla mustelina*

The lilting flutelike song of the wood thrush inspires bird watchers, naturalists, poets, musicians, and humankind in general. Few things are more beautiful than the evening song of the wood thrush as it echoes from deep within the forest. However, this species has suffered severe declines in population during the past thirty years due to loss of habitat, forest fragmentation, and nest parasitism from the brown-headed cowbird.

## All About

This medium-sized (7 3/4 inches in length) brown thrush has a bright rufous head and neck, olive-brown back and tail, and a white breast with large dark spots. Erect and robinlike in its posture, the wood thrush sings a multi-pitched and highly variable *eeeolay* song and utters a *whit-whit-whit* call when agitated. Wood thrush males do most of their singing at dawn and dusk, and usually from a midlevel perch in the forest.

## Habitat & Range

Wood thrushes only spend their summers with us in eastern North America, arriving as early as April, but departing for the tropics by mid-August or later. Many make the flight across the Gulf of Mexico in both spring and fall. During the breeding season, they can be found in mixed deciduous forests with tall trees and a thick understory. Fragmented forest plots or those with cleared understory (due to deer browsing or human landscaping) are far less attractive to wood thrushes.

## Feeding

Feeding much like a robin on the forest floor, the wood thrush sweeps aside leaf litter with its bill to uncover insects, larvae, millipedes, moths, ants, and even salamanders and snails. In fall, wood thrushes will feed in forest edge habitats to take advantage of fruits and berries.

## Nesting

The female wood thrush builds a cup-shaped nest out of grasses, leaves, and rootlets, usually held together with mud, in the fork of a tree branch within 20 feet of the ground. She lays three to four eggs and incubates them for about 12 days before they hatch. Young wood thrushes are ready to fledge two weeks later. Wood thrush nests in fragmented forest habitats are more likely to be parasitized by the brown-headed cowbird, which does not build its own nest, but rather lays its eggs in the nests of other songbirds—often at the expense of the host species.

## Backyard & Beyond

From spring through fall your best chance of locating a wood thrush is to listen for a male singing from patches of dense forest. Once you hear the song, patiently scan the upper, inner branches of the forest for this rusty-brown master singer. If you live in wooded habitat that is home to wood thrushes, be a good neighbor and keep pets restrained during breeding season.

# Veery
### *Catharus fuscescens*

The spiraling, almost unearthly song of the veery captivates most people who hear it. Actually seeing this shade-loving songbird is far more challenging. Although still a common nester in many areas, the veery has declined in many parts of its range, perhaps due to destruction of its winter habitat and, on its nesting grounds, from nest parasitism by cowbirds combined with the paring down of underbrush by surging deer populations.

## All About
Of all North American thrushes, the veery shows the greatest contrast between rich rustiness above and plainness below. A "typical" veery has a rusty wash on its breast and cheeks and a head lacking strong markings. Diffuse spotting punctuates the breast's rusty wash, but the remaining underparts are white. Western and Newfoundland birds are darker and more heavily spotted below, but the face is still plain, lacking the distinctive eye rings found on similar Swainson's and hermit thrushes.

## Habitat & Range
The veery nests across much of southern Canada, in the western mountains down to Colorado, across the Great Lakes states and throughout the Northeast, as well as in the Appalachians. Favored nesting habitat is moist deciduous forests with plenty of bushy undergrowth. In fall, most veeries migrate across the Gulf of Mexico and western birds apparently migrate through the East before taking this southbound flight. Veeries winter in tropical forests from Colombia to Brazil. Studies indicate that older second-growth forests are far more attractive to nesting veeries than those cut in the last decade or two.

## Feeding
The veery spends most of its time on or near the ground, feeding on a mix of berries and insects that it finds by hopping, flycatching, or flipping over dead leaves. Prey includes beetles, snails, ants, wasps, caterpillars, and spiders. Berries and other small fruits are particularly important in late summer and fall. The veery spends more than half the year outside the U.S. and Canada. Its diet during this time is not well documented.

## Nesting
A female veery builds a nest on or near the ground. Using dead leaves as a base, she later constructs a cup of small bark bits, weeds, and leaf mold. The female incubates her clutch of four, sometimes three or five, blue-green eggs, which hatch after 12 days. Young leave the nest about 12 days after hatching, and are fed by both parents.

## Backyard & Beyond
Migrating veeries put in appearances in backyards, not at feeders but often in berry-bearing shrubs and trees including spicebush, elderberry, dogwood, and blackberry. These birds migrate primarily at night and many die after colliding with tall buildings and communications towers.

# Gray Catbird

*Dumetella carolinensis*

Named for its mewing catlike call, the catbird is actually a multitalented singer that is almost comparable to the mockingbird in its vocal versatility. Able to operate both sides of its syrinx, or vocal organ, independently, it can actually sing two different songs at once, and it's a mimic, too—not a bad resume for an otherwise plain gray bird.

### All About
A slim, slate-gray bird about 9 inches long, the catbird is distinguished by a solid black cap and a bright chestnut patch under its tail. Because of its habit of cocking its tail, this patch is often visible. Catbirds are easy to recognize because—no matter what age, sex, or season—they all look the same. Very vocal, the male catbird makes an almost endless array of sounds, one after the other; some are his own and others are "stolen" from other birds or even from frogs, domestic animals, or mechanical devices heard in his travels. You can usually tell a catbird's song from that of other mimics, though, because each phrase is repeated only once, and the telltale *meouw* is thrown in from time to time.

### Habitat & Range
In most of its U.S. range, the catbird is migratory, moving southward in winter, away from the coldest weather. Flying at night, migrant catbirds are often victims of collision, striking tall buildings or communication towers with distressing frequency. A few avoid the dangers of migration by remaining in their northern territories, a tactic that works if they are well fed and the season is not overly harsh.

### Feeding
Foraging in thickets and brambles, the gray catbird eats mostly insects in spring and summer, adding small fruits as fall approaches. Favored insects include caterpillars, ants, aphids, termites, cicadas, and dragonflies. Among fruits it chooses grapes, cherries, and berries, followed by such late-lingering items as multiflora rosehips, catbrier, privet berries, bittersweet, and mountain ash.

### Nesting
Singing from deep within a thicket, the male catbird courts his female in spring. After mating, she builds a bulky cup of twigs, weeds, and leaves, sometimes adding bits of paper or string and then lining it with fine grasses or hair. She incubates her three or four eggs for about two weeks; both parents then feed the nestlings for 10 to 12 days until they fledge. Two broods are common.

### Backyard & Beyond
If a catbird remains in your neighborhood during winter it may be attracted by offerings of dried or fresh fruit, suet, doughnuts, peanut hearts, or table scraps. These birds are easily intimidated by other species, so they are more likely to respond to food scattered on the ground than concentrated in a small feeding dish.

# Brown Thrasher
*Toxostoma rufum*

The brown thrasher has a lush resounding voice, and sings a seemingly endless train of melodies—its own and others'—from one end of a spring day to the other, and it may stay hidden in a deep shrub all the while. The brown thrasher is common throughout its range, but not as well known as it ought to be. This mimic is a cheerful and friendly addition to any backyard.

## All About
Nearly a foot long, the brown thrasher is a strong and handsome bird, equally at home in woodland edges or shrubby backyards. Its upperparts are bright cinnamon, broken only by two, thin, white wing bars; its white breast is heavily streaked in brown. It has a long tail, a long slightly curved bill, and strong sturdy legs well suited to "thrashing" about on the ground. Beginning birders may confuse a thrasher with one of the thrushes, or perhaps a fox sparrow, but the thrasher is much larger, with a longer bill and tail. The thrasher's song is almost as rich and varied as a mockingbird's, and it is very similar in quality, but where the mocker usually sings its phrases three times each, the thrasher utters his only twice.

## Habitat & Range
Often seen on the ground, the brown thrasher is a bird of woodland edges, thickets, hedgerows, brushy riversides and parks, and shrubby backyards. It retreats from the northern reaches of its breeding range to spend the winter in less frigid areas, usually returning sometime in April. In most of the South, it is a year-round bird.

## Feeding
More than half the brown thrasher's diet consists of insects—beetles, grasshoppers, cicadas, and caterpillars—most of which it finds on the ground as it rummages with feet and bill among the leaf litter. Brown thrashers also eat fruits, nuts, seeds, and acorns.

## Nesting
The male brown thrasher sings vigorously upon first arriving at its breeding grounds, both to establish territory and to attract a mate. The mated pair builds a large, twiggy nest in deep cover, usually quite close to the ground. Both parents incubate four eggs for nearly two weeks. Chicks are fully feathered and ready to fly in just nine days, an adaptation to avoid predators, which are especially dangerous to low-nesting birds. Two and sometimes three broods are raised each year.

## Backyard & Beyond
Brown thrashers will visit feeding stations for seeds and grains that are scattered on the ground. Nuts are popular, as are suet mixtures, cornbread, doughnuts, and raisins. Thrashers are not particularly shy of humans, but do require some shrubs or hedges nearby where they can retreat if they feel threatened.

# European Starling
## *Sturnus vulgaris*

In 1889, there were no European starlings in North America, yet today—just over a century later—we have more than 200 million. Blame a fan of William Shakespeare. In 1890, a flock of a hundred starlings was released in New York's Central Park in an attempt to bring to America all the bird species mentioned in Shakespeare's plays. The adaptable starling soon spread westward in history's greatest avian population explosion.

## All About
Glossy black overall, with a yellow bill during breeding season, the starling is one of the most familiar birds—not only because it is so common, but because it almost always lives close to human settlements. In winter, starlings are duller overall, covered with white spots (little stars, or "starlings") and with a blackish bill. In all seasons, starlings are very vocal, displaying an astonishing ability to mimic other bird songs, sirens, voices, barks, or mechanical sounds. In flight, starlings flap their triangular-shaped wings rapidly.

## Habitat & Range
Starlings cover the entire North American continent year-round, except for the far North in winter. In fall they form gigantic, noisy flocks roaming in search of food and roosting sites. Every habitat type can host starlings, but they prefer those altered by humans (farmland, urban, and suburban areas) and tend to avoid remote, pristine habitats except where humans are present.

## Feeding
Insects, berries, fruits, and seeds are the starling's regular diet, but they are highly adaptable—as willing to eat French fries from a dumpster as they are to find bugs in our lawns or suet at our feeders. The starling's traditional foraging technique is to insert its long, sharp bill into the ground and then open it to expose beetle grubs and other prey.

## Nesting
Starlings are cavity nesters that cannot excavate their own holes, so they use existing cavities, such as woodpecker holes, pipes, crevices in buildings, and birdhouses. Sites are often usurped from other, less aggressive cavity nesters, such as bluebirds or purple martins. Once a male has a site, a female will help finish the nest—a messy affair of grass, feathers, paper, and plastic. Between four and six eggs are laid and incubated by both parents for about 12 days. Young starlings leave the nest three weeks later.

## Backyard & Beyond
Most Americans can see a starling simply by looking out their window. Many bird watchers consider them a pest at their feeders and birdhouses. To discourage starlings at your feeders, simply remove the foods they prefer: suet, peanuts, bread, and cracked corn. At nest boxes, an entry hole diameter of 1 9/16 inches or less will exclude starlings. Frequent removal of their nesting material will also discourage them.

# Cedar Waxwing
*Bombycilla cedrorum*

A beady, insectlike trill first alerts many bird watchers to the presence of cedar waxwings, so completely do they blend into canopy foliage. These wandering fruit-eaters appear and disappear seemingly without rhyme or reason, descending to strip a tree of its fruits, then whirling off to parts unknown. Fermented fruits may cause entire flocks to stagger about on the ground until the intoxication wears off.

## All About
"Sleek" is the word most often used to describe the silky fawn plumage of the cedar waxwing. A velvety-black bandit mask hides the eyes, and a bright yellow band tips the gray tail. Older birds have red tips on the secondary wing feather shafts, which look like shiny drops of sealing wax. Cedar waxwings are most often seen in flocks in fall and winter.

## Habitat & Range
The cedar waxwing's only real habitat requirement is the presence of fruit-bearing trees and shrubs; thus, it can be found everywhere except grasslands, deserts, and deep interior forests. Thought to be nomadic, the species does make a poorly understood migration that takes it as far south as southern Central America.

## Feeding
Cedar waxwings travel in tight flocks to locate and feed on small fruits. They may be completely hidden in leaves as they flutter and pluck fruit, only to explode out with reedy calls and a rush of wings when startled. In late summer, they may be seen in twisting, dodging pursuits of winged insects over water.

## Nesting
Though they defend no territory and in some places are semicolonial, cedar waxwings are monogamous. Both sexes help build a bulky, cup-shaped nest in the outer canopy of a tree. Leaves, straw, twigs, and string, often in a trailing mass, comprise the nest. The female lays four eggs and incubates them for 12 days, while the male feeds her. Young are fed on insects for the first two days, then solely on regurgitated fruits, leaving the nest around 15 days later. This fruit-based diet ensures that any parasitic brown-headed cowbirds hatching in their nests do not survive. Large flocks of immature birds (identifiable by their yellowish, streaked bellies) linger near breeding grounds for one or two months after the adults leave.

## Backyard & Beyond
Attracting cedar waxwings is best accomplished by planting the trees and shrubs they prefer—serviceberry, hawthorn, firethorn, dogwood, chokecherry, viburnums, native honeysuckles, blueberries, cedars, and others with small fruits. They may also visit birdbaths, especially those with moving water. Worldwide, there are only two other species of waxwing: the Bohemian and Japanese waxwings. Waxwings are related to silky flycatchers, a largely tropical family.

# Magnolia Warbler
*Dendroica magnolia*

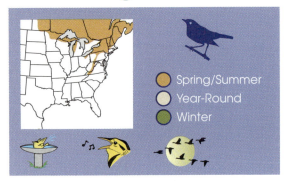

A small and active bird, the magnolia warbler (or "maggie" as some bird watchers call it) is a frequently seen spring migrant because it forages low in shrubby vegetation. The striking magnolia warbler has no particular association with magnolias—it was named in 1810 by early American ornithologist Alexander Wilson when he saw them for the first time in a stand of magnolias in Mississippi.

## All About
Magnolia warblers could be the poster bird for bird identification because they have one of everything: a dark mask, white eyeline, gray cap, white wing bars, a black necklace on a contrasting yellow breast, a yellow rump, and white tail panels. As they move about, magnolias almost seem to be trying to show you all of their markings. Adult males in fall plumage are a grayer version of their spring selves, but they retain the yellow breast and white tail panels. Male magnolias sing a highly variable song that sounds like *weeta, weeta, WEETA!* and is more recognizable for its soft delivery than for its rhythmic pattern.

## Habitat & Range
During the breeding season, magnolias are found at high elevations or in the far North in young scrubby pine, spruce, fir, and hemlock forests. In migration, magnolias can turn up almost anywhere, but they are most frequently seen in brushy areas with young deciduous trees. Because they are nocturnal migrants, magnolias are frequently seen first thing in the morning, actively feeding to refuel themselves after a night of travel.

## Feeding
Magnolias glean insects, spider eggs, aphids, and beetles from trees and vegetation. As they hop through a sapling, they check the branches, bark, and undersides of leaves for food items. They will also catch insects in midair and will hover briefly to nab an otherwise hard-to-get insect from beneath a hanging leaf.

## Nesting
In May and June, magnolia warblers are getting busy with breeding. Both sexes work to build the nest on the male's territory, and the site chosen is usually low and well concealed in a hemlock, spruce, or fir. The female lays three to five eggs and handles the 13-day incubation chores. Young magnolias leave the nest about 10 days after hatching, but the parents will continue to feed them for nearly a month after fledging.

## Backyard & Beyond
Magnolias are one of our most common warblers, perhaps due to their preference for habitats with young trees. Finding a maggie in spring is as easy as getting out during the peak spring migration period in late March, April, May, and June. Once the breeding season starts, you'll either need to visit high elevation coniferous forests or head north to the heart of the breeding range.

# Yellow-rumped Warbler
*Dendroica coronata*

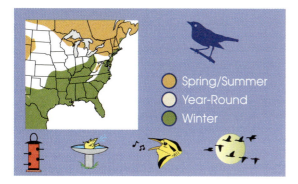

One of the best-known warblers in the United States—and easily the most widespread and numerous in winter—the yellow-rumped warbler is a paradox: Its plumage and its habitats are very variable; yet, it is relatively easy to identify whenever you find it. Eastern birds of this species used to be called "myrtle" warblers, while their western counterparts were known as "Audubon's" warblers. They are now all yellow-rumped warblers, despite differences in plumage and habitat. Trendy birders stick to their own favorite name: "butterbutt."

## All About
The yellow-rumped warbler is 5 to 6 inches long, with a sharp thin bill and slightly notched tail. In breeding plumage, the eastern male is blue-gray with a white throat and belly, black streaking on the back, a black face patch, two white wing bars, black bib, and yellow spots on the crown, shoulders, and rump. Spring females are browner and duller than their mates. Immatures and fall adults are brown above, with brown-streaked underparts and little or no yellow visible. The one constant in all plumages is the bright yellow rump. That, along with a frequent and distinctive *check!* note, will quickly identify these birds.

## Habitat & Range
Breeding in the far North, the eastern race of the yellow-rumped warbler is known in most of the country only as a migrant or winter resident. Migrants can be found in woodlands, hedgerows, thickets, and even along beaches as they stream through in large flocks. Winter birds congregate wherever they can find berries, their principal cold-weather food.

## Feeding
In Florida, yellow-rumps are known to drink the juice of broken or fallen oranges, and throughout their winter range they will consume weed seeds large and small. Some yellow-rumps come to backyard feeders where they eat a variety of fare.

## Nesting
For nesting, the yellow-rumped warbler selects conifer forests, generally spruce, pine, or cedar. The female builds the nest on a horizontal branch, anywhere from 5 to 50 feet high in the tree, using bark, twigs, weeds, and roots to create an open cup that is then lined with hair and feathers. The female incubates the four or five eggs for 12 to 13 days. When the chicks hatch, both parents feed them for 10 to 12 days until fledging, and then the male feeds them for a time afterward. There are usually two broods per year.

## Backyard & Beyond
In winter, yellow-rumped warblers may visit feeders to eat suet, hummingbird nectar, orange halves, or grape jelly. It is possible to lure them with sprigs of bayberry or other wild fruits. Away from home, look for them where natural foods are plentiful, such as in bayberry thickets or stands of wax myrtle.

# American Redstart

## *Setophaga ruticilla*

If you make spishing *or* pishing *noises around a mixed flock of migrating warblers, one of the first birds to pop up for a closer look may be this flashy little bird. The American redstart is a wood warbler that was named after a European member of the thrush family. But the American redstart is a true American original, even if its name derives from elsewhere.*

## All About

Like Europe's redstarts, the American flashes not red but orange in its tail, as well as on its wings and the sides of its breast. Otherwise, this warbler is black with a white belly. Birders call females and immatures "yellowstarts" because of similarly distinctive flashes of yellow (or in first-spring males yellow-orange) on the tail, wings, and the sides of the breast. Even seasoned birders can be thrown by the redstart's high-pitched, variable song, although some versions are easily recognized, such as *sweet-sweet-sweet-sweet-WHERE.*

## Habitat & Range

Within its extensive breeding range across eastern and northern North America, American redstarts nest in a variety of wooded habitats (deciduous or mixed) with an understory of young trees. In mountainous areas, they are common nesters in regrowing forests or at the forest edge. During migration, American redstarts are among the most visible migrating warblers. They primarily winter from Mexico south to northern South America and in the Caribbean, although small numbers winter in Florida and more rarely in Texas and Louisiana.

## Feeding

Spiders, caterpillars, and a wide variety of other small invertebrates wind up between the thin mandibles of the flittering redstart. The birds mostly seek insect prey, which they pick off leaves or capture in midair sallies, but redstarts also sometimes eat berries and seeds.

## Nesting

The female redstart twines together grasses and other plant materials and spider webs to make its cup nest, which is placed in young trees, often no higher than 15 feet above the ground. The female usually lays four eggs, which she incubates for about 12 days. Both parents feed their young. Before they are 10 days old, the young leave the nest but are attended by either parent.

## Backyard & Beyond

Among the most common migrant warblers, American redstarts frequently turn up in backyard trees during spring and fall. You can increase your odds of finding them at home by planting small native trees or shrubs where these insectivorous birds can seek insects. Shallow birdbaths or pools attract redstarts and other warblers; take care to situate water sources near shady cover that will still allow birds to see approaching cats.

# Ovenbird
## *Seiurus aurocapilla*

The ovenbird is a warbler that looks like a small speckled thrush. This deep forest bird only thrives where forests remain in large blocks, probably because if clearings are nearby, there are more nest predators and parasitic brown-headed cowbirds. Although spotting the forest-dwelling ovenbird takes patience, the bird's TEAcher-TEAcher-TEAcher-TEAcher *song* is distinctive and rings through the woods in spring and summer.

## All About
A good look at the ovenbird's head will help you differentiate it from larger thrushes and same-sized waterthrushes. The wide, white eye ring is the first clue. The waterthrushes lack this, having instead a white stripe (*supercilium*) running from above the eye to the back of the head. Several species of brown-backed thrushes have eye rings that are not as pronounced. These birds are also much larger and have heavier bills than the ovenbird. Thrushes hop and feed, at one moment still, then dashing; the ovenbird walks methodically. The ovenbird has neat "stripes" of spots running down its breast, while the thrushes are more randomly speckled underneath. While not always visible, the ovenbird's black-bordered, orange crown patch is a diagnostic field mark.

## Habitat & Range
Ovenbirds nest in mature deciduous or mixed deciduous and pine forests, but they can appear in any habitat during spring and fall migration. Most winter in Mexico, Central America, and on Caribbean islands. Forests that host nesting ovenbirds have a thick layer of dry leaf litter beneath them, providing the birds with feeding and nesting opportunities.

## Feeding
The ovenbird quietly chugs along the leafy forest floor, walking and looking for insects, spiders, and other invertebrates (such as earthworms and snails) among the leaves littering the ground.

## Nesting
This bird is named for its domed nest, which usually sits on the ground and is so well camouflaged with dead leaves that you can easily walk past without noticing it. Although leaves help conceal the nest, the female ovenbird constructs this structure using grasses, bark, and other materials. There is a side entrance for stealthy exit and entry. Inside, the female lays four or five eggs and incubates them for up to two weeks. Both parents feed the young. They leave the nest after about a week, but they are still fed by the adults for about two weeks afterward.

## Backyard & Beyond
If you have a well-treed backyard with ample leaf litter, you may spot a foraging ovenbird walking in your woods during migration. If you hear the ovenbird's loud song, watch for it on a low- to mid-height perch or foraging on the ground.

# Common Yellowthroat

*Geothlypis trichas*

This charming bird may be the most popular warbler in North America. It is certainly one of the most widespread and well known. Its repetitive song, written as *witchety-witchety-witch* actually does sound like that, and beginners trying to learn bird songs find that the yellowthroat's is one of the easiest to master.

## All About

Averaging about 5 inches in length, the common yellowthroat packs a lot of personality into a very small frame. Males are olive on top with a lemon-yellow throat and upper breast, white belly, yellow patch under the tail, and a bold black mask across the eyes, thinly bordered in white on top. The female is similar, but lacks the black mask. These are very active little birds and seem to be less timid than most warblers, possibly because they are nearly always low to the ground and therefore relatively easy to view. Their distinctive song continues well into the heat of summer.

## Habitat & Range

Only in the dry southwestern states is the common yellowthroat hard to find during the breeding season. Everywhere else this little bird has no trouble locating the moist, shrubby, brushy conditions it needs for nesting. Even a relatively small patch of suitable habitat will do for a single pair, while large areas may host many nests. In winter and on migration, yellowthroats extend their interests to include shrubby backyards, dry woodland edges, and similar sites.

## Feeding

Yellowthroats are almost exclusively insect-eaters, though they will add a few small seeds to their diet from time to time. Some favored insects are moths, aphids, leafhoppers, small caterpillars, mayflies, grasshoppers, and grubs. Foraging is done low to the ground, in dense cover.

## Nesting

Female yellowthroats build a bulky cup nest quite low to the ground in thick weeds, using grasses, sedges, and other materials taken from the surrounding area. After lining it with fine grasses and hair, she lays three to five eggs and incubates them for 12 days. Her mate will bring her food during this time, and will then help her feed the nestlings for up to 10 days until fledging. The family stays together longer than most warblers, as the adults continue to feed the dependent young. Common yellowthroats are frequent victims of cowbird nest parasitism and do not seem to have an adequate defense against it.

## Backyard & Beyond

In breeding season, thickets, hedgerows, marsh edges, and abandoned and overgrown farm fields are good places to look for common yellowthroats. Listen for their *witchety* song from spring through fall. They may be hard to find, but their loud, scolding *chuck* notes will often give them away.

# Black-throated Green Warbler
*Dendroica virens*

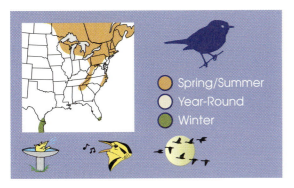

Easy to identify both by sight and by voice, the black-throated green warbler brings spring, summer, and fall cheer to many birders. Listen for its wheezy zoo-zee zoo zoo zee *or* zee zee zee zoo zee *song. Both male and female black-throated greens are colorful and easy to identify.*

## All About
This bird often appears in trees high above your head, but even a quick side or belly view reveals important identification clues, such as the bright yellow head framed from below by sharply contrasting black on the breast (and throat in male) and from above by an olive crown. The sides are streaked in black and the birds sport two white wing bars. They also have a yellow bar that runs across their white under-tails, or vents.

## Habitat & Range
The black-throated green warbler breeds primarily in coniferous and mixed forests from as far west as British Columbia, east through the Northeast, and down into the Appalachians. A few winter in southern Florida and southern Texas, but most black-throated green warblers migrate to Mexico and Central America for winter. During migration, black-throated green warblers are among the most conspicuous migrant warblers, actively foraging along woodland edges.

## Feeding
While nesting, black-throated green warblers eat insects, particularly caterpillars. They capture prey by snatching it from leaves but also by hovering at the tips of branches to locate and grab insects. During migration, poison ivy berries are among the fruits eaten. While on tropical wintering grounds, black-throated greens have been observed feeding on secretions that hang in globules from a commonplace tree called the cecropia.

## Nesting
Male and female black-throated green warblers share nest-building duties, making a cup of grassy stems and twigs, spider webs, and bark, which they line with softer materials such as feathers. This construction may take up to eight days and the female seems to choose the nest site, which is frequently between three to nine feet off the ground in a conifer, where two or more branches meet the trunk. Only the female incubates the four (sometimes three or five) eggs, usually for 12 days. The eggs are grayish or whitish drizzled with reddish brown markings. Females feed the young initially, joined after a number of days by the male. Young leave the nest after about 11 days, following one of the parents for about a month.

## Backyard & Beyond
This common migrant warbler retains most of its key field marks in its non-breeding plumage. During migration, scour chickadee and titmouse flocks and you may find black-throated green and other warblers in the treetops with these active feeders.

# Yellow Warbler
## *Dendroica petechia*

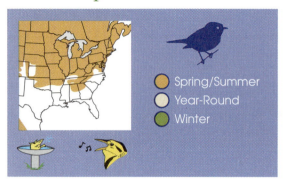
- Spring/Summer
- Year-Round
- Winter

One of North America's most familiar and widespread wood warblers, the yellow warbler's *sweet-sweet-I'm-so-sweet song* can be heard across the continent, from Alaska down to Mexico. In all, there are about forty different subspecies of the yellow warbler. Unlike many other wood warblers, population of the yellow warbler does not seem to be declining.

## All About
To many beginning birders, the yellow warbler is the "ambassador of warblers" because it is often one of the first to be identified, thanks to its colorful plumage, easy field marks, and wide breeding range. Males are bright yellow all over, their underparts streaked with rays of orange. Females are also yellow overall, including their undertails and underwings, but they lack bold streaking. The yellow warbler's song varies somewhat and is not always easily distinguished from that of chestnut-sided warblers.

## Habitat & Range
Yellow warblers are often found nesting in small trees or shrubs that grow at the edges of marshes, swamps, streams, lakes, and rivers. They sometimes set up housekeeping in drier deciduous forests, orchards, and thickets as well. On tropical wintering grounds, yellow warblers do not favor dense forest, but prefer partially open landscapes. In North America, the breeding range extends from Alaska through Canada, across the northern half of the U. S., as well as along the southern California coast and parts of Arizona down into western Mexico. North American birds winter from Mexico into northern South America.

## Feeding
Yellow warblers pick prey off leaves and grab flying insects in midair. Midges, caterpillars, spiders, mayflies, moths, and beetles are among the small invertebrates they capture. They also will eat an occasional berry or two.

## Nesting
A female yellow warbler usually builds an open cup nest in the fork of a young tree or shrub. The nest is fashioned from weed stalks, grasses, and bark shreds, but lined with finer materials such as plant fluff and hair. She usually lays between four and five greenish, dark-spotted or speckled eggs, which hatch after 12 days of incubation. After hatching, young are fed by both parents before they fly off when they are between 9 to 12 days old. Brown-headed cowbirds often lay their eggs in yellow warbler nests; to thwart this, the yellow warbler sometimes builds a new level onto the nest to cover the cowbird eggs, then lays a new clutch of eggs.

## Backyard & Beyond
Large properties backing up to water may host nesting yellow warblers, as long as waterside thickets are preserved. Yellow warblers also appear in backyard gardens during migration. They seem to show a particular preference for foraging in willow trees, so watch and listen for them there.

# Rose-breasted Grosbeak
*Pheucticus ludovicianus*

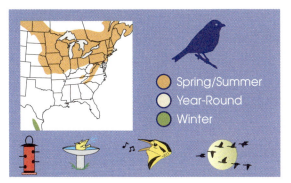

With its triangular scarlet breast patch and somewhat penguinlike pied plumage coloration, the male rose-breasted grosbeak is a North American beauty. This gorgeous songbird remains plentiful in a variety of habitats. The male's robinlike song is breezier and punctuated by a *chip* sound like a squeaky sneaker that, once learned, gives the bird away every time.

## All About
It is hard to mistake a male rose-breasted grosbeak. No other bird has a black head and back, a triangular rose-red breast patch, and clear white belly. Equally striking in flight, the male flashes rose-red under his wings with a wide, rectangular white wing patch. The female has a dramatically difference appearance. Looking like an overgrown brown and white finch, she is streaked below and has a broad white line both above her eye and below her dark ear patch. In fall, immature males look similar but have an orangey wash across the underparts. Especially near the western edge of the breeding range, care should be taken when identifying females and immatures, which strongly resemble those of the closely related black-headed grosbeak, a western species.

## Habitat & Range
The rose-breasted grosbeak breeds from far northwestern Canada, throughout the Midwest and Northeast, and at high elevations in the Appalachians. It prefers to nest in open woodlands or at the forest edge. These requirements are often met in neighborhood parks, along wooded roadsides, and sometimes in suburban neighborhoods. At its wintering grounds in the tropics, this bird also tends to occur in semi-open situations, sometimes with just scattered trees.

## Feeding
With its versatile, heavy bill, the rose-breasted grosbeak feeds both on vegetable and animal matter. During fall migration, it mostly eats berries and seeds, including sunflower seeds offered at feeders. Insect prey in spring and summer can include beetles (including the Colorado potato beetle), bees, ants, bugs, and caterpillars.

## Nesting
A female grosbeak builds her nest in a tree or tall shrub, usually between 5 and 20 feet above the ground. Assisted a bit by the male, she works twigs, weeds, and leaves into the loosely woven open cup nest, then usually lays four eggs. Both parents incubate for about two weeks, then feed their nestlings, which leave the nest between 9 to 12 days after hatching.

## Backyard & Beyond
At the feeder, rose-breasted grosbeaks will eat sunflower and safflower seeds and shelled peanuts. Elderberry, juneberry, raspberry, blackberry, and mulberry are among the shrubs and small trees that can be planted to attract migrant rose-breasted grosbeaks, which also feed on a variety of weed seeds.

# Scarlet Tanager
*Piranga olivacea*

The male scarlet tanager in spring plumage ranks among the most stunningly beautiful birds in North America. One glance at his neon-bright plumage can turn even the most disinterested person into a confirmed bird watcher. Oddly, this dazzling bird's song has been compared to "a robin with a bad cold." A distinctive *chick-burr* call is often the first clue of a scarlet tanager's presence.

## All About
The male scarlet tanager in spring plumage has a solid-red body and jet-black wings and tail, with a black-button eye and bone-gray bill. The female is dull olive above with dark wings and pale yellow underparts. Immatures resemble females, and in late summer the adult males take on the muted olive-yellow plumage. In all plumages, the scarlet tanager's wings are darker than those of the summer tanager. At just 7 inches long, scarlet tanagers are the smallest of the four North American tanager species.

## Habitat & Range
Preferring deciduous forests with oaks, maples, and beeches, scarlet tanagers generally inhabit areas farther north (or, in the South, at higher elevations) than summer tanagers. They arrive in April or May and depart by midautumn. Flocks of early migrants are sometimes decimated by sudden late-spring snowfalls or ice storms, which cause them to starve or freeze to death. Sometimes being the early bird is not such a good idea.

## Feeding
Basically insectivorous, the scarlet tanager moves quietly about in the upper canopy of deciduous trees in search of prey. Small summer fruits—such as blueberries and mulberries—are also taken, as are fall staples, such as poison ivy berries and sumac fruits. Scarlet tanagers occasionally engage in flycatching, or hovering behavior, to obtain food. Early or late in the season, cold weather may force them to the ground to forage for bugs in sheltered microhabitats.

## Nesting
Typically, the scarlet tanager nests in a large, unbroken, wooded tract and high in a deciduous tree—often, but not always—an oak. It will be situated well out from the trunk on a horizontal limb. Made by the female alone, it is shallow and loosely constructed of twigs, rootlets, weeds, and other plant material. Three to five eggs are laid, and the female incubates them for up to two weeks until hatching. Both parents feed the young during the 9- to 14-day nestling period and for two weeks more after fledging occurs.

## Backyard & Beyond
Scarlet tanagers are not common at bird feeders, but they do—on occasion—respond to offerings of bread, doughnuts, orange halves, or a peanut butter-cornmeal mixture. They will also eat small fruits and, in fall migration, may be a regular sight along tangled hedgerows overrun by poison ivy or multiflora rose.

# Northern Cardinal
## *Cardinalis cardinalis*

Cardinals are the familiar and beloved "redbird" found all across the eastern United States. This bird's popularity is such that seven U.S. states and countless sports teams have chosen the cardinal as their official emblem. In spring and summer, cardinal pairs can be found together, often with the male perched high above, singing his what-cheer-cheer-cheer *song*. In fall and winter, cardinals can be found in large loose flocks, especially during harsh weather.

### All About
A black face and a long red crest smartly set off the bright red plumage of the male cardinal. Females are a muted, brownish version of the male. Strongly territorial, mated cardinal pairs will vigorously defend their nesting turf from rivals, even going so far as to attack their own reflections in windows, mistaking the image for another cardinal. One of the cardinal's most notable behaviors is the "courtship kiss" in which a male feeds a bit of food to a female he is wooing.

### Habitat & Range
Found in a variety of habitats—from deserts to wetlands to manicured backyards, cardinals prefer an *edge habitat*—a place where woodland and open space meet. They are resident (nonmigratory) and thriving throughout their range, which has expanded northward in recent decades—thanks in part to the availability of food at bird feeders.

### Feeding
Cardinals forage on or near the ground. During warm weather, insects, berries, buds, and seeds are their primary diet. Gardeners appreciate cardinals for eating grubs, beetles, caterpillars, and other garden pests. In winter, cardinals shift to a greater reliance on seeds, nuts, and wild fruits. At bird feeders cardinals prefer sunflower seeds, but will also eat mixed seeds, suet, fruits, and peanuts.

### Nesting
Female cardinals choose thick cover—vine or rose tangles or shrubs—in which to weave their shallow, cup-shaped nests out of grasses, rootlets, twigs, and bark strips. Into this nest, the female will lay three to five eggs and incubate them for nearly two weeks before they hatch. Both parents feed the youngsters for about 10 days before they fledge. In summer, young cardinals can often be seen following a parent around, begging to be fed. Males will take on this duty while the female starts a second brood.

### Backyard & Beyond
You can enjoy cardinals all year long in your backyard by offering them the four things they need to survive: food, water, a place to roost, and a place to nest. A few bird feeders, a chemical-free lawn and garden, and some thick brushy cover will suit their requirements nicely. Watch for cardinals early and late—they are often the first birds active at dawn and the last ones to "turn in" at dusk.

# Indigo Bunting
## *Passerina cyanea*

Appearing all black against the light, a male indigo bunting properly lit is an unforgettable sight. A persistent late-season singer, he sings a jingly song comprised of paired notes that are often described as: *Fire! Fire! Where? Where? Here! Here! Put it out! Put it out!* Much of what we know about celestial navigation in songbirds derives from work with captive indigo buntings at the Cornell Lab of Ornithology.

## All About
The breathtaking, all-blue male indigo bunting, with his silvery conical bill, is unmistakable. Females and immatures are a warm cocoa-brown overall. This bunting has a habit of twitching its tail to the side, and its *spit!* note is characteristic. Males change their blue feathers for brown in autumn, which makes for some interestingly mottled specimens. They molt again on the wintering grounds and return in spring, blue once more.

## Habitat & Range
This species is common on roadsides and disturbed areas where "trashy" vegetation flourishes. Power line cuts, old fields, landfills, railroads, and hedgerows ring with the songs of indigo buntings, especially as summer reaches its fullest. Indigo buntings are strongly migratory, wintering in Central and northern South America.

## Feeding
The indigo bunting takes insects when they are available, especially to feed its nestlings. Weed seeds are its mainstay, supplemented by berries and small fruits. It forages on or near the ground, as well as in low shrubs and trees. Watch for them in autumn, bending grass stems and flicking their tails side to side as they forage in weedy patches.

## Nesting
Indigo buntings have a rather loose definition of monogamy, with extra-pair copulations being quite frequent. Males visit females in neighboring territories, and females visit males. Males vary in their tendency to feed young; some are attentive parents, whereas others leave most of the chick rearing to their mates. The nest is bulky but compact, cup-shaped, and constructed of bark strips, grass and weed stems, and skeletonized leaves, all bound with spider webs. It's often low in blackberry, sumac, or other brushy vegetation. These birds nest quite late in the season, reflecting their dependence on late-maturing weed seeds. Three to four eggs are incubated by the female for about 12 days, and the young leave the nest from 8 to 14 days later.

## Backyard & Beyond
Lucky is the one who hosts indigo buntings! Spring arrivals are most often first seen feasting on dandelion seeds. Later, black-oil sunflower seeds and millet mixes prove attractive. The growing popularity of "meadows in a can" make for rich feeding grounds for indigo buntings, which flock to coneflower, Mexican hat, cosmos, coreopsis, and especially foxtail grasses.

# Eastern Towhee
*Pipilo erythrophthalmus*

Drink your TEA! *sings the towhee throughout the brushy woodlands of the eastern United States. Formerly called the rufous-sided towhee (a much more descriptive name), this large (8½ inches long) sparrow is boldly patterned and spends nearly all its time on the ground scratching among the leaf litter, looking for food. The name towhee comes from the bird's call, which has also been transcribed as* chewink. *Many people know this bird as the chewink instead of towhee.*

## All About
Clean, flashy colors have given the towhee the nickname "Hollywood robin." In flight, the bird's white wing and tail spots are noticeable. Female eastern towhees replace the male's black plumage areas with chocolate brown. Towhees' preference for thick cover and brushy habitat make them harder to see than other common species. The loud scratching of a foraging towhee sounds like a large animal walking through dry leaves; this is often your first clue to a towhee's presence.

## Habitat & Range
Widespread across the eastern half of the United States and southern Canada, towhees in the northern part of the range are migratory, but those in the southern half are resident (nonmigratory). During mild winters, towhees may linger until harsh weather forces them to migrate or to seek the cover of wooded valleys and hollows. Brushy woodland thickets and edge habitats are preferred, but towhees are also found in older woodlands and suburban backyards.

## Feeding
Towhees eat just about anything found on the woodland floor, including insects, seeds, fruits, and even snails, spiders, and millipedes. They prefer to scratch the ground under feeding stations for mixed seeds, cracked corn, and sunflower seeds (which they crack with their powerful bill).

## Nesting
Towhees nest on or near the ground in a well-concealed spot. The female weaves a cup-shaped nest out of rootlets, bark strips, and grass. She also handles all the incubation duty, which typically lasts about 12 days. Normal clutch size is three to four eggs; young towhees fledge in about 10 days. Both towhee parents feed the youngsters, which allows the female to start a second—and sometimes a third—brood.

## Backyard & Beyond
Spring is the best time to find an eastern towhee. Male towhees are especially vocal during the breeding season and will leave deep cover to sing from a high perch within their territory. Make your feeders much more attractive to towhees by adding a brush pile nearby to help these shy birds feel more at home. In summer, recently fledged towhees can be confusing and hard to identify with their streaky, gray-brown coloring. Their white tail spots and ground-scratching habits will give them away.

# Field Sparrow
## *Spizella pusilla*

The field sparrow's clear whistled notes on a single tone is an easy bird song to learn and remember. Listen throughout the day, even in summer, for this persistent singer. Its rhythmic pattern resembles a ping-pong ball being dropped onto a table. A subtly beautiful sparrow of farm pastures and shrubby old meadows, the field sparrow is familiar to bird watchers in rural habitats.

## All About
The field sparrow is a small bird (5 3/4 inches long) with a biggish bill and long tail, but the first field marks most birders notice are the pink bill, plain face, and white ring surrounding the dark eye. Telling the field sparrow apart from chipping or tree sparrows is a matter of noting the field's unmarked buffy-gray breast and indistinct head stripes of brown and gray.

## Habitat & Range
As its name suggests, the field sparrow is found in fields, but it prefers brushy, older fields that have the beginnings of reforestation—saplings, small shrubs, and large thick clumps of grass. Field sparrows are found all across the eastern United States, but—unlike many of our migrant songbirds—they may only migrate a few hundred miles to spend the winter. In spring and summer, males do their singing from an exposed perch within their territories.

## Feeding
Throughout the year, the field sparrow's diet is grass seeds and other small plant seeds; in spring and summer the diet shifts to insects. Moths, grasshoppers, flies, and other grassland insects make up half of their summer diet, with most of the insects being found on or near the ground. In winter, as flocks of field sparrows forage together, a single bird will perch on top of a tall grass stem, letting its weight bend the stalk to the ground where the seeds can more easily be eaten.

## Nesting
In early spring (April to May) field sparrow nests are built on the ground, near a grass clump or small shrub. Later nests (June to July) may be in taller shrubs or vegetation, but the construction is the same—a loosely woven outer cup of grass lined with fine, soft grasses, all built by the female. Three to six eggs are laid and incubated by the female for about 12 days. Like other ground nesters, young field sparrows develop quickly and may leave the nest within a week. Flight is attained in two weeks and independence from the parents two weeks later.

## Backyard & Beyond
Within the breeding range, any older farm field should host field sparrows. Look for males perched on top of saplings or fenceposts. Field sparrows will come to cracked corn, mixed seeds, and eggshell bits scattered on the ground beneath bird feeders.

# Chipping Sparrow
*Spizella passerina*

A close look at this natty little bird reveals much to admire in its quiet and confiding ways. As common as it is around dooryards and gardens, we know surprisingly little about the chipping sparrow's mating systems. One Ontario study showed males not to be monogamous, as assumed, but to mate freely.

## All About
A rusty beret and bold, white eyeline are the best field marks of this slender little sparrow. Plain gray underparts, a streaked brown back, and a small, all-black bill set off its striking head markings. It is an under-appreciated bird, perhaps because it is so small and unobtrusive. Rather dry, monotonous trills, as well as its signature chipping notes, are the ambient sounds of a chipping sparrow's territory.

## Habitat & Range
Before the massive expansion of suburbs, the chipping sparrow was limited to open, grassy coniferous forests and parklike woodlands with shrubby understories. Our suburban habitats have just the right mix of short grass, shrubbery, and conifers that chipping sparrows need, so we enjoy their company on doorsteps and sidewalks. Although northern populations are strongly migratory, southern birds flock up but tend to stay near their breeding grounds.

## Feeding
Chipping sparrows forage primarily on or near the ground, feasting on weed and grass seeds and some smaller fruits. They feed insects to the young, however, sometimes flycatching on the wing. Winter flocks of up to 50 birds perch in trees, descending *en masse* to the ground to peck for seeds, then adjourning to treetops before the next feeding bout. At feeding stations, they'll peck on the ground or perch on hopper feeders.

## Nesting
Female chipping sparrows weave lovely little nests of thin twigs and weed stems, with a center composed of animal hair. These are often concealed in low trees and shrubs, but are easily located by the shrilling of older nestlings. Females incubate the four eggs for around 12 days, and the young leave the nest about 9 to 12 days later. Streaky, brown, and nondescript, they're fed by their parents for three more weeks before forming juvenile flocks.

## Backyard & Beyond
Chipping sparrows eagerly accept mixed seeds and suet dough mixtures offered on or near the ground. They're fond of rolled oats, and live mealworms will be taken straight to the young. They greatly appreciate baked and crushed eggshells strewn on a sidewalk. But it's most fun to offer them human or pet hair clippings. A trip to any salon can net a season's worth, and you may have the pleasure of finding a used nest lined with your own hair—the ultimate vanity piece for the discerning gardener.

# White-throated Sparrow
## *Zonotrichia albicollis*

Old Sam Peabody, Peabody, Peabody *is the sweet whistled song of the white-throated sparrow. In Canada, where this species spends the breeding season, the song is transcribed as* Oh sweet Canada, Canada, Canada—*but there's no arguing that the white-throated sparrow's song is easy to recognize. From September to March these northern breeders are with us, in loose flocks with other sparrows, brightening winter days with their cheery sounds.*

## All About
The first field mark most bird watchers notice on the white-throated sparrow is not the white throat, but the black-and-white striped head pattern with a yellow spot between the eyes and bill. Even at a distance this striking pattern is obvious. Some white-throated sparrows have tan-striped heads and a tannish throat. These belong to the tan-striped variety of the species, though many ornithologists formerly thought these were young birds not yet in adult plumage. This medium-sized ($6^{3}/_{4}$ inches long) sparrow has a gray breast and a brown, lightly patterned back.

## Habitat & Range
Spending most of the summer in the boreal coniferous forests of the far North and New England, the white-throated sparrow spends fall and winter to the south, where it is a regular at bird feeders and in brushy edge habitat. It prefers a habitat with thick underbrush and is found near the edge of the woods, along hedgerows, and in brushy thickets in parks and backyards.

## Feeding
White-throated sparrows prefer to feed on the ground. In spring and summer, the white-throated sparrow's diet is focused on insects—ants, grubs, and spiders—that it uncovers as it scratches through the leaf litter, much like a towhee does. In fall the diet shifts to include berries; in winter it includes mostly seeds from grasses. At bird feeders they are attracted to mixed seed, cracked corn, and sunflower or peanut bits offered on the ground or on a platform feeder.

## Nesting
White-throated sparrows nest on or near the ground in a well-concealed spot. The cup-shaped nest is built by the female from grass, pine needles, and twigs and lined with soft material, such as rootlets or fur. The female incubates the four to five eggs for about two weeks; the male assists her in feeding the nestlings for the nine days prior to fledging. The young birds rely on the parents for food for about another two weeks.

## Backyard & Beyond
Look for white-throated sparrows on the ground beneath your feeders from late fall through early spring. If your feeders are some distance from cover, consider moving them closer to the woods' edge, or add a brush pile nearby to make woodland birds (such as white-throated sparrows) feel more at home.

# White-crowned Sparrow
*Zonotrichia leucophrys*

The striking black-and-white stripes on the head of the adult white-crowned sparrow are a field mark that is hard to ignore. Flocks of white-crowned sparrows are fairly common in winter across the Midwest and during spring and fall migrations as the birds travel to and from their breeding range in the far North.

## All About
A large sparrow with a badger-striped head, the white-crowned sparrow has a pale gray breast, brown flanks and rump, and two white wing bars on the brown wings. Bill color varies by population from yellow to orange-pink. The white-crowned sparrow's song is a beautiful mix of clear whistled introductory notes, followed by a series of buzzy trills. It can be heard singing on sunny days during winter and prior to spring migration.

## Habitat & Range
The white-crowned sparrow breeds in the boreal forest edges, brushy thickets, and scrub of the far North but is also a year-round resident in many parts of the mountainous West. It winters across the southern two-thirds of the U.S. along woodland edges, in brushy fields, hedgerows, and in suburban parks and backyards. In the non-breeding season (September through April) it can often be found in feeding flocks with other sparrow species.

## Feeding
The diet of the white-crowned sparrow is composed mainly of plant seeds, which it finds as it forages on the ground. In spring, its diet includes tree buds, fruits, and some insects, especially during breeding season. White crowneds will visit feeding stations, especially if brushy thickets are nearby, preferring to scratch for seed bits on the ground below the feeders.

## Nesting
White-crowned sparrows nest on or near the ground, with the females weaving the cup-shaped nest out of grasses, rootlets, twigs, and strips of bark. A grass or animal hair lining holds the four or five eggs as they are laid and helps insulate them during the nearly two-week incubation by the female. Both parents care for the young, which leave the nest within two weeks. In areas where the white-crowned is a year-round resident there may be as many as four broods per year.

## Backyard & Beyond
White-crowned sparrow and the closely related white-throated sparrow are common backyard birds in fall and winter across the Midwest. Listen for their high, sweet, whistled songs and their sharp *pink!* call at dawn and dusk from thick brushy habitat. Scatter some mixed seed under your feeders and beneath your shrubs and brush pile to offer these ground feeders something to eat.

# Song Sparrow
## *Melospiza melodia*

Persistent singing, often year-round, makes this a well-named species. If there's a resident song sparrow in your yard, you'll probably hear its cheery notes at first light—as reliable as, but more pleasant than, a rooster's. One of the best-studied birds in North America, the song sparrow was the subject of Margaret Morse Nice's groundbreaking behavioral study in the 1930s. Much of what we understand about songbird territoriality began with this study.

## All About
The classic "little brown job," the song sparrow has a heavily streaked white breast marked with a messy central spot. A grayish, striped face and crown and warm-brown upperparts complete the description. Flight is low and jerky, with the tail twisting distinctively. Three introductory notes leading to a variable jumble of trills and chips distinguish its song. Males and females look similar.

## Habitat & Range
Though song sparrows occupy a wide range of habitats, they are most often found in shrubbery near water, from small streams to beach habitats. Song sparrows tend to be migratory in northern climes and year-round residents in the southern United States; this varies by population. The song sparrow is one of the most variable songbirds known. Populations in the Pacific Northwest, for example, are larger, darker, heavier-billed, and virtually unrecognizable compared to southeastern coastal populations.

## Feeding
The song sparrow's diet varies seasonally, with insects being its primary prey in spring and summer and with seeds and fruits dominating in fall and winter. Most of the song sparrow's foraging takes place on the ground, where it will scratch and kick about in leaf litter and grasses for weed seeds and insects.

## Nesting
The persistent singing of song sparrows is linked to strong territorial behavior; where they are resident year-round, they tend to defend territories year-round. Territory boundaries are quite stable from year to year. Both sexes defend their territory, and they tend to stay with one mate. Females construct a bulky nest of bark strips and weed and grass stems, well hidden deep in a dense shrub. Small, ornamental evergreens are irresistible to song sparrows. The female incubates three to five eggs for about 13 days. Young leave the nest at only 10 days and may be fed by the parents for the next 20 days before they are fully independent.

## Backyard & Beyond
Song sparrows readily visit feeders for sunflower seeds, cracked corn, and mixed seeds, preferring to feed on the ground. Peanut butter-based suet mixes are a favorite food, and song sparrows will appear to beg at windows for such fare. They are fond of water and will often nest near a water garden or backyard pond.

# Dark-eyed Junco
*Junco hyemalis*

The dark-eyed junco is often called the "snowbird," because it seems to show up at our feeders and in our backyards at the same time as the first snows begin falling over much of the country. But even in the Deep South, this member of the sparrow family is a familiar winter visitor to backyards, gardens, parks, pastures, and feeding stations.

## All About
Juncos are medium-sized (6¼ inches long) sparrows, but unlike most sparrows, their plumage lacks streaking. Dark-gray above and white below (or "gray skies above, snow below"), the junco has a conical, pinkish bill and flashes its white outer tail feathers in flight. Male juncos in the East are a darker gray than the brownish-overall females. Western junco forms show a variety of plumage colors, and many of these color forms were considered separate species until recently. Now they are all lumped into a single species: dark-eyed junco. Juncos make a variety of sounds, all of them high-pitched tinkling trills, especially when flushed from cover.

## Habitat & Range
Few bird species' ranges cover North America more thoroughly than that of the dark-eyed junco. In winter it can be found in every state. Spring migration begins as early as March and continues through early June. During breeding season, juncos retreat to the far north woods and to coniferous and mixed woodlands at high elevations. Fall migration begins in mid-August through October. Their winter habitat preferences run to brushy edge habitat along woods, fields, and suburban backyards and parks.

## Feeding
Juncos find their food on the ground. They are often seen scratching through the leaf litter, grass, or snow when foraging. In spring and summer the junco eats mostly insects, including spiders, caterpillars, ants, grasshoppers, and weevils, but it will also eat berries. In fall and winter the diet shifts to grass and weed seeds, along with birdseed gleaned from the ground beneath feeders.

## Nesting
The junco's nest is a simple, open cup of grasses and leaves, loosely woven and lined with finer grasses, fur, or feathers. Nests are normally located on the ground in a concealed spot and built by the female. She incubates her three to five eggs for almost two weeks; the male helps with feeding chores once the young hatch. Within two weeks the young birds leave the nest, and the parents are free to start another brood if the season permits.

## Backyard & Beyond
Where there is one junco, there is almost surely a flock. Seek them along the edges of woodlots, old pastures, and in areas with a thick growth of underbrush. Watch for the flashing white in the tail and listen for the juncos' trilling calls.

# Eastern Meadowlark
*Sturnella magna*

Our two meadowlark species (the second being *western meadowlark*, Sturnella neglecta) are indistinguishable visually, but their songs are different. The eastern meadowlark's sweet whistled song—*spring of THE year!*—and the western meadowlark's low, descending, whistled and gurgled *Swing low sweet chariot!* are both signs of spring's arrival.

## All About
Familiar birds of rural farm fields, meadows, and grasslands, the eastern and western meadowlarks are known by their distinctive field mark: a bright yellow breast with a "V" of black. Meadowlarks will sing from the ground and in flight, but they often use an elevated perch, such as a fencepost, tree, or power line. In flight, the meadowlark looks chunky and shows white outer tail feathers. A series of shallow, stuttering wingbeats followed by a short glide (sometimes accompanied by a song or chatter) is the typical flight pattern.

## Habitat & Range
Eastern meadowlarks prefer grassy meadows, prairies, and pastures with good grass cover. Westerns seem to favor shorter, drier grasslands. Both can also be found along golf courses, in hayfields, and in the grassy margins of airports. As their names suggest, the eastern meadowlark is primarily an eastern bird and the western primarily a western bird, but their ranges overlap significantly in the Midwest. These birds can apparently tell they are different species, because they almost never interbreed.

## Feeding
The meadowlark is a ground feeder that searches vegetation in spring and summer for insects, such as crickets, grasshoppers, grubs, and caterpillars. In winter, the diet shifts to seeds, grains, and some fruits. In fall and winter, both meadowlarks often form large single-species flocks, with dozens of birds foraging together in the same field.

## Nesting
Meadowlarks nest on the ground in thick grass. The nest is well concealed in a depression on the ground and is woven out of dried grasses. Two to six eggs are laid and incubated for about 14 days. Youngsters fledge about 10 days later. Both parents feed the young. For nesting, meadowlarks seem to prefer grasslands that are cut only once every three to five years. Even so, many meadowlark nests are lost to agricultural activity, predation, and pesticides.

## Backyard & Beyond
To find a meadowlark you must locate a suitable habitat, which usually means locating a rural spot with hayfields and pastures. During spring and summer, meadowlarks sing throughout the day, but do so most actively early in the morning. Listen for the slurring whistled song and the sputtering blackbird-like calls. Scan the wires, treetops, and fenceposts for the singing adult bird. Its handsome lemon-yellow-and-black breast should catch your eye.

# Brown-headed Cowbird
*Molothrus ater*

The cowbird's habit of laying its eggs in the nests of other, smaller songbirds makes the brown-headed cowbird a nest parasite. Cowbirds learned this behavior over centuries of following roaming herds of buffalo. The buffalo stirred up insects, the cowbird's main food. But all the movement made it impossible to stop, build a nest, and wait for the young to grow. So the cowbirds did the most convenient thing—laid their eggs in any nest they could find along the way.

## All About
The cowbird is a small (7 1/2 inches long) blackbird. Males have a glossy black body and a dark brown head, while females are a dull gray-brown overall. The short, conical bill and pointed wings help to distinguish the brown-headed cowbird from larger blackbirds. The cowbird's song is a series of liquid gurgles followed by a high, thin whistle.

## Habitat & Range
Cowbirds are found in a variety of habitats, but they prefer woodland edges, brushy fields, and old pastures, though they are equally at home in city parks and suburban backyards. Forest fragmentation has allowed the cowbird to parasitize the nests of woodland species, such as thrushes and vireos. In winter cowbirds often join flocks of other blackbirds—red-winged blackbirds, grackles, and European starlings—foraging in fields and grasslands and roosting *en masse* in large woodlots.

## Feeding
The diet of the cowbird consists of weed and grass seeds, along with insects, especially grasshoppers and beetles. Nearly all food is taken from the ground.

## Nesting
Male cowbirds court females with a variety of songs, bows, and sky-pointing displays. When she is ready to lay an egg, she finds a nest that often already contains the eggs of the nest's owner. This "host" nest is most frequently that of a smaller songbird—yellow warblers, song sparrows, red-eyed vireos, and chipping sparrows seem to be frequent victims—and the female cowbird may even remove one of the host's eggs before depositing her own. Hatchling cowbirds are almost always larger than their nestmates, and are able to out-compete them for food, enhancing the cowbird's chances of survival. Some bird species have evolved to recognize cowbird eggs and will build a new nest on top of the old one or will remove the cowbird egg.

## Backyard & Beyond
Finding cowbirds is almost never a problem, but limiting their impact on our songbirds can be problematic. One way to discourage cowbirds is to stop offering mixed seed and cracked corn during spring when they show up at bird feeders before many migratory songbirds return. If you see a songbird feeding a fledgling that is larger than itself, the fledgling is likely a cowbird.

# Red-winged Blackbird
## *Agelaius phoeniceus*

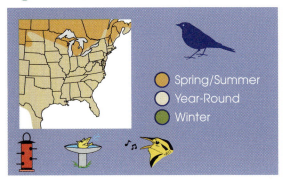

The red-winged blackbird's name succinctly describes the male's handsome plumage; yet, the females of this ubiquitous species have baffled many a bird watcher. Their streaky brown plumage is confusingly sparrowlike. Studies have shown that one dominant male red-winged blackbird may have many adult females nesting on his territory.

## All About
The *conk-a-ree* call of the male red-winged blackbird fills the air over marshes and fields all across North America. As he gives this call, announcing himself loudly to rivals and potential mates alike, he spreads his shoulders just so, showing bright red and yellow epaulets against his black wings. Redwings are medium-sized (8 3/4 inches long) blackbirds with an all-black body, an orange-red and yellow patch on the shoulder, and a nearly conical black bill. Females are streaky brown overall, but their longer bill helps separate them from the sparrows (which have stouter bills).

## Habitat & Range
Wet meadows, cattail marshes, upland grasslands, and pastures are all breeding habitat for red-winged blackbirds. In fall and winter, they may join with other blackbird species to form huge flocks. Northern-nesting redwings migrate (starting in September and October) to the southern U.S., while southern-nesting birds are nonmigratory. Fall blackbird flocks move during the day in oblong, loose clouds of birds. These flocks forage by day in agricultural fields and are often persecuted as a nuisance species for the crop damage they inflict. Spring migration begins in mid-February and continues through mid-May.

## Feeding
The red-winged blackbird's diet is mostly plant matter—weed seeds, grain, sunflower seeds, and tree seeds—along with some insects, all of which are gleaned from the ground. They will also visit feeding stations for sunflower seeds, cracked corn, peanuts, and suet. Surprisingly, they are able to use a variety of feeder types.

## Nesting
Nesting starts early for the red-winged blackbird, with males singing from an exposed perch on their territories as early as February in the South, later in the North. Females choose a nest site on a male's territory and build cup-shaped grass nests that are suspended from vertical supporting vegetation. Mud forms the foundation of the nest and soft grasses are the inner lining. Clutch size is three to four eggs, and the female alone incubates them for 10 to 13 days. Both parents care for the nestlings for about two weeks, until they are ready to leave the nest.

## Backyard & Beyond
Red-winged blackbirds are present continent-wide for most of the year. Wet meadows, swamps, and salt marshes are common habitats for these birds, especially in spring and summer. Listen for the male's loud *conk-a-ree* song.

# Common Grackle
## *Quiscalus quiscula*

Grackles are large, conspicuous, and noisy birds that are equally at home in a town or country setting. This species benefited greatly from the European settlement of North America as forests were turned into farm fields and new feeding and nesting opportunities emerged for the common grackle. Residential areas and farmland are particularly attractive to grackles.

## All About
Nearly half of the common grackle's 12 1/2-inch length is its tail. The grackle's black plumage is glossy and can show bright purple, bronze, or green highlights, especially on the head. Adult common grackles show a pale yellow eye, contrasting sharply with the dark head. The powerful bill is long and sharply pointed. In flight, grackles hold their long tails in a "V", much like the keel of a boat. Males and females are very similar in appearance. Grackles utter a variety of harsh, metallic tones.

## Habitat & Range
Common grackles are found in almost every habitat in eastern North America; though, in winter the population is more concentrated in the eastern and southern United States. Grackles prefer edge habitat and open areas with scattered trees or shrubs. From late summer to early spring, grackles gather in large roosts with other blackbirds. These roosts can contain as many as half a million birds, and are notable both for their noise and their droppings. Spring migrants may reach breeding territories as early as mid-February. Fall migration begins in September and peaks in October.

## Feeding
During breeding season, grackles eat mostly insects, but they are opportunists and will take nestling birds or eggs, small fish, mice, and frogs. In winter the diet shifts to seeds and grain. The impact of foraging winter flocks on crops has earned the common grackle a reputation as an agricultural pest. Most of the grackle's foraging is done on the ground, where the birds toss aside leaves and rubbish to uncover their food.

## Nesting
Grackles prefer to nest in dense conifers, close to rich foraging habitat. The large, open-cup nest is built by the female from grass, twigs, and mud and is lined with soft grass. She incubates the four to five eggs for about two weeks. The male joins her in feeding the nestlings an all-insect diet until fledging time arrives about 20 days later.

## Backyard & Beyond
Look for long dark lines of migrating common grackles during the day, especially in fall. Migrating flocks can contain thousands of birds and may stretch from horizon to horizon. At feeders grackles relish cracked corn and sunflower seeds most of all. Grackles are also known to take hard, stale pieces of bread and dunk them in a birdbath to soften them up.

# Baltimore Oriole
## *Icterus galbula*

- Spring/Summer
- Year-Round
- Winter

The colorful Baltimore oriole, like many long-distance migrants, leads three flamboyant lives: backyard, park, and forest nester in North America; winter nectar, fruit, and insect-eater in the tropics; and long-distance wanderer while transiting between its two homes. Named for the colonial family that settled Maryland—the family crest of which sported the bird's striking orange and black colors—the Baltimore oriole is one of only two widespread eastern orioles.

## All About
At rest and in flight, the male Baltimore oriole is a fireball of citrus orange blazed with black. The bird's head, back, and much of its wings and tail are black. In flight, a bright orange shoulder and white wing bars flash, as do its orange tail corners. The female Baltimore oriole is also colorful, lacking the entirely black head of the male but having vibrant orange-yellow underparts. The Baltimore oriole's unusually rich song and two-note whistle often reveal its presence.

## Habitat & Range
The Baltimore oriole breeds in open parklike woodlands, at forest edges—including along waterways—as well as in suburbs and city parks. This bird favors tall, mature deciduous trees, often in very open, widely scattered stands. During migration and on its wintering grounds, it is similarly adaptable, inhabiting forests, hedges, gardens, shade coffee and cacao plantations, and even pastures with scattered trees. Baltimore orioles nest from central Canada, across the southeast of the country, then south through much of the eastern U.S. north of Texas and the southeastern coastal plain. Most of the population winters from Mexico south to northwestern South America and in the northern Lesser Antilles, including Cuba. Some winter in Florida. Each winter, individuals pop up along many other parts of the East Coast and even in southern California.

## Feeding
During warm months, Baltimore orioles feed on a wide variety of insects, including caterpillars—at times tearing open tent caterpillar nests. Fruits are also eaten, including some cultivated varieties. In winter, Baltimore orioles eat berries, insects, and nectar, which they extract from flowers with their bristly tongues.

## Nesting
A female Baltimore oriole constructs a pendulous nest, sometimes with the help of her mate. Woven of plant fibers, string, and other materials, the nest hangs near the end of a large branch, usually between 20 and 30 feet off the ground. Within the enclosed nest, the female lays four or five bluish or grayish eggs, which are marked with brown and black. She incubates the eggs about two weeks, then both parents feed the nestlings, which leave the nest about two weeks after hatching.

## Backyard & Beyond
Halved oranges and sugar water in special feeders often entice Baltimore orioles to visit yards.

# House Finch
## *Carpodacus mexicanus*

Bird watchers who rely on an eastern field guide that is more than thirty years old may be forgiven for some confusion. This bird won't be in it! The house finch, native to the West, is a well-established, but recently arrived resident of the eastern United States. Released upon the passage of protective legislation forbidding trade in native wild birds, a small population of the so-called "Hollywood linnets" began breeding on Long Island in 1940, and they have now blanketed the eastern United States with their progeny.

### All About
People who feed birds are familiar with the house finches that sometimes cover feeders with fluttering, tweeting flocks. It's easy to see why they were kept as cage birds; the male's cheery, rich song, marked by a few harsh notes, tumbles brightly down the scale. Females are streaky, pale brown birds with white undersides; males have a rich pinkish-red rump, head, and upper breast. By comparison, male purple finches have an overall "dipped in wine" look, with a reddish suffusion to their back and wings, while female purple finches are much more boldly streaked with brown and white than are female house finches.

### Habitat & Range
As its name suggests, the house finch prefers nesting and feeding near homes. It's a thoroughly suburban bird in the East, but in its native West, it is found in undisturbed desert habitats as well. This species appears to be developing migratory behavior in the East, with a general movement toward the South in winter.

### Feeding
Most of the house finch's diet is vegetarian, and it spends a great deal of time feeding on the ground. Weed seeds, buds, and fruits are its mainstays away from feeding stations.

### Nesting
House finch nests are shallow twig platforms with a finely woven inner cup composed of rootlets, grass, feathers, and string. They are tucked into dense ornamental evergreens, hanging baskets, ledges, ivy-covered walls, and other nooks where there is an overhanging structure. Two to five eggs are incubated by the female, while the male feeds her. Young are fed regurgitated seeds and fledge from 12 to 16 days later.

### Backyard & Beyond
For most feeding station proprietors, the question is not how to attract house finches, but how to discourage them. Even attractive birds with pleasant songs wear out their welcome when they descend in dozens, monopolizing feeders. Black-oil sunflower seeds are a favorite, closely followed by Niger and mixed seeds. Some people resort to removing perches from tube feeders, thus discouraging house finches, which are poor clingers.

# Purple Finch

*Carpodacus purpureus*

The male purple finch is a rich raspberry-red (not purple) color and is often confused with the much more common male house finch (which is orange- or brick-red). Purple finches travel in flocks during the non-breeding seasons, and may descend on feeding stations for a few hours or weeks as they roam in search of a winter food source.

## All About

"Like it was dipped headfirst in raspberry wine" is how many bird watchers describe the color of the male purple finch, and it's an apt description, because the raspberry color completely encircles the bird's upper body. On the similar male house finch, the red covers only the head, face, and breast. The house finch's back and wings are brown and streaky. Large-headed with a stout bill, the purple finch is hard to miss, often announcing its arrival with a loud *pik!* call. Their song, which is sung beginning in late winter, is a loud, rich warble delivered from a treetop perch. Females are brown-backed with dark brown and white face patterns and dark cheek patches. Their white breasts are boldly streaked with brown.

## Habitat & Range

Purple finches breed in a variety of woodland habitats from cool coniferous woods to deciduous forests, orchards, and edge habitat. During migration and in winter, they can be found almost anywhere in the eastern United States from woodland edges to weedy fields and backyard feeding stations. They go wherever food is available and purple finch "invasions" in winter are often caused by shortages of natural food supplies in the North.

## Feeding

Seeds, blossoms, buds, and fruits comprise the purple finch's diet, with some insects also being consumed. Favorite food trees include elms, tulip poplars, maples, sweet gums, sycamores, and ashes. Typical foraging involves a flock of purple finches ranging amid the upper branches, grabbing and eating young buds. Sunflower seed is their preferred food at feeders.

## Nesting

Female purple finches do most of the nest building after the pair chooses a site in the outer branches of a large conifer tree. She weaves together bark strips, rootlets, and twigs into a cup and lines it with animal hair and fine grass. Three to seven eggs are deposited and incubated by the female for about two weeks. Both parents feed hatchlings until fledging time, about two weeks later.

## Backyard & Beyond

You may have both purple finches and house finches at your feeders, which means you have a great opportunity to learn to tell them apart. Once you see the differences in plumage (on males check the distribution of the red, on females check the facial pattern) you'll find that it's not that hard after all.

# Pine Siskin
## *Carduelis pinus*

This slender, streaky little finch is often overlooked—mistaken for a female house finch or a winter-plumaged goldfinch. But a closer look reveals a slender-billed, finely streaked finch adorned with yellow in its wings and tail.

### All About
Your first clue to a pine siskin's presence may be its loud, descending *Tzeeeew!* call as a flock drops into your backyard trees. Siskins also give a rising *Zweeeeet!* sound and sing a jumbled twitter of notes similar to a goldfinch's song. Fine brown streaks cover the pine siskin's body, but as the bird moves its yellow wing stripes and tail spots flash—a surprise bit of color on this otherwise drab bird.

### Habitat & Range
Across the Midwest and eastern U.S. the pine siskin is a winter visitor. It nests in the coniferous forests of the far North and throughout the West, but makes nearly annual appearances throughout eastern North America. During spring and summer, pine siskins are never far from conifers, alders, and the mixed woodlands in which they breed and forage. In winter, siskins often move southward—sometimes in great numbers—in search of food. They forage in weedy fields, hedgerows, pine woods, and at backyard feeding stations.

### Feeding
Siskins eat grass and weed seeds, especially wild thistle seeds, plus tree buds, pine seeds, berries, and some insects. Expert clingers, siskins will hang upside down on a catkin clump, pinecone, or weed stem and pry seeds loose with their finely pointed bills. Caterpillars, insect larvae, and spiders are also consumed. At feeders, siskins relish sunflower bits (they are unable to crack open the whole seeds themselves) and thistle (Niger) seed.

### Nesting
Male siskins begin courting females in late winter, before reaching their breeding grounds, as the winter feeding flocks are dispersing. Siskins are known to nest in loose colonies in conifer or mixed conifer-deciduous forests. The female builds the cup-shaped nest out of weed stems, grasses, bark strips, vines, and rootlets and lines it with soft material such as animal fur, feathers, thistledown, or moss. She lays three to five eggs and incubates them for about two weeks, during which time the male may bring her food. Both parents feed the nestlings, which leave the nest about 15 days after hatching.

### Backyard & Beyond
Add a thistle feeder and seed to your backyard offerings and you'll increase your chances of attracting siskins. Sunflower bits are another attractant, as is a source of open, moving water. Listen for the sharp, zippy calls of siskin flocks as they fly over. And be sure to look carefully at your flocks of drab winter goldfinches—a siskin may be accompanying them.

# American Goldfinch
## *Carduelis tristis*

The bright canary-yellow and black plumage of the breeding male American goldfinch has earned this species the nickname "wild canary." It is a familiar visitor to bird feeders at all seasons, especially in winter. The goldfinch's undulating flight is accompanied by a twittering call of *perchickoree* or *potato chip!*

## All About
American goldfinches appear very different in summer and winter. The male's brilliant yellow body and black cap in summer give way to a drab, olive-brown plumage in winter. Female goldfinches, though never bright yellow, also lose most of their color. Both sexes retain their black wings and tail year-round. The sweet, high-pitched, warbling song of the male is often given in early spring, just as these small (5 inches long) birds are beginning to show their first bright yellow feathers.

## Habitat & Range
Weedy fields, brushy woodland edges, and open habitats with scattered shrubs are the American goldfinch's normal habitats. In the breeding season, they prefer weedy fields with thistles and other seed-producing plants. In winter, goldfinches roam in noisy flocks, seeking food in fields, gardens, and at feeding stations.

## Feeding
Goldfinches are seedeaters in all seasons, consuming a huge variety of weed, grass, and plant seeds as well as tree buds. In goldfinch nests parasitized by brown-headed cowbirds, young cowbirds are unable to survive the all-seed diet fed to nestling goldfinches. Goldfinches are agile birds, able to exploit seed sources that other finches cannot, by hanging upside down from seedheads, plant stalks, and bird feeders.

## Nesting
Goldfinches' nesting season begins late, a timing adaptation so that nesting occurs when there is the greatest natural abundance of seeds, as well as the soft thistle down that goldfinches use to line their nests. Late June is the earliest nesting time, but peak nesting season is late July, though some nesting occurs as late as September. The nest site is in a shaded spot in a sapling or shrub and is selected by the pair. The female builds the open-cup nest from twigs (attached with spider web), rootlets, and plant stems, and she lines it with soft thistle down or a similarly soft material. Four to six eggs are incubated by the female for about two weeks, with the male bringing food to her on the nest. Both parents tend the nestlings for 12 to 17 days before they fledge.

## Backyard & Beyond
The twittering calls of goldfinches will alert you to the presence of these energetic songbirds. At bird feeders, goldfinches especially like thistle seeds (sometimes called Niger seeds), sunflower seeds and bits, and peanut bits. Goldfinches love to drink and bathe in shallow birdbaths and are especially attracted to moving water.

# House Sparrow
*Passer domesticus*

Introduced to North America in the early 1850s from England to help control wireworms, the house sparrow population spread across the continent in just 50 years. The house sparrow enjoys a close association with humans, almost always nesting and living in proximity to our settlements. It is one of the world's most successful and widespread species.

## All About
The chunky little house sparrow is known for its constant *cha-deep, cha-deep* calls and for the male's black bib in breeding plumage. Breeding males have a black bill and a contrasting black, gray, and brown head and face pattern. Winter males are a muted version of the breeding plumage. Females are drab gray-brown overall and lack the bib. House sparrows are constantly chirping and are aggressive competitors at feeders and nest sites.

## Habitat & Range
House sparrows are year-round residents. It's easier to describe where you *won't* find house sparrows because they are utterly ubiquitous. Pristine natural habitats—forest, grassland, or desert—that are lacking human development will also lack house sparrows. Historically, the house sparrow associated with horses (and the seeds and insects in their droppings) and other livestock. Today, house sparrows are found in the most urban of habitats, living on food scraps and nesting in building crevices—though they are still a common inhabitant of horse barns, farmyards, and feedlots.

## Feeding
Seeds and grains will be on the house sparrow's normal menu throughout the year. In spring and summer, they take advantage of bountiful insect populations. At any time, house sparrows are quick to take food at bird feeders or scraps of food offered directly or indirectly by humans in parks, picnic areas, fast food restaurants, and strip malls. Cracked corn, sunflower seeds, peanut bits, and bread products are favorite foods.

## Nesting
Males choose a cavity and sing by it to attract the female. Both build the messy nest of grass, weed stems, feathers, paper, and string. House sparrows will appropriate nest boxes from bluebirds, swallows, and purple martins (forcing many nest box landlords to use controls and special housing to discourage house sparrows), and they may even kill nest box competitors. The female lays between three and six eggs, which are incubated by both parents for 10 or more days. The parents share feeding duties until the nestlings are ready to fledge at about two weeks.

## Backyard & Beyond
House sparrows are feeding station regulars, especially in towns and cities. To discourage house sparrows from dominating nest boxes, use boxes with interiors less than 5 inches deep, remove their nesting material regularly, and place nest boxes far from buildings and thick shrubbery.

# Solutions for Common Feeding Problems

## Lack of Birds

- During spring and summer, the diet of many of our seed-eating feeder visitors shifts to a greater reliance on insects, fruits, and other natural, abundant food sources. Even during the traditional fall and winter bird-feeding seasons, birds may not immediately find a feeding station. Once the first chickadee, goldfinch, or titmouse "tunes in" to your feeders, the word will spread quickly and other birds will show up. Temporary loss of birds at a feeder can be caused by the presence of a hawk, a cat, or by stale birdseed.

## Discouraging Squirrels

- It is a battle that has been going on for nearly a century: humans trying to keep squirrels from getting to bird feeders. There are many squirrel-proof feeders available, but squirrels figure out many of these after a time. Placing your feeders on baffled poles far from any tree, deck railing, or other potential launching pad that a squirrel could use seems to be the most successful strategy. Alternatively, offer the furry menaces some cracked corn (or ears of field corn) far away from your feeders. Keep squirrels happy elsewhere, and you may keep them off your feeders.

## Blackbirds, Pigeons, Jays, and Sparrows

- Certain birds can hog all the space and food at your feeders to the exclusion of the smaller, less aggressive species. You can limit the impact of these "feeder hogs" by removing their preferred food from the menu. For blackbirds, pigeons, and doves, limit the cracked corn and mixed seed; for jays and crows, limit the suet, peanuts, cracked corn, and table scraps; for sparrows, limit the cracked corn and do not feed bread. Larger birds (such as grackles, rock pigeons, and blue jays) can also be discouraged through the use of small tube feeders with short perches—small birds can use 'em, but big birds can't.

## Hawk at Feeders

- Cooper's hawks and sharp-shinned hawks are songbird specialists that can be attracted to the bird activity at your feeders. Their tactic is a quick surprise attack, scattering the feeder visitors and perhaps catching a slow, sick, or unwary individual. As unpleasant as it may seem, it is perfectly natural and is an important aspect of nature's balance.

## Cat at Feeders

- Place your feeders a short distance away from thick cover where hunting cats might lurk. Mount your feeders high enough (above 4 feet) that a leaping cat cannot reach feeding birds. A circle of short (1-foot-high) wire fencing can make it more difficult for charging cats to catch birds.

## Night Marauders

- If your feeders empty out overnight, you probably have a mammal making nocturnal visits to your feeder. This furry critter could be a raccoon, an opossum, a flying squirrel, deer, or even a bear! Feed only as much seed as can be eaten by your birds during a single day, and you'll discourage these late-night diners.

## Sick Bird at Feeders

- Sick birds often show up at feeders, desperate for an easy meal, and they usually succumb to their illness within a short while. Although most bird illnesses are not transferable to humans, it pays to be cautious. Contact your local wildlife officials about any sick birds you see at your feeders—they often monitor wildlife health trends. If you find a dead bird, avoid making direct contact with it (wear gloves or use a plastic bag to pick it up), and bury it or discard it in the trash. Clean your feeders thoroughly and consider halting your feeding for a few days to allow the healthy birds to disperse temporarily.

# Food and Feeder Chart

| Species | Food |
|---|---|
| Quail, pheasants | Cracked corn, millet, wheat, milo |
| Pigeons, doves | Millet, cracked corn, wheat, milo, Niger (thistle seed), buckwheat, sunflower, baked goods |
| Hummingbirds | Plant nectar, small insects, sugar solution |
| Woodpeckers | Suet, meat scraps, sunflower hearts/seed, cracked corn, peanuts, fruits, sugar solution, mealworms |
| Jays | Peanuts, sunflower, suet, meat scraps, cracked corn, baked goods |
| Crows | Meat scraps, suet, cracked corn, peanuts, baked goods, leftovers, dog food |
| Titmice, chickadees | Peanut kernels, sunflower, suet, peanut butter, mealworms |
| Nuthatches | Suet, suet mixes, sunflower hearts and seed, peanut kernels, peanut butter, mealworms |
| Wrens, creepers | Suet, suet mixes, peanut butter, peanut kernels, bread, fruit, millet (wrens), mealworms |
| Mockingbirds, thrashers, catbirds | Halved apples, chopped fruit, mealworms, suet, nutmeats, millet (thrashers), soaked raisins, currants, sunflower hearts |
| Robins, bluebirds, other thrushes | Suet, suet mixes, mealworms, berries, baked goods, chopped fruit, soaked raisins, currants, nutmeats, sunflower hearts |
| Kinglets | Suet, suet mixes, baked goods, mealworms |
| Waxwings | Berries, chopped fruit, canned peas, currants, dry raisins |
| Warblers | Suet, suet mixes, fruit, baked goods, sugar solution, chopped nutmeats |
| Tanagers | Suet, fruit, sugar solution, mealworms, baked goods |
| Cardinals, grosbeaks | Sunflower, safflower, cracked corn, millet, fruit |
| Towhees, juncos | Millet, sunflower, cracked corn, peanuts, baked goods, nutmeats, mealworms |
| Sparrows, buntings | Millet, sunflower hearts, black-oil sunflower, cracked corn, baked goods |
| Blackbirds, starlings | Cracked corn, milo, wheat, table scraps, baked goods, suet |
| Orioles | Halved oranges, apples, berries, sugar solution, grape jelly, suet mixes, soaked raisins, dry mealworms, currants |
| Finches, siskins | Thistle (Niger), sunflower hearts, black-oil sunflower seed, millet, canary seed, fruit, peanut kernels, suet mixes |

# Nest Box Chart

| Species | Interior Floor Size of Box (inches) | Interior Height of Box (inches) | Entrance Hole Diameter (inches) | Box Mounting Height (feet) | Habitat for Box Placement |
|---|---|---|---|---|---|
| Chickadees | 4x4 | 9–12 | 1 1/8 – 1 1/2 | 5–15 | Open woods and edges |
| Prothonotary Warbler | 4x4 | 12 | 1 1/4 | 5–12 | Wooded areas, swamps and streams |
| Titmice | 4x4 | 12 | 1 1/2 | 5–12 | Wooded areas and edge habitat |
| White-breasted Nuthatch | 4x4 | 12 | 1 1/2 | 5–12 | Wooded areas and edge habitat |
| Carolina Wren | 4x4 | 9–12 | 1–1 1/2 | 5–10 | Old fields and thickets |
| Eastern Bluebird | 4x4 | 12 | 1 1/2 | 5–6 | Open land with scattered trees |
| Tree Swallow | 5x5 | 10–12 | 1 1/2 | 5–10 | Open land near pond or lake |
| Purple Martin | 6x6 | 6 | 2 1/8 | 15–25 | Open country near water |
| Great-crested Flycatcher | 6x6 | 12 | 1 3/4 – 2 | 6–20 | Open woods and edges |
| House Finch | 5x5 | 10 | 1 1/2 | 5–10 | Backyards and porches |
| Downy Woodpecker | 4x4 | 12 | 1 1/2 | 5–20 | Forest openings and edges |
| Hairy Woodpecker | 6x6 | 14 | 1 1/2 | 8–20 | Forest openings and edges |
| Red-bellied Woodpecker | 6x6 | 14 | 2 | 8–20 | Forest openings and edges |

# Nest Box Chart

| Species | Interior Floor Size of Box (inches) | Interior Height of Box (inches) | Entrance Hole Diameter (inches) | Box Mounting Height (feet) | Habitat for Box Placement |
|---|---|---|---|---|---|
| Red-headed Woodpecker | 6 x 6 | 14 | 2 | 8–20 | Forest openings and edges |
| Northern Flicker | 7 x 7 | 16–24 | 2 1/2 | 10–20 | Farmland, open country |
| Pileated Woodpecker | 12 x 12 | 24 | 4 | 15–25 | Mature forest |
| Bufflehead | 7 x 7 | 17 | 3 | 5–15 | Wooded lakeshores, swamps |
| Wood Duck | 12 x 12 | 24 | 3 x 4 oval | 5–20 | Wooded swamps, bottomland |
| Hooded Merganser | 12 x 12 | 24 | 3 x 4 oval | 5–30 | Wooded swamps, bottomland |
| Goldeneyes | 12 x 12 | 24 | 3 1/4 x 4 1/4 oval | 15–20 | Wooded lakeshores, swamps |
| Common Merganser | 12 x 12 | 24 | 5 x 6 oval | 8–20 | Wooded lakeshores, swamps |
| Saw-whet Owl | 7 x 7 | 12 | 2 1/2 | 8–20 | Forest clearings and edges |
| Eastern Screech-owl | 8 x 8 | 18 | 3 | 8–30 | Farmland, orchards, woods |
| Barred Owl | 14 x 14 | 28 | 8 | 15–30 | Mature bottomland forest |
| Barn Owl | 12 x 36 | 16 | 6 x 7 oval | 15–30 | Open farmland, marshes |
| American Kestrel | 9 x 9 | 16–18 | 3 | 12–30 | Farmland |

# A Glossary of Common Bird Terms

- **Avifauna:** The community of birds found in a given region or habitat type.

- **Cavity nester:** A bird that nests inside an enclosed area such as a hollow tree, an old woodpecker hole, or a bird house.

- **Crown:** The top of a bird's head.

- **Diurnal:** Active during daylight hours.

- **Edge habitat:** A place where two or more habitats come together, such as where woodland meets an old meadow. Edge habitat typically offers a rich diversity of birds.

- **Endemic:** A breeding species that is unique to a given geographical region.

- **Extinct:** A bird that no longer exists in the wild. The Carolina parakeet is an example of an extinct species.

- **Extirpated:** A bird that once was present in a given area but no longer is. It does exist in other areas, however. For example, the red-cockaded woodpecker has been extirpated from much of its original range throughout the South, but remains in small pockets of its former range.

- **Eyeline:** Refers to a line of contrasting colored feathers over or through a bird's eye, often used as a field mark for identification.

- **Field mark:** An obvious visual clue to a bird's identification. Field guides are based on describing field marks of birds.

- **Fledgling:** A bird that has left the nest, but may still be receiving care and feeding from a parent.

- **Hotspot:** A location or habitat that is particularly good for bird watching on a regular basis.

- **Juvenile/Juvenal:** *Juvenile* (noun) refers to a bird that has not yet reached breeding age. *Juvenal* is an adjective, referring to the plumage that a juvenile bird wears.

- **Life bird:** A bird seen by a bird watcher for the first time is a life bird. Life birds are usually recorded on a birder's life list, a record of all the birds he or she has seen at least once.

- **Lores:** The area between a bird's bill and its eyes.

- **Migrant:** A bird that travels from one region to another in response to changes of season, breeding cycles, food availability, or extreme weather. Many of our warbler species that spend the spring and summer in North America *migrate* to Central or South America for the winter.

- **Mimic:** A term used to describe birds that imitate other sounds and songs. Three common bird species are mimics: the northern mockingbird, gray catbird, and brown thrasher.

- **Nape:** The back of a bird's neck, often referred to in reference to a field mark for identification.

- **Neotropical migrant:** Refers to migratory birds of the New World, primarily those that travel seasonally between North, Central, and South America.

- **Nestling:** A bird that is still being cared for in the nest.

# A Glossary of Common Bird Terms

- **Peeps:** A generic term for groups of confusingly similar small sandpipers.

- **Pishing (or spishing):** A sound made by bird watchers to attract curious birds into the open. Most often made by repeating the sounds *spshhh* or *pshhh* through clenched teeth.

- **Plumage:** Collective reference to a bird's feathers, which can change both color and shape through the process of seasonal molt. During a molt, a bird loses some or most of its old worn-out feathers and grows new healthy feathers to replace them. Breeding plumage is worn by birds during the breeding season and this is often when a bird is at its most colorful. Non-breeding or winter plumage is worn during fall and winter, generally, and is often less colorful than breeding plumage.

- **Primary feathers (primaries):** The long flight feathers originating from the "hand," or end, of a bird's wing.

- **Raptor:** A term used to refer to a bird of prey, including hawks, owls, osprey, and vultures.

- **Resident:** A non-migratory species—one that is present in the same region all year.

- **Spotting scope:** A single tube optical device mounted on a tripod and used to look at distant birds. Most birding scopes are between 15x and 60x in magnification power.

- **Suet:** The large chunks of hard, white fat that form around the kidneys of beef cattle. Suet is used by bird watchers as a high-energy winter food for birds.

- **Tail spot:** Spots, usually white, on a bird's tail, often used as a field mark for identification.

- **Underparts:** A term referring to the lower half of a bird (breast, belly, undertail), often used in relation to a field mark.

- **Upperparts:** A term referring to the upper half of a bird (crown, back, top of tail), often used in relation to a field mark.

- **Vagrant:** A bird that wanders far from its normal range.

- **Wing bars:** Obvious areas of contrasting color, usually whitish, across the outer surface of a bird's wings.

# Frequently Asked Questions

## General

**Q.** There is a bird in my backyard that not only sings throughout the day, but also *all night long!* This particular bird has many, many songs. Do you have any idea what kind of bird this is?

**A.** Your bird is most likely a northern mockingbird. Don't worry, male mockingbirds only perform this nocturnal singing in the spring and summer, during the time of the full moon. Try running an electric fan (to create a buffer of sound) or using your earplugs on those nights when the male mockingbird is singing. Having a mocker around is a good thing—some would even consider you lucky!

**Q.** A female robin recently built a nest in a tree on my patio. On May 10, she started laying her eggs—four in total. How long before they hatch, and how long after that do they still need the nest?

**A.** Robins incubate their eggs for 12 to 14 days. Once hatched, the nestlings remain in the nest for another 14 to 16 days before fledging. Two weeks is normally the incubation period for most songbirds. Another two weeks is an average time before the young leave the nest.

**Q.** Many times I have seen hawks being mobbed by American crows. Is this a common phenomenon, and why does it occur?

**A.** Mobbing behavior by crows is common. The crows are reacting to the potential threat that the hawk poses as a predator to the adult crows and their offspring. The mobbing often serves to harass the hawk into leaving the area. Occasionally, a mobbed hawk will turn the tables and attack and kill a crow.

**Q.** A woodpecker is pecking holes in my house siding. Is there anything I can do to get it to stop?

**A.** A woodpecker drilling on your wooden house is only doing what comes naturally—drilling into wood in search of shelter or food. Most house-wrecking woodpeckers do their damage in fall, which is when they begin making their winter roost holes. Try mounting a nest box with an appropriately sized hole over the drilled area. Fill the house with wood chips, and you may divert the bird's attention and gain a tenant.

Woodpeckers also use wood and sometimes metal parts of houses as drumming sites. They drill their bills against the surface in a rapid staccato beat. This drumming noise is a territorial announcement and a method for attracting a mate. Drumming happens most regularly in spring. There are several things you can try; one of them may work.

1. Place some sheet metal or heavy aluminum foil over the area the bird is using.
2. Hang some aluminum pie plates around the affected area. Make sure they move in the wind (to scare the bird away).
3. Place a rubber snake near the drilling area (to scare the bird away).
4. Repeatedly frighten the bird by yelling or clapping when it lands on your house.
5. If nothing else works, call your local wildlife official to see if someone can come to your house to remove the offending bird.

# Frequently Asked Questions

**Q.** Is seeing a robin a true sign of spring's arrival? Where do they go in winter?

**A.** American robins are surprisingly hardy as long as they have access to their winter food sources: fruits. They switch over in winter from their mostly insect-based summer diet. As such, robins are *facultative migrants*. This means that they will migrate only as far south as they need to or are forced to by bad weather or food shortages. During ice storms, when fruits are covered in a thick coating of ice, many robins flock together and move south. In the same way, if a robin spends the winter in your region, it's probably because there's enough food to see it through.

The idea that robins are the first true sign of spring is somewhat mythical. In much of northern North America, a few robins overwinter, but they stick to woods and thickets where they can find fruit. Most backyard bird watchers do notice the robins' return when these birds appear on lawns with the onset of warm weather, seeking their warm-weather food: earthworms, grubs, caterpillars, and other insects.

**Q.** Do all birds mate for life?

**A.** No. Some species have unusually strong pair bonds between mated birds. These species include some eagles, cranes, swans, geese, and ravens. Being mated "for life" means, really, for as long as both birds are alive. When one of the pair dies, the other will take a new mate. Most North American bird species pair up primarily to reproduce, and then go their separate ways soon after they have nested. In some species, the pair bond is brief. In the case of ruby-throated hummingbirds, the pair bond lasts only as long as courtship and copulation. The male has nothing to do with the incubation or raising of the young birds.

**Q.** Do all birds migrate?

**A.** Not all bird species migrate, but most do. Migration in North America is defined as the seasonal movement of birds, northward in spring from the wintering grounds, and southward in fall from the breeding grounds. Among the birds that are *resident*, or that do not migrate, are many grouse, ptarmigan, and quail species; many owl species; pileated, red-bellied, downy, and hairy woodpeckers along with white-breasted nuthatch, Carolina wren, northern cardinal, wrentit, ring-necked pheasant, Townsend's solitaire, common raven, gray jay, and northern mockingbird.

## Bird Care

**Q.** Is it true that if you find a baby bird out of the nest, you should not touch it because the parent birds will detect your scent and abandon the nest?

**A.** No, most birds do not have a well-developed sense of smell. However, most mammalian predators (skunks, foxes, raccoons, weasels, and so forth) do have a good sense of smell and may follow your scent trail to a bird's nest. If you are going to handle a baby bird be sure to place it out of harm's way, back in the nest or in an open-topped cardboard box propped in a tree. Many bird species are equipped to survive outside the nest at a very young age. These species include many shorebirds, gamebirds, and birds such as robins and wrens.

**Q.** If I find a baby bird that has fallen from a nest, what should I do?

**A.** Try to place the nestling back in its nest if at all possible. This will be the baby bird's best chance at a normal life. If you can't find the nest or a place to put the nestling out of harm's way, you will need to get the bird to a licensed rehabilitator as soon as possible.

# Frequently Asked Questions

Baby birds are unable to *thermoregulate* (regulate their body temperature), and so must be kept in a protected area with a heat source. A soft nest made of tissues inside a small cardboard box, placed on a heating pad set on LOW temperature, is a good example of a temporary home. A moist sponge placed in the box will add a touch of desired humidity. This will warm the bird.

Try to contact a wildlife rehabilitator as soon as possible. Your state fish and wildlife officers are responsible for licensing and regulating the activities of rehabilitators and have listings for those in your region. Make sure anyone else giving you advice is familiar and current with the specialized needs of wildlife.

**Q.** I found an injured bird. What should I do with it?

**A.** A person must have special permits from the federal, state, or provincial government to handle injured or dead non-game bird species. While your first instinct may be to call your local veterinarian, many vets are unwilling to care for "wildlife cases." In many situations, the best thing to do is to let nature take its course. Birds and other creatures are part of nature's natural cycle of life and death. An injured or dead bird may be a meal for another animal. If you feel you *must* do something to help an injured bird, call your local wildlife office, department of the environment, fish and game, or extension office. Your local vet may take rehabilitation cases—or may know of a licensed rehabilitator in your area.

## Window Strikes

**Q.** A bird is flying from window to window, butting its head against the glass while looking into the house. Can you explain this behavior?

**A.** Your bird is fighting its reflection in the windows, thinking that the reflection is a rival bird. The behavior will last through the breeding season. One solution is to place screens over the outside of the window. Plastic wrap stuck to the outside will also work—anything that will break up the reflection will do. You may also offer your bluebirds places to perch, such as snags and posts, far from windows. Bluebirds love a perch in the middle of a lawn or field. This has worked to distract the birds from windows.

**Q.** How can I keep birds from flying into my windows?

**A.** Silhouettes of flying hawks or falcons do work, but they perform best when applied on the outside of the glass. Hanging ornaments such as wind chimes, wind socks, and potted plants also helps. Misting the outside of the window with a very weak detergent or soda solution will eliminate the reflection, but will also impair visibility for you. Awnings, eave extensions, and window screens will eliminate reflection and stop the collision problem. Plastic cling wrap applied to the outside of the window can also be effective. One of the most effective solutions we have found is FeatherGuard, a series of bright-colored feathers strung on fishing line and hung over the outside surface of the glass.

## Bird Feeding

**Q.** What is the best seed to offer birds?

**A.** Black-oil sunflower seed is the most universally eaten seed at bird feeders. But there are many other seeds and foods to offer birds. What is most popular with your birds depends on where you live and what birds are present.

# Frequently Asked Questions

**Q.** What is the best feeder for bird feeding?

**A.** There is no single best feeder for bird feeding. A well-rounded feeding operation will include a platform feeder, a tube feeder, a hopper feeder, a suet feeder, and a peanut feeder. And don't forget the birdbath!

**Q.** I recently purchased a bird feeder, but have yet to see any birds. What am I doing wrong?

**A.** You're not doing anything wrong. It takes time for birds to locate a new feeding source. A spell of bad weather always drives birds to concentrate at feeders. Try putting your feeder in a new location far from your house and the portion of your yard where you are active. Put the feeder in or near a tree that the birds regularly use.

**Q.** Do birds that eat at feeders lose their ability to find food naturally? If I stop feeding them, will they starve?

**A.** No. Birds are not totally reliant on the food offered at your feeding station. Birds are programmed by instinct to forage for food, and they have evolved over millions of years to be very mobile in their food-finding habits. Because they can fly, birds are efficient at going to where the food is. Though feeding stations have been linked to slightly improved survival rates for birds in harsh weather conditions, overall bird feeding does not drastically affect the birds' survival. Also, when warmer weather comes, many of the seed-eating birds that frequented your feeders during winter switch to an insect-based diet in spring.

**Q.** How do I keep squirrels away from my bird feeders?

**A.** Baffling your feeders (preventing squirrels from gaining access to the feeders) is the best way. Feeders can be strung from a thin wire, far from any object from which the squirrels can leap. String the wire with empty 35mm film canisters (with the lids on) or short lengths of 1-inch PVC pipe, which will spin and dump the squirrels off. There are many squirrel-proof feeders on the market. These may give the squirrels a small electric shock, may prevent them from reaching the seed, or may rotate or bounce to dump the squirrels off. But be forewarned: Squirrels have been known to outsmart the most ingenious of the squirrel-proof inventions.

And if you can't beat 'em, join 'em! Feed squirrels ears of dried corn, but place the corn away from your bird feeders. Given the choice, squirrels will always go for the easiest food, and they *love* corn.

**Q.** What can I do to protect the birds in my yard from cats?

**A.** Hang feeders at least 5 feet above the ground. For ground-feeding birds, arrange ornamental border fencing in two or three concentric circles about 16 inches to 2 feet apart, to disrupt a cat's ability to leap at feeders or to spring on birds. Harass offending cats with a spray of water to train them to avoid your yard. If all else fails, use a live trap to catch the cats and take them to the local animal shelter. If the cats belong to your neighbors, ask them to restrain their pets from accessing your yard.

# Frequently Asked Questions

## Hummingbirds

**Q.** What is the best ratio of water to sugar to use for feeding hummingbirds?

**A.** Four parts water to one part sugar (a 4:1 ratio) has been shown to be the closest to the sucrose content of natural flower nectar. Concentrations stronger than this (such as a 3:1 ratio or stronger) are readily consumed by hummers, but no scientific evidence exists regarding the potential helpful or harmful effects on hummingbirds.

**Q.** Can I use molasses or honey instead of sugar to make my hummingbird nectar?

**A.** No. White table sugar is the only human-made sweetener that, when mixed with the right amount of water, closely resembles natural flower nectar. Resist the urge to use other sweeteners, which spoil quickly and may not be good for hummingbirds to consume.

**Q.** Is the red dye found in premixed solutions bad for hummingbirds?

**A.** Though no conclusive scientific evidence exists showing harmful effects of red food dye on hummingbirds, this chemical additive is certainly not a necessary ingredient in hummingbird solution.

Many commercially available brands of hummingbird solution contain red food coloring that is meant to be attractive both to hummingbirds and to shopping bird watchers. Brightly colored flowers are nature's way of attracting the eye of a foraging hummingbird, so the red solution in feeders is aimed at attracting hummingbirds. Bright red feeder parts (which most hummer feeders have) or a bright red ribbon hung near the feeder can be just as attractive as red-dyed solution. Red dye or food coloring may or may not be harmful to hummingbirds, but it is completely unnecessary.

**Q.** How do I foil a "bully" hummer?

**A.** Many hummingbird species defend feeding territories, and assemblages at feeders usually develop hierarchies. The behavior exemplifies natural selection at work, and you should do nothing except enjoy it.

If you're worried about hungry hummers, put up several more feeders near your original one. The bully will be overwhelmed by the sheer numbers of other birds and will quit being so territorial.

**Q.** Do hummingbirds migrate on the backs of Canada geese?

**A.** No. This is either a Native American myth or just an old wives' tale. Hummingbirds are excellent, strong-flying migrants. A healthy ruby-throated hummingbird can easily handle the 500-mile flight across the Gulf of Mexico.

**Q.** Is it true that hummingbirds at my feeder will not migrate if I leave my feeder up in the fall?

**A.** No. This is another in a long line of bird myths. Birds are genetically programmed to migrate when their internal "clocks" tell them to do so. They will depart when the time is right—whether your feeders are up or not. However, leaving your feeders up in fall, and getting them up early in spring may help early or late migrants that are passing through your area.

# How to Build a Simple Birdhouse

These plans are designed to help you build a simple birdhouse—one that is easy to put together and will attract a number of species. The 1 1/2-inch entrance hole will allow birds as large as bluebirds to enter the house, but even tiny house wrens and chickadees will find this house appealing.

Before you begin the building process, read through this entire plan. This will make the building go more smoothly and should prevent costly, frustrating errors. Study the instructions and drawings together. The letters in the instructions refer to the drawing that illustrates a particular section of directions.

Now, let's look at materials. Cedar will last, but it can be expensive. Pound for pound, cedar is the most durable, weather resistant, and provides the best insulation—so if your budget permits it, cedar is the best wood to use for birdhouses. After years of weather, nails in cedar can become loose, so I suggest using screws in place of nails for cedar construction. Pine is easy to nail and does not split easily, but it will decay unless preservatives are used (on the outside of the box only).

An excellent alternative material is 5/8-inch thick exterior plywood. It is tough, weathers well, and will not split along the edge if you use nails of the proper size, usually four-penny galvanized box nails. Called T 1-11, this wood has vertical grooves to resemble boards and is often used for exterior siding on homes. Most lumber yards and home centers sell T 1-11 in large 4-x-8-foot sheets. When assembling a birdhouse using exterior plywood, always remember to keep the weather surface of the wood on the outside of the birdhouse. It is an obvious point, but one that is easily forgotten in the midst of the building process.

Unless otherwise instructed, use four-penny galvanized box nails for nailing house parts together. Remember to use screws when using cedar or pine or when you feel extra strong binding is necessary.

It's impossible to predict which bird species is most apt to settle in your new birdhouse. Half a dozen cavity-nesting birds prefer a box with a single slant roof and a 1 1/2-inch-diameter entrance. Depending on your location, it could be tree swallows, hairy or downy woodpeckers, or perhaps titmice, chickadees, Carolina or house wrens, or even bluebirds.

Good luck with your building—and with being a landlord to the birds!

## Materials:

western red cedar, exterior plywood, or T 1-11 siding scraps (5/8 inch thick, 31 × 14 inches), which will be cut into the following pieces:

**bottom:** 5 × 5 inches
**sides (cut 2):** each 10 × 9 × 5 inches
**back:** 12 × 6 1/4 inches
**front:** 9 1/2 × 6 1/4 inches
**roof:** 8 1/4 × 8 1/4 inches

four-penny galvanized box nails
right-angle screw hook, about 1 1/2 inches long
caulking compound
sixteen-penny galvanized framing nails
2 galvanized siding nails (or wood screws), 1 3/4 inches long

## Tools:

square
ruler
pencil
saw
plane
drill or brace, with 1 1/2-inch expansion bit and 1/2-inch diameter bit
2 C clamps (optional)
rasp
hammer
wood blocks of various sizes
drill, with assorted small bits

# How to Build a Simple Birdhouse

## Instructions:

**A**

1. On the weather surface of the plywood, measure and mark with a pencil the exact outlines of each piece. Be sure the grain of the wood runs vertically on the two side pieces, the back, and the front. The T 1-11 siding has a vertical groove running down it. This won't hurt anything—but when laying out the parts, keep the groove away from the edge of each piece to avoid problems with nailing later on.

2. Lay out the two side pieces with a common line along the 9-inch dimension so that the tops angle toward the center line, making a shallow V. In this way, when you assemble the house, the weather surface will end up on the outside.

3. After checking the measurements once more, carefully saw or cut out all the parts. Trim the rough edges with a plane to knock off splinters. You won't need to sand anything—this is going to be rustic!

4. Lay the parts on the workbench and mark them, just to keep track. There are six parts—two sides, a roof, a bottom, a front, and a back.

5. To accommodate the roof slant, you will need to bevel the top edges of the front and back panels with a plane. Set the two pieces in front of you, just as they will be when assembled. On the weather surface of the front panel and on the inside surface of the back, draw a horizontal line 1/8 inch down from the top. Then bevel off 1/8 inch from each piece individually.

6. On the front panel, center a vertical line running 3 inches down from the top. Put a cross

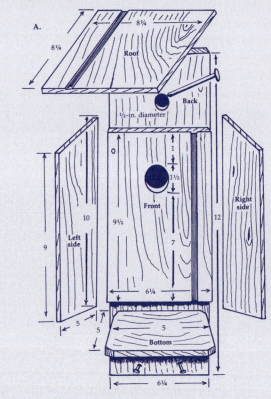

A Simple Birdhouse

Note: Dimensions are in inches

mark on the line, 1 3/4 inches from the top. Open the expansion bit to precisely 1 1/2 inches, then test it on a scrap board and measure the hole. Now, to ensure a clean cut, clamp the panel tightly to a board. Center the bit on the cross mark and drill the hole. (If you have no C clamps, lay the panel on a board and drill halfway. Turn it over and drill through the other side.) Round off the sharp edges with a rasp.

7. On the bottom piece, measure 3/8 inch in on each side of each corner and mark. Place a ruler diagonally across each corner and connect the two marks. Saw off the four corners at these points. The resultant openings in the finished house will allow adequate drainage and air circulation for the birds.

# How to Build a Simple Birdhouse

8. On the back panel, with the weather side up, center a vertical line—2 inches long—down from the top. At the bottom of the line, drill a 1/2-inch hole.

9. Mark a line across the weather surface of both side panels, 1 inch up from the bottom. On the right panel, extend the bottom line across the edges. Mark a line across the face of the front panel, 1 inch up from the bottom. It, too, should extend across the edges.

10. Now, mark a line across the weather surface on the back panel, 2 1/2 inches up from the bottom, and extend it across the edges.

**B**

1. You are now ready to start putting things together. Lay the right-hand side panel (the one on the right when the entrance of the completed birdhouse faces you), weather surface up, on the bench. Start two nails, each 1 1/2 inches in from the edge and 1/4 inch below the bottom line. Drive them in until they barely peek through the other side. Be sure they are straight.

2. Place the bottom panel (weather side toward you) on edge and at a right angle to the bench, against a flat wall or solid surface. (When the corners are cut off, it is easier to get the side and bottom flush when both are pressed against a flat wall.) Lay the right side panel (weather side out) across the upper edge of the bottom piece, matching the line on the side panel with the interior surface of the bottom. (Place a block under the other end of the right panel.) Drive the nails in part way—just enough to hold.

**C**

1. Turn the assembled pieces over so the right side faces you. Place two nails in the weather surface of the back panel, 1/4 inch below the line you marked earlier and 1 1/2 inches from the ends of the bottom panel. Drive them in until they begin to show on the other side.

2. Put the back piece on the two pieces that you assembled. Make sure that the lines marked on the bottom match, and that the edges are flush with the outside of the side panel.

B.

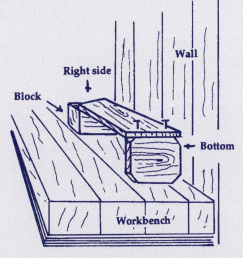

C.

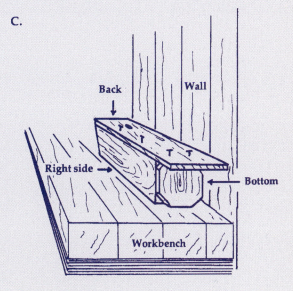

# How to Build a Simple Birdhouse

D.

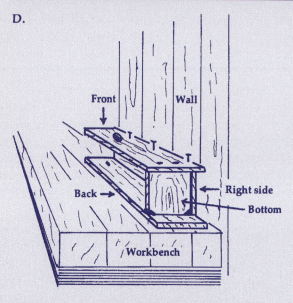

2. Put the front in place, matching the lines marked at the bottom with the interior surface of the bottom panel. There should be about a 1/2-inch gap at the top of the right side when the roof is on.

3. Drive the nail into the bottom, nearest the enclosed side, until the nail holds. Then start a nail 2 inches down from the top of the front panel and 1/4 inch in from the edge. Make sure that the front panel edge and the side are flush. Drive the nail in part way. Spring the bottom corner into alignment, and drive the nail near the open edge part way into the bottom. Start another, 2 inches up from the bottom, and drive it in part way. If everything looks good, pound in all the nails.

3. Drive the nail into the bottom, nearest the side panel, enough to hold. Start another nail along the edge of the back panel, 2 inches down from the top and about 1/4 inch from the edge. Check to see that the back panel edge and the side are flush. Drive the nail in part way.

4. Now check the bottom. Its outer corner may be sprung slightly. Press it into alignment with the back panel marks, hold, and drive the other bottom nail in part way. Check it over to see if the bottom is lined up. If so, place one more nail along the edge, 4 inches up from the bottom of the back panel, and drive in all the nails.

E.

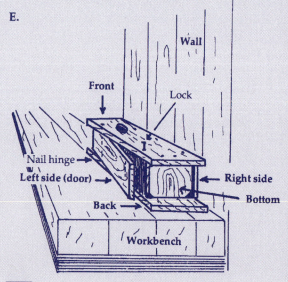

## D

1. Turn the unit on its back. Lay out the front panel, weather side up—racing stripe dazzling your eyes—and start two nails 1/4 inch below the bottom line and 1 1/2 inches in from each edge. Be sure the points have just come through the other side.

## E

1. Fit the left-hand side panel into position. If it is tight, plane down the edge for a looser fit. You want this "door" to open easily even when the wood swells in wet weather, so you can inspect the nest and clean out the house at the season's end.

# How to Build a Simple Birdhouse

**2.** Check for about a $1/2$-inch gap at the top. Drive two nails—one into the bottom and one into the front, halfway up—part way in to hold temporarily. (They will be removed later.)

**3.** On the left edge of the front panel, make a mark 1 inch from the top. Using a square, draw a horizontal line across the left side panel on the mark. At one end of this line, drive a nail through the front panel into the edge of the left panel. At the other end of the line, drive a nail through the back panel into the edge of the left panel. These nail hinges will allow the "door" to be opened.

**4.** Put a mark on the front panel 2 inches up from the bottom and centered over the edge of the door. Drill a small hole, about 2 inches deep, at the mark. Use a right-angle screw hook twisted into place as a lock nail. It is not likely to fall out of the hole, as a nail might, when the box is tipped forward. Remove the temporary nails and test the door.

### F

**1.** On the roof, start two nails, each $1/4$ inch in from the back or top edge of the roof, and about 2 inches in from the left and right sides. Remember that the roof slants, and you want the nail angled so it goes straight into the edge of the back panel. Stand the box upright with a block under the front. Run a strip of caulking compound along the top edge of the back panel. Place the top on, with the wood grain running down the slant, not across it.

**2.** Adjust the roof for equal overhang on each side. It should be flush with the back. Drive the nail in part way.

**3.** Sight along the front and drive two more nails—gingerly—into the top edge of the front panel until they hold. If it looks right, hammer them in.

### G

**1.** Now for hanging the birdhouse. If there are predators in your area, resist the temptation to hang your house on a tree or fencepost. If your area is predator-free (and not many areas are in North America), trees or fenceposts may be acceptable. To be safe, I suggest baffling all of your bird houses.

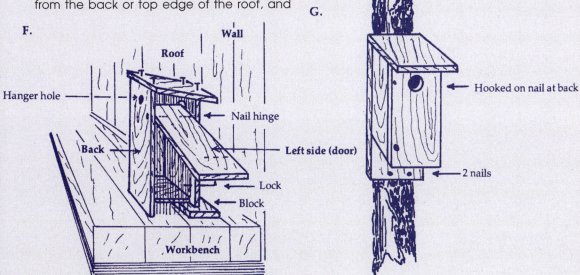

F.

G.

161

# Bird-Friendly Plants for Your Yard

## TREES

| Common Name | Latin Name | Good For/Other Notes |
|---|---|---|
| Apples | *Malus* spp. | Fruit, insects, cavities |
| Ashes | *Fraxinus* spp. | Seeds, insects, cover |
| Aspens | *Populus* spp. | Seeds, insects, cover, cavities |
| Birches | *Betula* spp. | Seeds, insects, cover |
| Cedars | *Juniperus* spp. | Fruit, year-round cover |
| Cherries | *Prunus* spp. | Fruit |
| Chokecherry, common | *Prunus virginiana* | Fruit |
| Cottonwoods | *Populus* spp. | Cavities, shelter |
| Crabapples | *Malus* spp. | Fruit, insects |
| Dogwoods | *Cornus* spp. | Fruit |
| Firs | *Abies* spp. | Year-round cover |
| Hackberries | *Celtis* spp. | Fruit, cover |
| Hawthorns | *Crataegus* spp. | Fruit, cover, nesting |
| Hemlocks | *Tsuga* spp. | Seeds, insects, shelter |
| Hollies | *Ilex* spp. | Fruit, year-round cover |
| Junipers | *Juniperus* spp. | Year-round cover |
| Larches | *Larix* spp. | Seeds |
| Madrones | *Arbutus* spp. | Fruit |
| Maples | *Acer* spp. | Seeds, cover |
| Mesquites | *Prosopis* spp. | Shelter |
| Mountain ashes | *Sorbus* spp. | Fruit |
| Mulberry, red | *Morus rubra* | Fruit |
| Oaks | *Quercus* spp. | Acorns, cover, insects |
| Pines | *Pinus* spp. | Year-round cover, insects |
| Poplars | *Populus* spp. | Cavities, shelter |
| Sassafras | *Sassafras albidum* | Fruit, cover, cavities |
| Shadbush, or serviceberry | *Amelanchier laevis* | Fruit, flowers |
| Spruces | *Picea* spp. | Year-round cover |
| Sycamores | *Platanus* spp. | Cavities, shelter, insects |
| Willows | *Salix* spp. | Cavities, shelter, insects |

# Bird-Friendly Plants for Your Yard

## SHRUBS

| Common Name | Latin Name | Good For/Other Notes |
|---|---|---|
| Arrowwood viburnum/Viburnums | *Viburnum dentatum*/*Viburnum* spp. | Fall fruit. Tolerates shade |
| Bayberry, northern | *Myrica pensylvanica* | Fruit. Male & female plants needed for fruit |
| Blackberry, American | *Rubus allegheniensis* | Fruit, dense cover, nesting |
| Blueberry, highbush | *Vaccinium corymbosum* | Fruit, flowers, cover. Needs acid soil |
| Chokeberry, red | *Aronia arbutifolia* | Fruit. Moist soil preferred |
| Cranberry, highbush | *Viburnum trilobum* | Fruit. Shade tolerant |
| Dogwoods | *Cornus* spp. | Fall fruit, dense cover |
| Elderberry, American | *Sambucus canadensis* | Fruit, dense cover |
| Hercules' club | *Aralia spinosa* | Fruit |
| Hobblebush | *Viburnum alnifolium* | Fruit. Shade tolerant |
| Hollies, deciduous | *Ilex decidua, Ilex* spp. | Winter fruit. Male & female plants needed for fruit |
| Huckleberry, black | *Gaylussacia baccata* | Fruit. Sandy soil preferred |
| Inkberry | *Ilex glabra* | Fruit. Thicket-forming. Needs acid soil |
| Mahonia | *Mahonia aquifolium* | Fruit, year-round cover |
| Manzanitas | *Arctostaphylos* spp. | Early fruit, thick cover |
| Nannyberry | *Viburnum lentago* | Fruit. Shade-tolerant |
| Pokeweed | *Phytolacca americana* | Fall fruit. |
| Roses | *Rosa* spp. | Winter fruit. Summer flowers |
| Shadbushes | *Amelanchier* spp. | Early fruit |
| Spicebush | *Lindera benzoin* | Fruit. Needs moist soil |
| Sumacs | *Rhus* spp. | Fruit available all winter |
| Winterberry, common | *Ilex verticillata* | Fruit. Male & female plants needed for fruit |
| Yews | *Taxus* spp. | Year-round cover. Some fruit |

## VINES

| Common Name | Latin Name | Good For/Other Notes |
|---|---|---|
| Ampelopsis, heartleaf | *Ampelopsis cordata* | Fruit. Resembles a grape vine |
| Bittersweet, American | *Celastrus scandens* | Fruit. Avoid Asian species. |
| Grapes, wild | *Vitis* spp. | Fruit attracts 100 species, cover |

# Bird-Friendly Plants for Your Yard

## VINES

| Common Name | Latin Name | Good For/Other Notes |
|---|---|---|
| Greenbriars | *Smilax* spp. | Fruit, thick cover |
| Trumpet honeysuckle | *Lonicera sempervirens* | Nectar, fruit, cover. Avoid Asian species |
| Trumpet vine | *Campsis radicans* | Nectar, summer cover |
| Virginia creeper | *Parthenocissus quinquefolia* | Fruit attracts 40 species |

## FLOWERS

| Common Name | Latin Name | Good For/Other Notes |
|---|---|---|
| Asters | *Aster* spp. | Flowers attract butterlies, seed |
| Bachelor's button | *Centaurea cyanus* | Seed |
| Black-eyed Susan | *Rudbeckia serotina* | Seed |
| Blazing star | *Liatris* spp. | Seed, flowers attract butterflies |
| California poppy | *Eschscholzia californica* | Seed |
| Coneflower, purple | *Echinacea purpurea* | Seed, flowers attract butterflies |
| Coreopsis | *Coreopsis* spp. | Seed, flowers attract butterflies |
| Cornflower | *Centaurea cyanus* | Seed |
| Cosmos | *Cosmos* spp. | Seed |
| Daisy, gloriosa | *Rudbeckia* cv. | Seed |
| Goldenrods | *Solidago* spp. | Flowers for butterflies, winter cover |
| Joe-Pye weeds | *Eupaorium* spp. | Flowers for butterflies, winter cover |
| Marigolds | *Tagetes* spp. | Seed |
| Penstemons | *Penstemon* spp. | Nectar, seed |
| Poppies | *Papaver* spp. | Flowers attract butterflies, seed |
| Primroses | *Oenothera* spp. | Seed |
| Sedums | *Sedum* spp. | Flowers attract butterflies, seed |
| Sunflowers | *Helianthus* spp. | Seed |
| Thistles, globe | *Echinops* spp. | Flowers, seed, nesting material |
| Zinnias | *Zinnnia elegans* | Seed, flowers attract butterflies |

# Bibliography

American Bird Conservancy. 2003. *Guide to the 500 Most Important Bird Areas in the United States*. New York: Random House.

American Ornithologists' Union. 1998. *Check-List of North American Birds*. 7th edition. Washington, DC: American Ornithologists' Union.

Choate, E. A. 1985. *The Dictionary of American Bird Names, Revised Edition*. Boston: Harvard Common Press.

Ehrlich, P. R.; Dobkin, D. S.; and Wheye, D. 1988. *The Birder's Handbook*. New York: Fireside Books.

Kaufman, K. 1996. *Lives of North American Birds*. Boston: Houghton Mifflin Co.

Kaufman, K. 2000. *Birds of North America, A Kaufman Focus Guide*. Boston: Houghton Mifflin Co.

National Geographic Society. 1999. *Field Guide to the Birds of North America*. 3rd edition. Washington, D.C.: National Geographic Society.

Peterson, R. T. 1996. *A Field Guide to the Birds* (Eastern). Boston: Houghton Mifflin Co.

Poole, A., and Gill, F., eds. 1992–2002. *The Birds of North America*. Philadelphia, PA: American Ornithologists' Union/Birds of North American, Inc.,

Sibley, D. A. 2000. *The Sibley Guide to the Birds*. New York: Alfred A. Knopf, Inc.

Stokes, D., and Stokes, L. 1996. *Stokes Field Guide to Birds: Eastern Region*. Boston: Little, Brown and Co.

Terres, J. K. 1995. *The Audubon Encyclopedia of North American Birds*. New York: Wings Books.

Thompson III, B. 1995. *An Identification Guide to Common Backyard Birds*. Marietta, OH: Bird Watcher's Digest Press.

Thompson III, B. 1997. *Bird Watching For Dummies*. New York: John Wiley & Sons.

Thompson III, B. 2003. *The Backyard Bird Watcher's Answer Guide*. Marietta, OH: Bird Watcher's Digest Press.

Zickefoose, J. 1995. *Enjoying Bird Feeding More*. Marietta, OH: Bird Watcher's Digest Press.

Zickefoose, J. 2001. *Natural Gardening for Birds*. Emmaus, PA: Rodale Organic Living Books.

# National Organizations for Bird Watchers

## National Organizations

### American Bird Conservancy
P.O. Box 249
The Plains, VA 20198
(540) 253-5780
www.abcbirds.org

### American Birding Association
P.O. Box 6599
Colorado Springs, CO 80934-6599
800-850-2473
www.americanbirding.org

### Cornell Laboratory of Ornithology
Attn: Communications
159 Sapsucker Woods Road
Ithaca, NY 14850
800-843-2473
www.birds.cornell.edu

### National Audubon Society
700 Broadway
New York, NY 10003
(212) 979-3000
www.audubon.org

### National Wildlife Federation
11100 Wildlife Center Drive
Reston, VA 20190-5362
800-822-9919
www.nwf.org

### The Nature Conservancy
4245 North Fairfax Drive, Suite 100
Arlington, VA 22203-1606
800-628-6860
www.tnc.org

## Field Guides to Birds

Griggs, J. L. 1997. *All the Birds of North America*. New York: Harper Collins.

Kaufman, K. 2001. *Birds of North America (Kaufman Focus Guides)*. Boston: Houghton Mifflin Co.

National Geographic Society. 1999. *National Geographic Field Guide to the Birds of North America, 3rd edition*. Washington, D.C.: National Geographic Society.

Peterson, R. T. 2002. *A Field Guide to the Birds of Eastern and Central North America (Peterson Series). 5th ed*. Boston: Houghton Mifflin Co.

Robbins, C. S., et al. 1983. *Birds of North America: A Guide to Field Identification (Golden Field Guide Series)*. Revised edition. New York: Golden Press.

Sibley, D. A. 2000. *The Sibley Guide to the Birds. New York:* Alfred A. Knopf, Inc.

Stokes, D., and Stokes, L. 1996. *Field Guide to the Birds of North America*. Boston: Little, Brown and Co.

## Audio Guides to Birds

Elliott, L. 2004. *Know Your Bird Sounds, volumes 1 and 2.* Mechanicsburg, PA: Stackpole Books.

Elliott, L.; Stokes, D.; and Stokes, L. 1997. *Stokes Field Guide to Bird Songs: Eastern Region (Stokes Field Guide to Bird Songs).* New York: Time Warner Audio Books.

Peterson, R. T. 2002. *A Field Guide to Bird Songs of Eastern and Central North America. Revised edition.* Boston: Houghton Mifflin Co.

Walton, R. K., and Lawson, R. W. 1989. *Birding By Ear, Eastern and Central North America (Peterson Field Guide Series).* Boston: Houghton Mifflin Co.

Walton, R. K., and Lawson, R. W. 1994. *More Birding By Ear (Peterson Field Guide Series).* Boston, MA: Houghton Mifflin Co.

## Periodicals for Bird Watchers

### The Backyard Bird Newsletter
P. O. Box 110
Marietta, OH 45750
800-879-2473
www.birdwatchersdigest.com

### Bird Watcher's Digest
P. O. Box 110
Marietta, OH 45750
800-879-2473
www.birdwatchersdigest.com

### Living Bird
Cornell Laboratory of Ornithology
159 Sapsucker Woods Road
Ithaca, NY 14850
800-843-2473
www.birds.cornell.edu

# Photography Credits

**Arthur Morris/Birds as Art:** Pages 35, 46, 47, 48, 49, 50, 51, 52, 53, 54, 55, 56, 59, 61, 63, 64, 65, 66, 67, 68, 69, 70, 73, 74, 75, 76, 77, 79, 82, 85, 87, 88, 89, 91, 93, 95, 96, 98, 99, 101, 102, 103, 104, 106, 107, 109, 111, 112, 113, 114, 115, 116, 117, 119, 122, 125, 127, 129, 131, 132, 133, 134, 135, 136, 137, 138, 139, 140, 141, 144, 145

**Bird Watcher's Digest:** Pages 34, 37, 38 (both photos), 39 (both photos), 40, 41

**Tom Vezo:** Pages 60, 72, 80, 81, 92, 108, 118, 130

**Maslowski Photography:** Pages 78, 84, 86, 142, 143

**Robert McCaw:** Pages 71, 90, 100, 105, 123

**Cliff Beittel:** Pages 57, 62, 124

**Brian Henry:** Pages 94, 110, 121

**Barth Schorre:** Pages 120, 126

**Julie Zickefoose:** Pages 43, 176

**Ron Austing:** Page 83

**Bill Bevington:** Page 128

**Randall Ennis:** Page 33

**Charles Melton:** Page 42

**Gary Meszaros:** Pages 58

**Marie Read:** Page 97

# Index

**A**cadian flycatcher, 92
*Accipiter cooperii*, 60
*Actitis macularia*, 70
*Agelaius phoeniceus*, 138
*Aix sponsa*, 52
American
    coot, 67
    crow, 99
    goldfinch, 42, 144
    kestrel, 65
    redstart, 120
    robin, 93, 110, 111
    woodcock, 71
*Anas discors*, 54
*Anas platyrhynchos*, 53
*Archilochus colubris*, 84
*Ardea herodias*, 49
Audubon's warbler, 119
August teal, 54
*Aythya affinis*, 56
*Aythya collaris*, 55

**B**aeolophus bicolor, 104
bald eagle, 63
Baltimore oriole, 35, 140
barn swallow, 39, 103
barred owl, 79
beebird, 95
belted kingfisher, 85
bittern, least, 50
black-billed cuckoo, 77
blackbird, 137, 138
    red-winged, 137, 138
black-capped chickadee, 105
black duck, 53
black-headed grosbeak, 125
black-throated green
    warbler, 123
blue
    heron, great, 78
    jay, 98, 99
bluebird, 39, 102, 107, 110,
    116, 145
    eastern, 110
blue-gray gnatcatcher, 109
blue-winged, 54
    teal, 54

Bohemian waxwing, 117
*Bombycilla cedrorum*, 117
Bonaparte's gull, 72
*Branta canadensis*, 51
broad-winged hawk, 61
brown-headed
    cowbird, 112, 121, 137, 144
    nuthatch, 106
brown thrasher, 115
*Bubo virginianus*, 78
bunting, 128
    indigo, 128
    snow, 100
*Buteo jamaicensis*, 61
*Butorides virescens*, 50
butterbutt, 119

**C**anada goose, 51
Canadas, 51
canary, wild, 144
*Caprimulgus vociferus*, 81
cardinal, 42, 104, 127
    northern, 109, 127
*Cardinalis cardinalis*, 127
*Carduelis pinus*, 143
*Carduelis tristis*, 144
Carolina
    chickadee, 105
    wren, 39, 42, 104, 107
*Carpodacus mexicanus*, 141
*Carpodacus purpureus*, 142
catbird, 114
    gray, 114
*Cathartes aura*, 59
*Catharus fuscescens*, 113
cedar waxwing, 117
*Ceryle alcyon*, 85
*Chaetura pelagica*, 83
*Charadrius vociferus*, 68
chewink, 129
chickadee, 36, 39, 104, 105,
    108, 123
    black-capped, 105
    Carolina, 105
chimney swift, 83
chipping sparrow, 130, 131, 137
*Chordeiles minor*, 82

chuck-will's widow, 81
*Circus cyaneus*, 62
clay-colored robin, 111
*Coccyzus americanus*, 77
*Colaptes auratus*, 91
*Columba livia*, 76
common
    grackle, 139
    loon, 48
    merganser, 58
    moorhen, 67
    nighthawk, 81, 82
    pond heron, 50
    yellowthroat, 122
*Contopus virens*, 92
Cooper's hawk, 60, 65
coot, American, 67
cormorant, 47, 72
    double-crested, 47
*Corvus brachyrhynchos*, 99
cowbird, 96, 113, 122, 137
    brown-headed, 112, 121,
        137, 144
crane, 49
crow, 99
    American, 99
cuckoo
    black-billed, 77
    yellow-billed, 77
*Cyanocitta cristata*, 98

**D**ark-eyed junco, 135
*Dendroica coronata*, 119
*Dendroica magnolia*, 118
*Dendroica petechia*, 124
*Dendroica virens*, 123
double-crested cormorant, 47
dove, 75
    mourning, 42, 75
downy, 88, 89
    woodpecker, 88, 89
duck, 52, 53, 54, 55, 56, 57,
    58, 67
    black, 53
    ring-necked, 55, 56
    ruddy, 57
    stiff-tailed, 57

wood, 52, 55
*Dumetella carolinensis*, 114

**E**agle, bald, 63
eared grebe, 46
eastern
    bluebird, 110
    flycatcher, 94
    kingbird, 95
    meadowlark, 136
    phoebe, 92, 93
    screech-owl, 80
    towhee, 129
    wood-pewee, 92
*Eremophila alpestris*, 100
European starling, 39, 86, 87, 101, 116, 137

**F**alco sparverius, 65
falcon, 65
    peregrine, 65
field sparrow, 130
finch, 125, 143
    house, 42, 141, 142, 143
    purple, 141, 142
fish hawk, 64
flicker, 60, 91
    northern, 91
    yellow-shafted, 91
flycatcher, 39, 92, 93
    Acadian, 92
    eastern, 94
    great crested, 94
    silky, 117
fox sparrow, 115
*Fulica americana*, 67

**G**allinule, purple, 67
*Gavia immer*, 48
*Geothlypis trichas*, 122
gnatcatcher, 109
    blue-gray, 109
goatsucker, 82
golden-crowned
    kinglet, 108
goldfinch, 143, 144
    American, 42, 144

goosander, 58
goose, 47
    Canada, 51
goshawk, northern, 60
grackle, 137, 139
    common, 139
gray catbird, 114
great
    blue heron, 49, 78
    crested, 94
    crested flycatcher, 94
    horned owl, 78
greater
    scaup, 55, 56
    yellowlegs, 69
grebe, 46, 72
    eared, 46
    horned, 46
    pied-billed, 46
green-backed heron, 50
green heron, 50
grosbeak, 125
    black-headed, 125
    rose-breasted, 125
gull, 72, 73, 74
    Bonaparte's, 72
    herring, 73, 74
    inland, 73
    ring-billed, 73, 74

**H**airy, 88, 89
    woodpecker, 88, 89
*Haliaeetus leucocephalus*, 63
harrier, 62
    northern, 62
hawk, 60, 78, 82
    broad-winged, 61
    Cooper's, 60, 65
    fish, 64
    marsh, 62
    red-shouldered, 61, 98
    red-tailed, 61, 98
    sharp-shinned, 60, 65
hermit thrush, 113
heron, 47, 49, 50, 78
    common pond, 50
    great blue, 49, 78

    green, 50
    green-backed, 50
    little, 50
    squat, 50
herring gull, 73, 74
high-hole, 91
*Hirundo rustica*, 103
Hollywood
    linnet, 141
    robin, 129
horned
    grebe, 46
    lark, 100
house
    finch, 42, 141, 142, 143
    sparrow, 110, 145
    wren, 107
hummingbird, 84, 90, 108, 109
    ruby-throated, 84, 90
*Hylocichla mustelina*, 112

**I**cterus galbula, 140
indigo bunting, 128
inland gull, 73

**J**apanese waxwing, 117
jay, blue, 98, 99
junco, 135
    dark-eyed, 135
*Junco hyemalis*, 135

**K**estrel, 65
    American, 65
killdeer, 68
kingbird, 95
    eastern, 95
kingfisher, 36, 85
    belted, 85
kinglet, 104
    golden-crowned, 108
    ruby-crowned, 108

**L**ark, horned, 100
*Larus argentatus*, 74
*Larus delawarensis*, 73
*Larus philadelphia*, 72
least bittern, 50

lesser
    scaup, 55, 56
    yellowlegs, 69
linnet, Hollywood, 141
little heron, 50
longspur, 100
loon, 48, 58
    common, 48

**M**agnolias, 118
magnolia warbler, 118
mallard, 53, 55
marsh hawk, 62
martin, 101
    purple, 39, 101, 116, 145
meadowlark, 136
    eastern, 136
    western, 136
*Megascops asio*, 80
*Melanerpes carolinus*, 87
*Melanerpes erythrocephalus*, 86
*Meleagris gallopavo*, 66
*Melospiza melodia*, 134
merganser, 58, 72
    common, 58
*Mergus merganser*, 58
merlin, 65
mockingbird, 109, 115
*Molothrus ater*, 137
moorhen, common, 67
mourning dove, 42, 75
*Myiarchus crinitus*, 94
myrtle
    swallow, 102
    warbler, 119

**N**ighthawk, 82
    common, 81, 82
northern
    cardinal, 109, 127
    flicker, 91
    goshawk, 60
    harrier, 62
nuthatch, 39, 106
    brown-headed, 106
    red-breasted, 106
    white-breasted, 106

**O**riole, 140
    Baltimore, 35, 140
osprey, 63, 64
ovenbird, 121
owl, 78, 79, 80
    barred, 79
    eastern screech, 80
    great horned, 78
    screech-, 80
    spotted, 79
*Oxyura jamaicensis*, 57

**P**andion haliaetus, 64
*Passer domesticus*, 145
*Passerina cyanea*, 128
pelican, 47
peregrine falcon, 65
*Phalacrocorax auritus*, 47
*Pheucticus ludovicianus*, 125
phoebe, 39, 42, 93
    eastern, 92, 93
*Picoides pubescens*, 88
*Picoides villosus*, 89
pied-billed grebe, 46
pigeon, 60, 76
    rock, 76
pine siskin, 143
*Pipilo erythrophthalmus*, 129
*Piranga olivacea*, 126
plover, 68
    semipalmated, 68
*Podilymbus podiceps*, 46
*Poecile atricapillus*, 105
*Poecile carolinensis*, 105
*Polioptila caerulea*, 109
*Progne subis*, 101
purple
    finch, 141, 142
    gallinule, 67
    martin, 39, 101, 116, 145

**Q**uiscalus quiscula, 139

**R**ail, 67
raincrow, 77
red-bellied woodpecker, 86, 87, 109
redbelly, 87

redbird, 127
red-breasted nuthatch, 106
red-eyed, 96
    vireo, 96, 97, 137
red-head, 86
red-headed woodpecker, 86, 87
red-shouldered hawk, 61, 98
redstart, American, 120
redtail, 61
red-tailed hawk, 61, 98
red-winged blackbird, 137, 138
redwing, 138
*Regulus calendula*, 108
ring-billed gull, 73, 74
ringneck, 55
ring-necked duck, 55, 56
robin, 39, 60, 70, 111, 112, 126
    American, 93, 110, 111
    clay-colored, 111
    Hollywood, 129
rock pigeon, 76
rose-breasted grosbeak, 125
ruby-crowned kinglet, 108
rubythroat, 84
ruby-throated hummingbird, 84, 90
ruddy duck, 57
rufous-sided towhee, 129

**S**andpiper, 70
    spotted, 70
sapsucker, 90
    yellow-bellied, 90
saw-bill, 58
*Sayornis phoebe*, 93
scarlet tanager, 126
scaup, 55, 56
    greater, 55, 56
    lesser, 55, 56
*Scolopax minor*, 71
screech-owl, 80
    eastern, 80
seagull, 74
*Seiurus aurocapilla*, 121
semipalmated plover, 68
*Setophaga ruticilla*, 120
sharp-shinned hawk, 60, 65
*Sialia sialis*, 110

silky flycatcher, 117
siskin, 143
   pine, 143
*Sitta carolinensis*, 106
snowbird, 135
snow bunting, 100
song sparrow, 134, 137
sparrow, 42, 43, 104, 129, 131, 132, 133, 135
   chipping, 130, 131, 137
   field, 130
   fox, 115
   house, 110, 145
   song, 134, 137
   tree, 130
   white-crowned, 133
   white-throated, 132, 133
*Sphyrapicus varius*, 90
*Spizella passerina*, 131
*Spizella pusilla*, 130
spotted
   owl, 79
   sandpiper, 70
squat heron, 50
starling, 110, 116
   European, 39, 86, 87, 101, 116, 137
stiff-tailed duck, 57
stork, 49
*Strix varia*, 79
*Sturnella magna*, 136
*Sturnella neglecta*, 136
*Sturnus vulgaris*, 116
summer
   tanager, 126
   teal, 54
Swainson's thrush, 113
swallow, 36, 39, 101, 103, 145
   barn, 39, 42, 103
   myrtle, 102
   tree, 39, 102, 107
swift, chimney, 83

*T*achycineta bicolor, 102
tanager, 126
   scarlet, 126
   summer, 126

teal, 54
   August, 54
   blue-winged, 54
   summer, 54
thrasher, 115
   brown, 115
thrush, 110, 111, 112, 113, 115, 120, 121
   hermit, 113
   Swainson's, 113
   wood, 70, 112
titmouse, 39, 104, 108, 123
   tufted, 104, 109
towhee, 129
   eastern, 129
   rufous-sided, 129
*Toxostoma rufum*, 115
tree
   sparrow, 130
   swallow, 39, 102, 107
*Tringa flavipes*, 69
*Troglodytes aedon*, 107
tufted titmouse, 104, 109
*Turdus migratorius*, 111
turkey, 66
   vulture, 59
turkey, wild, 63, 66
*Tyrannus tyrannus*, 95

**V**eery, 113
vireo, 96, 97
   red-eyed, 96, 97, 137
   warbling, 97
*Vireo gilvus*, 97
*Vireo olivaceus*, 96
vulture, turkey, 59

**W**arbler, 90, 96, 97, 108, 118, 119, 120, 121, 122, 123, 124
   Audubon's, 119
   black-throated green, 123
   magnolia, 118
   myrtle, 119
   yellow, 124, 137
   yellow-rumped, 119
warbling vireo, 97
waterthrush, 121

waxwing
   Bohemian, 117
   cedar, 117
   Japanese, 117
western meadowlark, 136
whip-poor-will, 36, 81
white-breasted nuthatch, 106
white-crowned sparrow, 133
white-throated sparrow, 132, 133
wild
   canary, 144
   turkey, 63, 66
wood
   duck, 52, 55
   thrush, 70, 112
woodcock, 71
   American, 71
woodpecker, 36, 39, 86, 87, 88, 89, 90, 91, 94, 104
   downy, 88, 89
   hairy, 88, 89
   red-bellied, 86, 87, 109
   red-headed, 86, 87
wood-pewee, 92
   eastern, 92
wren, 39
   Carolina, 39, 42, 104, 107
   house, 107

**Y**awkerbird, 91
yellow-bellied sapsucker, 90
yellow-billed cuckoo, 77
yellowhammer, 91
yellowlegs
   greater, 69
   lesser, 69
yellow-rumped warbler, 119
yellow-shafted flicker, 91
yellowstart, 120
yellowthroat, 122
   common, 122
yellow warbler, 124, 137

**Z**enaida macroura, 75
*Zonotrichia albicollis*, 132
*Zonotrichia leucophrys*, 133

# Sighting Notes

| Date | Species/Description | Location |
|------|---------------------|----------|
|      |                     |          |

# Sighting Notes

| Date | Species/Description | Location |
|------|---------------------|----------|
|      |                     |          |

# Sighting Notes

| Date | Species/Description | Location |
|------|---------------------|----------|
|      |                     |          |

# Meet Bill Thompson, III

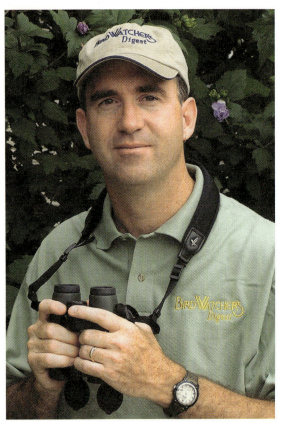

Bill Thompson, III is the Editor of Bird Watcher's Digest, the popular bimonthly magazine devoted to birds and bird watching. From an early age, Bill knew his life would be intertwined with birds and bird watching. One of his first words was "junco" and one of his early memories is of seeing a male cardinal in a tree. In 1978, his parents, Bill and Elsa Thompson, founded Bird Watcher's Digest in their living room, fulfilling their dream. It has been published continuously since its inception.

In addition to this book for Cool Springs Press, Bill Thompson is the author of the Southern series of state bird watching books for Cool Springs Press. He is the author of the best-selling book, Bird Watching for Dummies. He is also the author of many booklets published by Bird Watcher's Digest. His articles on bird watching have appeared in numerous books and magazines, including National Gardening. Bill is a frequent guest lecturer and speaker for many events. In addition, he is a longtime member of The American Birding Association and is a Director of the Ohio Ornithological Society.

Bill, his wife Julie Zickefoose (an acclaimed artist and nature writer), and their two children enjoy life on an 80-acre farm in Whipple, Ohio. One of their life dreams became a reality when they added a 50-foot-tall bird-watching observation tower to their home. To date, they have recorded sightings of more than 181 bird species. When he's not serving as an editor, traveling, lecturing, or writing books, Bill enjoys playing guitar in his band, The Swinging Orangutangs, with his wife, Julie, and brother, Andy.